Dissecting
the Unholy Trinity of
Dawkins, Harris, and Hitchens

THE
IRRATIONAL
ATHEIST

Vox Day

BENBELLA BOOKS, INC.
Dallas, Texas

BenBella Books, Inc.
6440 N. Central Expressway, Suite 503
Dallas, TX 75206
Send feedback to feedback@benbellabooks.com
www.benbellabooks.com

Printed in the United States of America
10 9 8 7 6 5 4 3 2

Library of Congress Cataloging-in-Publication Data

Day, Vox.
   The irrational atheist : dissecting the unholy trinity of Dawkins, Harris, and Hitchens / Vox Day.
      p. cm.
   ISBN 1-933771-36-4
   1. Atheism. 2. Dawkins, Richard, 1941—Religion. 3. Harris, Sam, 1967—Religion.
4. Hitchens, Christopher—Religion. I. Title.
   BL2747.3.D39 2007
   211'.8—dc22

                                                                    2007041413

Proofreading by Maggie McGuire, Emily Chauviere, and Yara Abuata
Cover design by Todd Michael Bushman
Text design and composition by John Reinhardt Book Design
Printed by Bang Printing

Distributed by Independent Publishers Group
To order call (800) 888-4741
www.ipgbook.com

For special sales contact Robyn White at Robyn@benbellabooks.com

Praise for *The Irrational Atheist*

"In a day when too few of the recently published 'New Atheists' get hoisted on their own petard, it is gratifying to see Vox Day undertake that assignment with warmth and enthusiasm."
—Douglas Wilson, *Christianity Today*

"Vox Day frags the New Atheism movement with the kind of logic and fact that Dawkins, Harris, Hitchens, and Onfray only claim to use. The important factor is that Day makes his challenging assertions without faith-based cross-waving."
—Dr. Johnny Wilson, Editor-in-Chief, *Computer Gaming World*

"The Vox is in the henhouse, with the scent of Dawkins's blood in his nostrils and a mouthful of Hitchens's feathers! Harris, alas, doesn't make it out of the book alive and the emergency team is still waiting to see if Dawkins will pull through after receiving one of the most visceral literary lobotomies ever inflicted in publishing. In the culture wars between New Atheism and The Rest of the World, *The Irrational Atheist* is 'must-read' material."
—Ian Wishart, *Investigate Magazine*

"Day's work is a healthy kick in the head to the comfortably numb. Using their own claims against them, he uses logic, reason, and rhetoric to reveal that atheists are the new fanatics, and that we should all—religious or irreligious—be very wary of their schemes. G. K. Chesterton once remarked that without God, there would be no atheists; Day updates this by showing how atheism itself is an evolutionary dead-end. A provocative, gutsy, and in-your-face book, but eminently enjoyable reading."
—Read Mercer Schuchardt, Assistant Professor of Communication, Wheaton College

"In *The Irrational Atheist*, Vox Day plays the card that the atheists consider their trump—reason—against them in a devastating and highly entertaining manner. With clarity and wit, he presents a wealth of evidence to demolish the arguments put forward by the leading 'brights' of the day."
—Chad the Elder, Fraters Libertas

DEDICATION

This is for those who walk The Way,
Weak and stumbling, poorly shod.
May they find strength in every day
To persist on the path to God.

This is for those still lost in night,
Angry, doubting, trapped in strife.
May they find answers in the Light
That leads to the eternal life.

This is for those who fall for Christ,
Faithful, fearless before Cain.
May they find courage to suffice
And know that they die not in vain.

ACKNOWLEDGMENTS

WITHOUT THE EXAMPLES AND INFLUENCE of my parents, Dr. Gregory Boyd, Tim Stahl, and Andrew and Marit Lunstad, this book would not exist. It is not always our strengths that testify to the truth, sometimes it is our flaws. I have been fortunate to enjoy the unrelenting support of my most faithful readers, the dread Ilk of Vox Popoli, whose encouragement, criticism, and general insanity have provided many ideas that have been incorporated, one way or another, into this text. I must also thank my sometime nemeses, especially Dark Window, Brent Rasmussen, and Dr. P. Z. Myers, for their forthright defense of their own beliefs and the sporadic clashes that have aided me in articulating my own position.

I am grateful to Jamsco, whose detailed perusal of the early drafts was invaluable. Thanks to readers Giraffe, SZook, and BAJ as well. Meredith Dixon helped with the Latin translations and HuckG provided a speedy and dependable procurement service in tracking down various required texts.

Special thanks to Mr. Frederick Dawe, Esq., who is equally reliable in contract negotiations and bar fights. And most of all, I am deeply appreciative of the love and support of the lovely Spacebunny, and am much obliged for her willingness to participate in the occasional midnight symposium on life, the universes, and everything.

CONTENTS

PREFACE

Get ready for the throw down....

—Tupac Shakur, "2 of Amerikaz Most Wanted"

"WHAT'S YOUR OBSESSION with these guys?" A reader e-mailed to ask after my fourth column addressing the intellectual sins of the three leading New Atheists was published on WorldNet-Daily, the independent news site where I write a weekly opinion column. After all, the Creator God of the universe is presumably capable of defending Himself, and the elephant is what it is, regardless of what I, Richard Dawkins, Sam Harris, Christopher Hitchens, or anyone else might imagine it to be based upon our different experiences of it.

When it comes to understanding God, are we not all blind men feeling up an oversized mammal?

And while I am a believer, a non-denominational evangelical Christian to be precise, my purpose in writing this book is not to

1

defend God, or even to argue for the truth of my particular religious faith. Instead, I intend to defend those who are now being misled into doubting their faith or are fooled into feeling more secure in their lack of faith on the basis of the fraudulent, error-filled writings of these three men. I do not make this triple charge of fraudulence lightly, nor is my doing so a fearful response to their churlish disregard for what to me and millions of other individuals is the central element of human existence.

There is simply no more fitting description of the cerebral snake oil that Dawkins, Harris, and Hitchens are selling to the unwary reader—and the media—under the false label of science and reason. I am confident that no one, not even the most purely rational, über-skeptical agnostic or card-carrying ACLU atheist, will take serious exception to my charge by the time they finish this book.

It took me some time to decide what this book should be titled. Part of the challenge was due to the fact that it addresses the philosophical and ideological arguments of three very different men. If the book were to solely address Sam Harris, I should likely have entitled it *The Incompetent Atheist*. In the case of Christopher Hitchens, I could have reasonably named it *The Irrelevant Atheist*. And given the way in which the eminent Richard Dawkins has apparently decided to abandon empirical evidence, the scientific method, and Reason herself in embracing a quasi-medieval philosophical ontology, *The Ironic Atheist* would surely have been most fitting.

In the end, I settled upon *The Irrational Atheist* for the following reason. This book is a direct challenge to the idea that atheism is the proper philosophical standard for human reason, that being an atheist is an inherently rational perspective, and that attempting to build a civilized society without religion is a rational object.

This is not a theological work. The text contains no arguments for the existence of God and the supernatural, nor is it concerned with evolution, creationism, the age of Earth, or intelligent design. It contains no arguments from Scripture; in attacking the arguments, assertions, and conclusions of the New Atheists, my only weapons are the purely secular ones of reason, logic, and historically documented, independently verifiable fact. This is not a book about God, it is about those who seek to replace Him.

At first glance, it may seem crazy that a computer game designer, one whose only significant intellectual accomplishment of note is to have once convinced Michelle Malkin to skip an opportunity to promote herself, should dare to dispute an Oxford don, a respected university professor, a famous French philosopher, a highly regarded journalist, and an ecstasy-using dropout who is still working toward a graduate degree at forty...okay, perhaps that last one makes sense. As Gag Halfrunt is reliably reported to have said of the immortal Zaphod Beeblebrox, I'm just zis guy, ya know?

But don't be tempted by the logical fallacy of the Appeal To Authority; after all, in this age of academic specialization, an evolutionary biologist is less likely to be an expert on the historical causes of war and religious conflict than the average twelve-year-old wargamer, and even a professor in the field of cognitive studies may not have spent as much time contemplating the deeper mysteries of intelligence as a game designer who has seen many a sunrise while experimenting with the best way to make the monsters smarter.

So, I should like to encourage you to think of this book as an intellectual deathmatch, keep track of the frags, and see if I don't manage to exorcise the Unholy Trinity of Richard Dawkins, Sam Harris, and Christopher Hitchens once and for all.

I

A PRIDE
OF ATHEISTS

Vox Dei, as every philosopher knows, cannot be trusted in science.

—CHARLES DARWIN, "Organs of Extreme Perfection and Complication"

I DON'T CARE IF YOU GO TO HELL.

God does, assuming He exists, or He wouldn't have bothered sending His Son to save you from it. Jesus Christ does, too, if you'll accept for the sake of argument that he went to all the trouble of incarnating as a man, dying on the cross, and being resurrected from the dead in order to hand you a Get Out of Hell Free card.

Me, not so much. I don't know you. I don't owe you anything. While as a Christian I am called to share the Good News with you, I can't force you to accept it. Horse, water, drink, and all that.

So, it's all on you. Your soul is not my responsibility.

I am a Christian. I'm also a libertarian. I believe in free will and in allowing you to exercise it. I believe that our free will is a gift from our Creator and that He expects us to use it. I believe in living and letting live. If you'll leave me alone, I'll be delighted to do you the courtesy of leaving you alone in return. I have no inherent problem with atheists or agnostics, I have no problem with Muslims or Jews or Hindus or Pastafarians, and I have no problem with the crazies who believe that humanity is the result of ancient alien breeding experiments. To be honest, I rather like the crazies—their theories are usually the most entertaining of the lot. I believe what I believe, you believe what you believe, and there's no reason why we shouldn't both be perfectly cool with that.

Richard Dawkins, Sam Harris, and Christopher Hitchens are not so much cool with that.

I'm not asking you to respect my beliefs. Why should you? Maybe you think I'm insane because I believe that Jesus is coming back one of these days, but does my insanity actually affect you in any material way? Is my religious madness really all that much more out there than my faith that the Minnesota Vikings will win the Super Bowl someday? Talk about the substance of things hoped for...Vegas will give you better odds on J.C. this year. As for your beliefs, I really don't care if you want to question God's existence or criticize the Pope or deny the Holocaust or declare that Jesus was an architect previous to his career as a prophet. Every member of humanity is at least a little bit crazy in his own special way, some just happen to make it a little more obvious than others.

Vox's First Law: Any sufficiently advanced intelligence is indistinguishable from insanity.

All I ask, all the vast majority of the billions of people of faith on the planet ask, is to be left alone to believe what we choose to believe and live how we decide to live. But the Unholy Trinity have no intention of leaving me alone. Richard Dawkins accuses me of child abuse because I teach my children that God loves them even more than I do. Sam Harris declares that I should not be tolerated and suggests that it might be ethical to kill me in preemptive self-defense. Christopher Hitchens asserts that I am a form of human Drāno, poisoning everything I encounter. A fourth New Atheist, the philosopher Daniel Dennett, is less judgmental, but even he, bless his heart, wants to save me from myself.

And now we have a problem.

That's why I'm writing this book. I'm not trying to convince you that God exists. I'm not trying to convince you to accept Jesus Christ as your Lord and Savior. I'm not even trying to convince you that religious people aren't lunatics with low IQs who should be regarded with pity and contempt. But I am confident that I will convince you that this trio of New Atheists, this Unholy Trinity, are a collection of faux-intellectual frauds utilizing pseudo-scientific sleight of hand in order to falsely claim that religious faith is inherently dangerous and has no place in the modern world.

I am saying that they are wrong, they are reliably, verifiably, and factually incorrect. Richard Dawkins is wrong. Daniel C. Dennett is wrong. Christopher Hitchens is drunk, and he's wrong. Michel Onfray is French, and he's wrong. Sam Harris is so superlatively wrong that it will require the development of esoteric mathematics operating simultaneously in multiple dimensions to fully comprehend the orders of magnitude of his wrongness.

You make the call.

THE CHURCHES OF ATHEISM

The idea that he is a devotee of reason seeing through the outdated superstitions believed by less intelligent beings is the foremost conceit of the atheist. This heady notion was first made popular by French intellectuals and deistic ur-atheists such as Voltaire and Denis Diderot, who ushered in the so-called Age of Enlightenment. That they also paved the way for the murderous excesses of the French Revolution and dozens of other massacres in the name of human progress is usually considered an unfortunate coincidence by their philosophical descendants.

Atheism is not new. It predates Christianity by at least 400 years according to the account of the trial of Socrates recorded by Plato in his *Apology* back in 399 B.C.[1] While the Athenian philosopher denied the charge of disrespecting the gods of Olympus, the fact that both Socrates and his accuser Meletus recognized the concept of *atheos* and argued over whether it was an accurate description of Socrates' beliefs or not is sufficient proof that there were those who did not

---

[1] Spare me that B.C.E. BS. You would think historians, of all people, would have some respect for historical tradition.

believe in divine beings long before Richard Dawkins left the lab at Oxford and took up his cross to follow Darwin.

In his review of the history of atheism, French atheologist Michel Onfray dates its explicit inception to 1729 and a book published posthumously by the Abbé Jean Meslier, the parish priest of Étrépigny in northeastern France.[2] His *Memoir of the Thoughts and Feelings of Jean Meslier: Clear and Evident Demonstrations of the Vanity and Falsity of All the Religions of the World* is less interesting for its historical noteworthiness than for the way it shows how little atheism has changed over the last 278 years. Meslier is perpetually indignant, he denies miracles, free will, and the soul, asserts the superiority of atheist morality, and looks forward to the "happy and great revolution" to come when reason replaces religion. According to Onfray, he even calls for an "international communalism." It's really quite extraordinary.

Still, one may be excused for not being aware of atheism's historic intellectual lineage, considering the copious media coverage that has been devoted to the discovery of the three men *Wired* magazine breathlessly dubbed "the New Atheists," Richard Dawkins, Sam Harris, and Daniel Dennett. With the recent addition of Christopher Hitchens, the New Atheists are nearly as inescapable these days as they are incestuous;[3] here Dawkins is lionizing Harris's "wonderful little book," there he is favorably quoting Dennett favorably quoting himself, while the works of Dawkins and Dennett top Harris's list of recommended reading. Only Hitchens, ever the iconoclast, doesn't join the endless circle jerk, keeping his references to the others at a minimum and showing the good sense to be embarrassed by the two professors' insistence on calling themselves "brights."

These days atheism is, like the atheist's ultimate destination, hot indeed. Not since the 1920s, when the faux scientific writings of Freud and Marx were inspiring European intellectuals and artists, and the latter part of the 1960s when the American intellectual elite

---

[2] Onfray, Michel. *In Defence of Atheism: The Case Against Christianity, Judaism and Islam*. London: 2007. 29.

[3] Dawkins, Richard. *The God Delusion*. London: Houghton Mifflin, 2006. In a book largely dedicated to attacking Christianity and the Bible, Richard Dawkins refers to the Books of Matthew, Mark, Luke, and John a total of twelve times. He cites Mr. Harris and Professor Dennett twenty-two times, only twenty times more than the influential Christian intellectuals G. K. Chesterton and C. S. Lewis.

belatedly caught up, has there been so much enthusiasm about the nonexistence of God. This is somewhat bewildering, as no one appears to be nearly as excited about a similar absence of belief in unicorns, vampires, werewolves, astrology, nation-building, or the Labor Theory of Value. Nor is anyone dedicating much of their time to writing books and giving speeches at universities and conferences with the avowed goal of convincing others not to believe in them, either. On the other hand, unicorn fanciers don't possess a great deal of influence with either of the two American political parties, vampire enthusiasts don't commit honor killings,[4] and astrologers are seldom known to launch global holy wars based on the relative positions of Mars and Venus.

So perhaps it's not entirely unreasonable that those concerned with the collective clout of the billions of individuals who believe in the spiritual sovereignty of a formerly deceased Jewish carpenter should seek to reduce that influence by undermining those beliefs. It is certainly in keeping with the best practices of Western intellectual debate; Adam Smith similarly attacked the French physiocrats by pointing out the divergence between their theoretical system and the way in which the various national economies had been observed to operate.[5]

However, it is not only nature that abhors a vacuum. The human intellect is not well-suited to stop believing in one thing without replacing that belief, nor is it comfortable for an individual to drop his self-identification without selecting an alternative. While the New Atheists express some faint hope of converting the religious faithful into disbelievers, this is not the primary focus of their works. Dawkins and Dennett both express a degree of skepticism that theists will ever start reading their books, let alone find the courage to finish them. The atheist evangelism of *The God Delusion*, *The End of Faith*, and *god is not Great* is directed at the irreligious reader; for all that *Letter to a Christian Nation* is nominally aimed at Christian readers,

---

[4] They do, however, commit rather more murders than one might suspect. And rather nasty ones, too.

[5] "*The great body of the party are commonly intoxicated with the imaginary beauty of this ideal system, of which they have no experience, but which has been represented to them in all the most dazzling colours in which the eloquence of their leaders could paint it.*" Smith, Adam. *The Theory of Moral Sentiments* (Oxford, 1976 ed.), 232.

the Sunday School theology it contains makes it clear that it is actually written for the benefit of atheists whose lack of faith is weak. New Atheism is a militantly fundamentalist call to arms intended to wake up the wavering, it is a godless jihad waged under a scarlet flag[6] with a cry of *Deus n'existe pas.*

But negation serves poorly for inspiration, so simply making the negative case against religion is not enough. To convert the godless into raging, red-letter infidels, the New Atheists attempt to make a positive case for something that goes well beyond not being something else. Not even the most ardent non-stamp collector is likely to take much action involving his hobby of not collecting stamps, after all. So, is there more to atheism than the simple meaning of the word, which literally means "without the belief in the existence of a god or gods"? The concept appears simple enough. A-Theism. Without theism. As Brent Rasmussen, an atheist who writes at Unscrewing the Inscrutable, describes it:

> Atheism describes a person in which god belief is absent. That's all. Nothing more. Black or white. On or off. There or not there.

This is a perfectly reasonable definition in theory, but in practice it's not quite that simple. As bizarre as it may sound, researchers have learned that nearly half of those who describe themselves as atheist or agnostic nevertheless believe in life after death as well as in Heaven and Hell, beliefs that have historically been considered to be a fairly strong indication of theism. The Christian pollster George Barna somewhat sardonically notes that given this apparent lack of consistency about their stated beliefs on the part of those questioned (this was far from the only serious contradiction revealed by the polling), the significance of the labels with which individuals identify themselves may not be as relevant as is ordinarily assumed.[7]

Barna's skepticism regarding self-identification appears to be justified, for it turns out that there are not only atheists who believe they will go to Heaven, there are also those who lack god belief but who

---

[6] The scarlet A is the symbol of Richard Dawkins's OUT campaign. It's like the Campus Crusade for Cthulhu, only sillier.

[7] "Americans Describe Their Views About Life After Death." The Barna Group. 21 Oct. 2003.

do not describe themselves as atheists. In fact, if one did not turn a jaundiced eye upon the presumed accuracy of religious self-identification, it would be very difficult to account for the large discrepancy between the number of self-identified atheists and the much larger group of people who keep turning up in polls under the group described as "no religion." Now, there are three ways to interpret these two data points: (1) there is a substantive difference between being an atheist and not being religious, (2) many people without religion still cling to a belief in God, or (3) there are a large number of individuals who simply don't know what to call themselves.

Given the large number of American voters, 26 percent in the 2004 election,[8] who cannot figure out if they are Democrats or Republicans even after making a selection between the two parties, Occam's Razor suggests that the third explanation is the one most likely to be correct. Richard Dawkins would surely concur, as one of the stated purposes of his book is to encourage those who are not avowed atheists to come forward and publicly identify themselves as such.[9] But this is likely to be a vain endeavor. Since the normal individual tends to put significantly more time into living his life instead of thinking about it and cataloging its abstract aspects, one can hardly expect him to devote the time and effort required to assemble an internally consistent belief system that is labeled correctly according to objective definitions approved by intellectuals.

The New Atheists themselves are of little help. They, too, muddy the water as they thrash about in their various denials of God. Richard Dawkins begins reasonably enough by suggesting that one's theistic tendencies may be viewed on a gradient of seven degrees, ranging from complete certainty in the existence of God to complete certainty in His nonexistence. However, he promptly disappoints the reader by rating himself a six, or an agnostic who believes there is a very low probability of God's existence. But how could this be? Why, it's as if the Archbishop of Canterbury were to declare that all Christians should doubt the existence of God![10]

---

[8] According to the 2004 CNN exit polls.

[9] "*The reason so many people don't notice atheists is that many of us are reluctant to 'come out.'*" Dawkins, *The God Delusion*, 4.

[10] Williams, Rowan. "Of Course This Makes Us Doubt God's Existence." Telegraph. 2 Jan. 2005.

While Richard Dawkins's confession of *de facto* weak atheism in the place of *de jure* strong atheism is a little surprising, coming as it does in a section entitled "The Poverty of Agnosticism," Dawkins's expressed doubt that there are many who would qualify for the perfect seven of the strong atheist is even more eyebrow-raising. This hedging, although commendable for its honesty, is in marked disharmony with the cocksure tone of *The God Delusion*, and indeed, Dawkins's public persona as the great evangelist of atheist pride.

Daniel Dennett's take on the matter is a simpler one, although his call for the need to conduct a proper scientific inquiry into various matters of faith does not amount to making a serious case against religion so much as it lays a structural foundation for someone else to begin assembling the information required for one. As for the alternative, Dennett is content to note that atheism is the negation of theism; he cannot be bothered to either delve into definitions or construct much of a positive argument for non-belief. Despite his complaint about the way in which debates about God "tend to take place in a pious fog of indeterminate boundaries," Dennett leaves it unclear whether his refusal to believe in lesser supernatural forces such as witches, Santa Claus, and Wonder Woman should properly be considered an aspect of his atheism or merely an adjunct to it.

The reader might well question any need for this distinction based on the assumption that atheists reject not only God, but all aspects of the supernatural as well, were it not for Sam Harris. While Harris rejects all gods and the entire concept of faith itself on the one hand, he embraces "spiritual possibilities" and harbors a personal dedication to the esoteric teachings of the Buddhist[11] faith on the other. One might assume that this would disqualify the man as an atheist even by his own lights, but Harris adroitly evades the apparent dichotomy by redefining Buddhism as a non-religion of faith, its many faithful adherents who believe otherwise notwithstanding.[12] This is a rather

---

[11] "*I have been very hard on religions of faith—Judaism, Christianity, Islam, and even Hindusim—and have not said much that is derogatory of Buddhism. This is not an accident. While Buddhism has also been a source of ignorance and occasional violence, it is not a religion of faith, or a religion at all, in the Western sense. There are millions of Buddhists who do not seem to know this. . . .*" Harris, Sam. *The End of Faith*. New York: W. W. Norton and Company, 2004. 293. I'm sure those millions of Buddhists must be deeply appreciative of a Jewish-American atheist informing them that their 2,500-year-old religion is not a religion at all.

[12] Harris's attempt to redefine Buddhism as a non-religion is also in conflict with Dennett's definition

neat trick, if more than a little intellectually shabby, and one wonders if the entire conflict between the New Atheists and the religious
folks who fill them with such fear could not be brought to a peaceful end by a similar redefinition of Judaism, Christianity, Islam, and
even Hinduism. After all, there is surely a higher percentage of Jews
who don't believe in a literal God of Abraham than Mahayana Buddhists who lack faith in the divine ability of the Amitabha Buddha
to aid them in their souls' journey to Sukhāvatī. However, the ongoing travails of the circus formerly known as the Episcopalian church
strongly suggest that redefining religion as a social club is unlikely to
prove a viable strategy in the long run.

Harris's own version of atheism conveniently encompasses his unusual beliefs, as he asserts that an atheist is nothing more than a
person who has read the Jewish, Christian, and Islamic scriptures,
considered the claims that they were written by an omniscient deity,
and found them to be ridiculous.[13] Happily for Harris, this leaves the
door open for atheists to devote themselves to beliefs culled from sacred texts such as the *Bhagavad Gita*, the Amitāyurdhyāna Sūtra, or
the Tibetan Book of the Dead while remaining godless in good standing. It seems as long as the atheist is only expanding his consciousness, transcendental meditation is laudable, although one assumes
the exercise must be stopped at once should any thought of salvation, celestial Buddhas, or reaching the Pure Land happen to enter
the mind of the meditator.

However, Harris offers a very different definition of atheism in his
Letter to a Christian Nation. Two different definitions, actually:

> *An atheist is simply a person who believes that the 260 million Americans*
> *(87 percent of the population) claiming to "never doubt the existence of*
> *God" should be obliged to present evidence for his existence—and indeed,*
> *for his benevolence, given the relentless destruction of human beings we*
> *witness in the world each day. An atheist is a person who believes that the*
> *murder of a single little girl—even once in a million years—casts doubt*
> *upon the idea of a benevolent God.*[14]

of religion: *"social systems whose participants avow belief in a supernatural agent or agents...."*

[13] Harris, Sam. "10 Myths—and 10 Truths—About Atheism." *The Los Angeles Times*. 24 Dec.
2006.

[14] Harris, Sam. *Letter to a Christian Nation*. New York: Knopf, 2006. 51. I note that by Harris's

The evidence also suggests that an atheist is not a person who subscribes to the concepts of consistency or precision, at least not if his name is Sam Harris. One wonders where these 260 million Americans will be expected to present their evidence, and to whom, especially in a democracy where 87 percent of the population presumably have some say in what they are obliged to do. But these mysteries notwithstanding, it should be obvious that even among the New Atheists, the nature of atheism varies somewhat depending upon the imagination of the individual infidel. And although atheism is neither a religion nor a philosophy in its own right, the attentive observer will notice that atheists can nevertheless be divided into a variety of "churches," each distinct from the other and yet as internally uniform and readily identifiable as any Christian denomination or Islamic sect.

THE HIGH CHURCH ATHEISTS

The middle-aged man enters the room at the top of the hour. He wears a sports coat with corduroy patches on the elbow. Beneath the sports coat are an open-collared shirt and a pair of faded jeans. His ponytail is streaked with gray and accentuates his receding hairline. The faint scent of bean curds on his breath hint at his vegetarian diet.

The room is crowded and takes little notice of his entrance. The middle-aged man takes his place at the front of the room. He will wait for the crowd to fall silent. A couple in the back row are talking about where they will go to the movies that night. The girl has decided she would like to go to see the new Nicole Kidman film, but her boyfriend worries that there will not be enough mindless violence for him to enjoy it. The students finally notice the middle-aged man standing behind the lectern. The professor smiles. Turning his back, he begins to sketch the outline of a forty-five-minute diatribe on the chalkboard, which, among other things, will touch on the wonders of socialized medicine in Holland, homophobic semiotics in modern American cinema, and the squamous evil of the Fox News channel. Despite the fact that this is supposed to be an English class, none of it has anything to

---

logic, the Archbishop of Canterbury is an atheist. Of course, given the current state of the Anglican church, it's entirely possible that Harris is correct.

do with the plays of William Shakespeare.

The middle-aged man's students quickly discern that their grades will depend upon telling him what he wants to hear. Although saddened to have lost an opportunity to learn anything about the classic English literary canon to which the course is nominally devoted, they feel a tremendous delight at the inflated grades he distributes. The man's professional peers envy his tenure, although they don't approve of the way he often spends his evenings with a sensitive gay studies major prone to wearing black fingernail polish.

These are the facts. This is all we know for certain about the middle-aged man. Is there anything else we can infer about him on the basis of his behavior? Was he good at sports? Is he left-handed or right-handed? Can he juggle? His actions leave no clue at all. Does he enjoy jigsaw puzzles? His behavior is simply mute on questions of this sort and hundreds like them. Why is it so easy, then, so trivially easy—you-could-almost-bet-your-life-on-it easy—to guess the middle-aged man's religion, or rather, his lack thereof?[15]

The fact is that a professor at an elite university is as likely to be an atheist as a suicide bomber is to be Muslim;[16] a 2006 paper by Neil Gross of Harvard and Solon Simmons of George Mason University reported that 72.9 percent of the professors they polled described the Bible as "an ancient book of fables, legends, history, and moral precepts," compared to 17.5 percent of the general population. In the same paper, 34 percent of all university professors described themselves as "not religious" and 31.2 percent specified "none" when asked about their current religious preference.

As any self-professed "bright" will be more than happy to inform you, those who call themselves atheists tend to be more intelligent, better educated, and wealthier than the norm, assuming that one equates education with pieces of paper collected from paper-selling institutions.[17] It is no coincidence, then, that the New Atheist triumvirate

---

[15] There's mediocre prose, there's bad prose, and then there's Sam Harris waxing creative. How he didn't win a Bulwer-Lytton award for that ghastly first page of *The End of Faith*, I'll never know. When he's not being self-consciously literate, his writing is all right, but light a candle to St. Darwin and pray that he never decides to inflict a novel on humanity.

[16] Until very recently, two-thirds of all historical suicide bombings had been perpetrated by the Tamil Tigers. Harris, unsurprisingly, declares this secular Marxist group to be religious despite their direct statements to the contrary. So, Buddhism ≠ religion, but secular Marxism=religion. Got it?

[17] As I shall demonstrate in the following chapters, an impressive academic pedigree does not nec-

should be comprised of two university professors and a third fellow working toward his doctoral degree.

Intelligence, education, and high incomes are not the only marks of the High Church Atheists. They are also extremely law-abiding, as there were only 122 atheists, two-tenths of 1 percent of the 65,256 prison population, being held in English and Welsh jails in 2000. They tend to lean politically left, often possess a marked interest in the sciences, and are overwhelmingly confident that the various fine-tunings of Darwin's theory of evolution over the years suffice to explain the origins of Man as well as a whole host of other mysteries.

And that's not all! Sam Harris is kind enough to inform us that self-professing atheists are not arrogant, dogmatic, lacking in a basis for morality, closed to spiritual experience, or responsible for the greatest crimes in human history.[18] American Atheists, a political organization set up to protect the civil rights of atheists, chimes in with alarming cheerfulness in its declaration that atheists are also "POSITIVE! . . . ECLECTIC! . . . INNER-DIRECTED! . . . INDEPENDENT! . . . HAPPY!"[19]

They certainly enjoy exclamation points, anyhow. But not every shared trait of the High Church atheist is quite as superlatively wonderful as atheists might have one believe. For example, fresh from a visit to England for an inspiring sermon from the High Church's own Archbishop of Oxford, Wired magazine writer Gary Wolf found himself noting that atheists are almost always enthusiastic, defiant men who "enjoy pissing people off."[20] Another Dawkins interviewer reached a similar conclusion: "I agree with virtually everything he says, but find myself wanting to smack him for his intolerance."

This is not unusual, as the High Church atheist's undeveloped social skills are often so dramatic as to be reasonably described as a form of social autism. The atheist tends to regard every statement

---

essarily indicate the possession of a decent education in the liberal arts and sciences, or even a basic ability to examine the available evidence and reach a rational conclusion.

[18] Harris, Sam. "10 Myths—and 10 Truths—About Atheism." It seems Harris is under the impression that Mao was a Methodist, Stalin an Evangelical Lutheran, and Pol Pot a secret 7th Day Adventist.

[19] http://www.atheists.org/visitors.center/intro.html.

[20] Wolf, Gary. "The Church of the Non-Believers:" Wired magazine, Nov. 2004. This explains Dawkins, Harris, and Hitchens, anyhow, as well as the complete absence of female writers addressing the subject.

with which he disagrees in much the same manner that a bull views a matador's red flag, viewing even the most cherished myths held by his friends and family as little more than imperative targets of opportunity. It is no wonder that the 2001 American Religious Identification Survey reported that atheists are one-third as likely to be married as the average American; these are the sort of men who believe that boring a woman with lengthy explanations of why her opinions are incorrect is the best way to her heart.

There is even evidence to suggest that in some cases, High Church atheism may be little more than a mental disorder taking the form of a literal autism. On one of the more popular atheist Internet sites, the average self-reported result on an Asperger Quotient test was 27.9.[21] The threshold for this syndrome, described as "autistic psychopathy" by its discoverer, Dr. Hans Asperger, is 32, whereas the average normal individual scores 16.5. In light of Wolf's observations, it is interesting to note that those diagnosed with Asperger's tend to be male, intelligent, impaired in social interaction, and prone to narrow, intense interests.

This idea may explain why the following pair of definitions have proven to be useful in distinguishing between the High Church atheist and the agnostic.

AGNOSTIC: I don't believe there is a God. Because I haven't seen the evidence.

ATHEIST: There is no God. Because I'm an asshole.

THE LOW CHURCH ATHEISTS

After the Protestant Reformation fractured Christendom, the various Christian churches were deeply divided as to the proper way to worship the Lord Jesus Christ. Because the Reformed Church, better known to us today as the Puritans, rejected the Catholic Church's

---

[21] "I'm mostly normal!" Pharyngula. http://scienceblogs.com/pharyngula/2007/08/im_mostly_normal.php#comments. 1 Aug. 2007. Fifty-nine readers volunteered their results on the AQ test; the average did not include several individuals who mentioned having been medically diagnosed with the syndrome but did not take the test. Obviously, an amount of scientific research would need to be done in order to establish any causal relationship between Asperger Syndrome and atheism, but it is an interesting hypothesis since a similar poll of 165 readers at my blog, Vox Popoli, revealed an average score of nineteen for theists and twenty for agnostics.

priestly model of worship, it saw no need for the liturgies, vestments, and ceremonial trappings that had become an integral part of Catholic ceremony over the centuries.[22] Churches that retain these formal elements, such as the Roman Catholic Church, the Church of England, and the Church of Sweden, are today known as High Church, while Puritans, televangelists, snake-handlers, Billy Graham crusaders in football stadiums, Jesus freaks, and Southern Baptists can all be described as Low Church.

And just as an Anglican bishop in his beautiful vestments has a tendency to look somewhat askance on the crazy evangelicals who open up their services with giant black singers backed by electric guitars and the preacher on the drums,[23] the High Church atheist isn't particularly keen on being lumped in with his godless brethren of the Low Church.

The contradictory relationship between the High and Low Churches of atheism can perhaps be best understood by looking at the makeup of the American Democratic Party. While Democrats are heavily favored by highly educated individuals[24] of the sort described at the beginning of the previous section, the party's support from society's least-educated individuals is not only every bit as strong, but is more electorally important. Voters with postgraduate schooling were only 25 percent more likely to vote for the Democratic Party presidential candidate in 2004;[25] while those who did not complete high school were 90 percent more likely to identify themselves as Democrats.[26] Since there are 75 percent

---

[22] This rejection of Popish vanity can in some ways be seen as a revival of the ascetic poverty doctrine of the Fraticelli, a broad label describing several groups of monks linked with the Franciscan order who were chiefly united in their harsh criticism of the Catholic Church, its corruption, and its wealth from the late thirteenth century until the middle of the fifteenth century. The more literarily inclined may recall that these "brothers of the poor life" played a significant role in a certain Umberto Eco novel.

[23] I was signed to both Wax Trax! and TVT Records at the end of their industrial heyday and only once have I ever seen a band rock harder than the Woodland Hills Church worship team in the late '90s. Norm, Greg, Tim, Slick, I miss you, guys!

[24] *"Of the 17 states (including D.C.) with an above average percentage of citizens with advanced degrees, 13 (76.5%) voted for Kerry. Of the 34 states with a below average percentage of citizens with advanced degrees, 27 (79.4%) voted for Bush."* About.com: "Educational Attainment and 2004 Vote." Attempting to characterize individual behavior by statewide statistics is a bizarre way to go about it, the only significant information here is the fact that according to the U.S. Census Bureau, the percent of the U.S. population holding advanced degrees in 2003 was 9.4 percent.

[25] *Kerry 55 percent, Bush 44 percent.* CNN Election 2004. http://www.cnn.com/ELECTION/2004/pages/results/states/US/P/00/epolls.0.html.

[26] *Republican 21 percent, Democrat 40 percent.* TRENDS 2005 The American Public: Opinions and

more Americans who have never completed high school (16.4 percent of adults over twenty-five) than who possess an advanced degree (9.4 percent) this means that despite their reputation for being the party of the most highly educated, Democrats are nevertheless more than twice as likely to be someone who has dropped out of high school than to be an individual with a master's degree.[27]

So while it's perfectly true to say that the Democratic Party is the party of the intelligent and the educated, such a statement doesn't tell the whole story and is more than a little misleading. The same is true of atheists.

The most easily identifiable factor separating Low Church atheists from their High Church brethren is neither educational nor liturgical, but eponymical. They simply don't describe themselves as atheists. Instead, they show up on various religious surveys as "no religion" or occasionally "secular."[28] Their beliefs are distinctly recognizable as atheistic, as they don't believe in God, they don't attend religious services, they don't believe in the supernatural, and they don't belong to religious organizations, but a failure to openly embrace an atheist identity is not the only significant distinction of the Low Church atheist.

I previously referenced the number of atheists being held by the prison system of England and Wales, where it is customary to record the religion of the prison population as part of the Inmate Information System. In the year 2000, there were 38,531 Christians of twenty-one different varieties imprisoned for their crimes, compared to only 122 atheists and sixty-two agnostics. As Europe in general and the United Kingdom in particular have become increasingly post-Christian, this would appear to be a damning piece of evidence proving the fundamentally criminal nature of theists while demonstrating that atheists are indeed more moral despite their lack of a sky god holding them to account.[29]

Values in a 51%–41% Nation.

[27] Note: I didn't vote for Bush or Kerry. I'm a libertarian, so I had no dog in that hunt.

[28] I am not describing those who call themselves agnostics here, as in most of the various surveys and polls, they tend to either be lumped in with atheists or as part of a separate "don't know" category.

[29] There are some silly bits of information floating around the Internet claiming to prove that Christians are fifty times more likely to go to prison than atheists. Of course, by cherry-picking this data, one could claim that English and Welsh Christians are 315 times more likely to go to prison

However, there also happened to be another 20,639 prisoners, 31.6 percent of the total prison population, who possessed "no religion." And this was not simply a case of people falling through the cracks or refusing to provide an answer; the Inmate Information System is specific enough to distinguish between Druids, Scientologists, and Zoroastrians as well as between the Celestial Church of God, the Welsh Independent church, and the Non-Conformist church. It also features separate categories for "other Christian religion," "other non-Christian religion," and "not known."

At only two-tenths of a percent of the prison population, High Church atheists are, as previously suggested, extremely law-abiding. But when one compares the 31.6 percent of imprisoned no-religionists to the 15.1 percent of Britons who checked "none" or wrote in Jedi Knight, agnostic, atheist, or heathen in the 2001 national survey, it becomes clear that their Low Church counterparts are nearly four times more likely to be convicted and jailed for committing a crime than a Christian.[30]

Studies have shown that those without religion have life expectancies seven years shorter than the average churchgoer,[31] are more likely to smoke, abuse alcohol, and be depressed or obese,[32] and they are much less likely to marry or have children. Their criminal proclivities strongly suggest that they are less intelligent on average than theists and High Church atheists alike, and they also outnumber their High Church counterparts by a significant margin, as the following table of various polls demonstrates:

---

than atheists and be superficially correct. One would have to be an intellectually dishonest ass to do so, though.

[30] 3.84 times more likely, to be precise. Census, April 2001, Office for National Statistics. While Christians account for 39.1 percent of the English and Welsh prison population, they make up 71.8 percent of the total population.

[31] "*Religious attendance is associated with U.S. adult mortality in a graded fashion: People who never attend exhibit 1.87 times the risk of death in the follow-up period compared with people who attend more than once a week.*" Hummer R., Rogers R., Nam C., Ellison C. G. "Religious Involvement and U.S. Adult Mortality:" Population Research Center, University of Texas at Austin. 1999.

[32] Although it seems that Baptist women who read Left Behind novels but don't go to church regularly are the most at risk for excess poundage. Krista M. C. Cline and Kenneth F. Ferraro, "Does Religion Increase the Prevalence and Incidence of Obesity in Adulthood?" *Journal for the Scientific Study of Religion* 2 (2006): 269.

Atheist	Agnostic	No Religion	Source	Scale	Year
2.9%	—	11.9%	Encyclopedia Brittanica	Global	2005
2.4%	—	12.5%	CIA World Factbook	Global	2004
0.4%	0.5%	13.2%	American Religious Identification Survey	U.S.A.	2001
10.4%	—	6.3%	What the World Thinks of God (BBC)[33]	U.K.	2004
—	—	18.0%	Eurobarometer[34]	E.U.	2005
32.0%	32.0%	—	Financial Times/Harris[35]	France	2006
—	—	11.7%	Federal Census[36]	Switzerland	2000

Data about religious beliefs are notoriously difficult to obtain with any degree of accuracy and can be complicated by government policies that dictate either an official religion or an official lack of religion, but the more polls one examines, the more a pattern becomes discernible. In most countries, the number of High Church atheists is similar to the number of self-declared agnostics, and the total of the two combined is but a small fraction of the number of Low Church atheists.

One interesting aspect of the European Union poll was its question about how often an individual thinks about the meaning and purpose of life. Those who don't believe in a god or life force were 27 percent less likely to say that they spent any time thinking about such things than those who do, which tends to support the idea that Low Church atheists are Low Church precisely because they are less interested in dwelling on their disbelief and its implications than High Church atheists, who seldom appear to be interested in anything else.

---

[33] This is a good example of the difference between High Church atheists and Low Church ones. High Church atheists would be very excited about a BBC show on God, Low Church atheists would rather watch *Eastenders*.

[34] Unfortunately, the question in the Science, Technology, and Social Values section wasn't very specific, as the individuals polled were offered three choices between (1) belief in God, (2) belief in some sort of spirit or life force, or (3) don't believe in any god, spirit, or life force.

[35] It is France, not any of the Scandinavian countries, that reliably shows up in various polls as the most atheistic country in the West, but there is good reason to be skeptical of the Harris poll numbers because the numbers of non-believers reported in it are between three and ten times higher than the number reported in other polls of the same countries. To give one example, the 64 percent sum of reported atheists and agnostics is almost twice as high as the number of French respondents answering that they did not believe in a god or life force in the Eurobarometer poll.

[36] This figure was confirmed by the 1998 Schweizer Arbeitsmarktsurvey which found 11.5 percent of the working population did not belong to a church or religious group.

AGNOSTICS: THE UNITARIANS OF ATHEISM

I once attended a friend's pagan wedding in a Unitarian church. It was both creepy and disappointing. I would have felt much more comfortable if we'd all stripped naked, painted our butts blue, and danced around a burning tree or something instead of sitting through what felt like a straight-faced parody of a Christian ceremony. Listening to the pastor appealing to our collective love for the couple to bless their union was like a religious stroll through the Valley of the Uncanny, wherein the very similarity between the imitation and the real thing is the cause of the creep factor.

Unitarianism offers religion without faith. In a similar manner, Agnosticism offers disbelief without arrogance. Whereas the atheist is always in the impossible position of trying to prove a negative, the agnostic is content to relax, kick back, and wait for others to demonstrate the proof of their assertions. And while agnostics have many things in common with High Church atheists, sharing both their disbelief in God and the supernatural as well as many of their secondary traits, it is nearly impossible to confuse the two types of nonbelievers.

The most obvious difference is that agnostics are not at war with anyone, whereas atheists are prone to aggressively attacking just about everyone, including agnostics. Sam Harris accuses them of not being intellectually honest,[37] while Richard Dawkins considers their views to be fence-sitting PAP, an acronym of his creation that stands for Permanent Agnosticism on Principle that also happens to be a word meaning "to lack substance." (How astonishingly witty!) Hitchens takes a more ecumenical approach to non-belief, viewing atheists, agnostics, and freethinkers all as one big faithless family, while Dennett is similarly open to allowing agnostics to join him and his fellow atheists in dubbing themselves "brights," should they be so inclined.

Since one of the primary factors distinguishing agnostics from atheists is their disinclination to go out of their way to annoy people, it's hardly a surprise that very few, if any, agnostics have taken the professor up on his gracious offer.

---

[37] http://www.truthdig.com/interview/item/20060403_sam_harris_interview/.

Agnosticism is actually a perfectly reasonable position, arguably the most reasonable position an individual can hold regarding things that cannot possibly be known with utter certainty by anyone at this point in the space-time continuum. Most atheists would be more accurately described as agnostics with personality problems, for as philosotainer Scott Adams points out on his Dilbert Blog, a "weak atheist" is simply an ideological label for literal agnostics who want to stake out an anti-religious position despite their admission of uncertainty regarding God's existence. The fact that even the world's leading atheist confesses an inability to take a "strong atheist" position tends to support Adams's conclusion.

I rather like self-identified agnostics. A conversation with an agnostic seldom causes anyone to get bent out of shape, and it's almost impossible to imagine an agnostic regime fighting over Holy Lands, interfering with people's lives, or slaughtering great quantities of people in order to destroy an existing society in an effort to create a utopian new one. No doubt it's annoying to the New Atheists that so many avowedly godless individuals should roll their eyes at atheist histrionics and decline to sign up for any angry anti-theist jihads, but really, there are far worse creeds to live by than shrug and let live.

The problem for agnostics is that the High Church unholy warriors tend to live by the reverse of the old Arab proverb. Agnostics, despite their skepticism, are quite willing to be on friendly terms with everyone, but for the militant atheist, the friend of his enemy is his enemy too. Atheists find the easy tolerance of the agnostic intolerable; to paraphrase Sam Harris, certainty about the absence of the next life is simply incompatible with tolerance in this one.

This is why agnostics so often regard theists with puzzled bemusement while viewing their godless cousins, with whom they superficially appear to have far more in common, with a mix of embarrassment and unadulterated horror.

THE APOCALYPTIC TECHNO-HERETICS

The award-winning[38] science fiction writer Bruce Bethke has a pet theory that science fiction, especially disaster-oriented hard science fiction, primarily exists to provide a mechanism for writing end-of-the-world stories sans theology. "Left Behind for atheists," he calls it, pointing to Greg Bear's deity-free apocalyptic novel *Forge of God* as being but one of many examples.

It sounds crazy, but then, it would be a mistake to discount the guy responsible for coining the term "cyberpunk," because we are reliably informed that the world will end in neither ice nor fire, but in an explosion of processing power.

Thus sayeth the prophet of the Singularity, science fiction novelist Vernor Vinge, who has been predicting that superintelligent computers will surpass human intelligence, become self-aware, and begin designing their even more intelligent successors since 1993, when he published his famous essay "The Coming Technological Singularity: How to Survive in the Post-Human Era." And while the Singularity sounds suspiciously like the plot line of the Terminator movies, it's actually based upon an application of Moore's Law, which states that the number of transistors on an integrated circuit doubles every two years.

Because increased transistor counts translate directly into processing power measured in millions of instructions per second, this means that more transistors means smarter computers. The Intel 4004 had only 2300 transistors executing 0.06 MIPS in 1971, while the Intel Core 2 Duo processor in the laptop with which I am now typing these words possesses 291 million transistors executing 21,418 MIPS. Exactly how many MIPS are required before a machine will awaken and become self-conscious remains unknown, but in his essay, Vinge wrote that he expected it would happen before 2030, if it happened at all.

Ray Kurzweil, on the other hand, gives humanity until 2035.

Ken MacLeod, a Scottish science fiction author, describes the Singularity as "the Rapture for nerds" and in the same way Christians

---

[38] Mr. Bethke won the Phillip K. Dick award for distinguished science fiction published in paperback original form in the United States in 1995. He would really appreciate it if you would avoid making the obvious pun.

are divided into preterist, premillennialist, and postmillennialist camps regarding the timing of the *Parousia*,[39] Apocalyptic Techno-Heretics can be divided into three sects, renunciationist, apotheosan, and posthumanist. Whereas renunciationists foresee a dark future wherein humanity is enslaved or even eliminated by its machine masters and await the Singularity with the same sort of resignation that Christians who don't buy into Rapture doctrine anticipate the Tribulation and the Antichrist, apotheosans anticipate a happy and peaceful amalgamation into a glorious, godlike hive mind of the sort envisioned by Isaac Asimov in his Foundation novels. Posthumanists, meanwhile, envision a detente between Man and Machine, wherein artificial intelligence will be wedded to intelligence amplification and other forms of technobiological modification to transform humanity and allow it to survive and perhaps even thrive in the Posthuman Era.[40]

Although it is rooted entirely in science and technology,[41] there are some undeniable religious parallels between the more optimistic visions of the Singularity and conventional religious faith. Not only is there a strong orthogenetic element inherent in the concept itself, but the transhuman dream of achieving immortality through uploading one's consciousness into machine storage and interacting with the world through electronic avatars sounds suspiciously like shedding one's physical body in order to walk the streets of gold with a halo and a harp.

Furthermore, the predictions of when this watershed event is expected to occur rather remind one of Sir Isaac Newton's tireless attempts to determine the precise date of the Eschaton, which he finally concluded would take place sometime after 2065, only thirty years after Kurzweil expects the Singularity.

So, if they're both correct, at least Mankind can console itself that the Machine Age will be a short one.

---

[39] Or the Second Coming of Jesus Christ, if you prefer. Preterists think he came back already in 70 A.D., premillennialists believe he's coming after the Tribulation ends to establish his 1,000-year reign, and postmillennialists believe that he will come back after the forces of evil have already been vanquished and the Kingdom of God has been established gradually over time.

[40] *Accelerando* by Charles Stross and the Culture novels of Iain M. Banks are excellent novels and possibly the best explications of the posthuman possibilities. If the Singularity ever actually takes place, blame Scotland.

[41] And, one can't help but suspect, a certain amount of chemical inspiration.

THE ATHEIST CREED

In 325 A.D., Christian leaders found it necessary to convene a council at Nicaea in order to provide all Christendom with an ecumenical statement of Christian faith. Amazingly, they were successful, for despite the subsequent splintering of Christianity into hundreds, if not thousands, of churches and denominations, each with their own idosyncratic customs and exotic dogmas, the Nicene Creed still serves very well to distinguish the Christian from the not-Christian.

Atheism has no such creed but it could certainly use one. Given the variety of atheisms already mentioned, we need one to serve as a legitimate and reasonable basis for discussing atheism throughout the course of this book. Fortunately, American Atheists has provided a clear and unambiguous statement that ecumenically encompasses the various core beliefs of the vast majority of atheists, High Church, Low Church, and Heretic alike, which I have taken the liberty of having translated into Latin in order to give it the proper magisterial grandeur.

> *Praeter res naturales, nihil exstat.*
> *Cogitatio est proprietas materiae.*
> *Singula animalia omninoque irrevocabiliter mors terminat.*
> *Sunt nullae vires, nullae res, nulla entia, quae distant natura,*
>   *vel extra naturam sunt.*
> *Sunt nullae vires, nullae res, nulla entia, quae natura superant.*
> *Sunt nullae vires, nullae res, nulla entia, quae supra naturam sunt.*
> *Nec fieri possunt.*[42]

As the creed indicates, atheism of all variants requires a focus on material phenomena. High Church atheists, agnostics, and apocalyptics tend to enjoy contemplating some of the more esoteric manifestations, while Low Church atheists are inclined to focus on quotidian ones such as cars, clothes, and the stereo system next door. But because the New Atheists are uniformly High Church, their anti-theistic arguments are invariably intertwined with Man's primary method for comprehending and utilizing material phenomena, which is to say, science.

---

[42] *"Nothing exists but natural phenomena. Thought is a property or function of matter. Death irreversibly and totally terminates individual organic units. There are no forces, phenomena, or entities which exist outside of or apart from physical nature. There are no forces, phenomena, or entities which transcend nature. There are no forces, phenomena, or entities which are supernatural. Nor can there be."*

II

DEFINING SCIENCE

Where there is shouting there is no true science.

—LEONARDO DA VINCI

IN THE SUMMER OF 1992, my band was scheduled to play on the second stage at the Chicago Lollapalooza, one slot ahead of Temple of the Dog. As it turned out, we never ended up taking the stage thanks to our singer who stayed at a different hotel, managed to get lost, and didn't show up until the end of the day. But the afternoon was far from a complete loss, as we spent a happy afternoon underneath a blazing hot sun, drinking, shaking the girl tree, and watching the Jesus and Mary Chain, Pearl Jam, and Soundgarden warm up the crowd for the apocalyptic show that Ministry put on at sunset.

What I remember most about that summer day wasn't the Red Hot Chili Peppers or any of the big-name bands, it was the Jim Rose Circus Sideshow. It wasn't any of the painful feats performed by the Torture King or the Amazing Mr. Lifto that burned their way into my brain, either, but Jim Rose enthusiastically bellowing "It is science!"

every time cinder blocks were attached to nipples or broken glass was devoured. "It is science!"

But torture, even public self-torture, is not generally considered to be genuine science, no matter how entertaining its observers might find it to be. The National Academy of Sciences does not recognize torture as one of its thirty-one disciplinary sections and its practitioners have not historically been admitted as members, at least not on that sole basis. Nor can every act performed by a genuine scientist be legitimately described as science; if the bear's proverbial actions in the woods are not classified as science, the scientist's should not be, either.[1]

This is a book about religion and atheism, not science. But it is impossible to entirely separate atheism from science, because scientific materialism has such an influence on atheistic thinking even in matters where science is not directly involved. For some atheists, such as Richard Dawkins, science played an important role in causing them to abandon their former faiths but now serves primarily as a foundation for an ongoing intellectual journey. For others, it is a religion substitute that provides them with purpose and a secular priesthood to whom they look for answers. Due to the frequent entanglement of atheism and science, it is crucial to distinguish between that which is science and that which is not science at all before one can seriously examine the New Atheists' arguments.

The need to separate real science from non-science can also be seen in the way that the phrase "studies show" has become a secular form of making a vow, a useful means of reassuring the skeptical listener that the speaker is swearing to the truth of his words despite any doubts that the listener might harbor. Another problem is the increasing appearance of metastudy abuse in the news media, a bizarre, pseudo-scientific variant of attempting to determine the truth by means of a democracy wherein each quasi-scientific study gets a vote.

Now that "studies show" is no longer considered sufficiently conclusive, "nine out of ten studies show" is supposed to be more convincing. But this is chewing-gum advertising, not science. So, what is

---

[1] Unless, of course, the scientist is occupied with testing a hypothesis by observing precisely what it is that bears do in the woods and how much of it they are doing. Or something to that effect.

science, if it is not self-skewering, timber-littering, or vote-counting?

Richard Dawkins, who has devolved from spending his time performing genuine science in the field of evolutionary biology to performing in public as a professional science propagandist,[2] is surprisingly unhelpful in this regard, especially considering that it is his job to help the public better understand science. While he leaves the reader with no doubt that he likes science very much indeed, his description of it in *Unweaving the Rainbow* bears more similarity to the Apostle Paul's description of love recorded in his first letter to the Corinthians than to anything approaching a useful definition.

Science is "hard and challenging," science is "wonderful." Science "can pay its own way," even if "it doesn't have to." Science is "fun," it is "the very opposite of boring." Science should never be "dumbed down," for it "can enthrall a good mind for a lifetime." Those best qualified to appreciate science are "real poets[3] and true scholars of literature." Science does not have an "anti-poetic spirit," it is never "dry and cold," it is not "cheerless" nor is it "overbearing." Science allows "mystery but not magic" and "strangeness beyond imagining" but no "cheap and easy miracles." It "ought to be motivated by a sense of wonder," and is "occasionally arrogant," but then, "it has a certain amount to be arrogant about."[4] It "progresses by correcting its mistakes" and "makes no secret of what it still does not understand."

In the humble philosophical tradition of Socrates, its "very essence" is "to know what we do not know." And even if "there are dangers of becoming intoxicated," we can rest assured that the "feeling of awed wonder that science can give us is one of the highest experiences of which the human psyche is capable."

If, at this point, the reader is beginning to wonder if Dr. Dawkins has perhaps more than a little in common with Dr. Timothy Leary or fellow evolutionary theorist Terence McKenna,[5] he may be assured

---

[2] I mean that literally. He holds the Charles Simonyi Chair for the Public Understanding of Science at Oxford University.

[3] *"By poets, of course, I intend artists of all kinds."* Dawkins, Richard. *Unweaving the Rainbow*, New York: 1998. 21. Why he should write "poets" in the place of "artists" when poetry is but a small subset of art remains a mystery. As will become increasingly clear to the reader, Dawkins is an entertaining writer but he isn't exactly what one would be tempted to describe as a precise one.

[4] Ibid., 26. Dawkins is actually quoting Lewis Wolpert here.

[5] McKenna theorized that spoken language and other aspects of human consciousness evolved as

that he is not alone. After all, it wasn't prayer and fasting that produced lysergic acid diethylamide.

But if Oxford's most famous professor never quite gets around to answering the question, the *Oxford English Dictionary* does not shirk from the task. It defines science as "the intellectual and practical activity encompassing the systematic study of the structure and behavior of the physical and natural world through observation and experiment. (—ORIGIN Latin *scientia*, from *scire* "know.")

There, was that so hard? Science is systematic study done through observation and experiment. Therefore, if the study is not systematic, or if observation and experiment are not involved, it is obviously not science by this definition.

This is a key point. *If observation and experiment are not involved, then it is not science!*

Unless, of course, one is defining it differently, as some scientists are wont to do. One of the more famous alternate definitions, and one to which both Dawkins and Hitchens make reference, is that provided by the Austrian Karl Popper, a professor at the London School of Economics who is considered to have been one of the leading philosophers of science. Popper's primary criterion for distinguishing between science and not-science is the concept of falsifiability. For a hypothesis to be falsifiable, it must be theoretically possible to make an observation that would disprove the subject. Atheists are particularly fond of this definition, as the difficulty involved in falsifying a supernatural God allows them to argue that religion cannot be science.[6] But can Popper's concept of falsifiability really be taken seriously as a dividing point between science and not-science? It appears more than a little flawed to me. Let's begin with postulating that a study of the language of the gods is not proper science, whereas a study of the color of swans is.

I base this premise on the classic example of a falsifiable proposition, the statement that "all swans are white." The fact that one

---

a result of devouring psilocybin-containing mushrooms that grew in the fecal matter of prehistoric herds of ur-cows, which our primate ancestors are supposed to have followed after climbing down from the trees. This is known as the "Stoned Ape" theory of evolution. It will probably not come as a big surprise to learn that McKenna was known for consuming extremely large quantities of hallucinogenic chemical agents himself.

[6] I note that it's not difficult to falsify Christianity, however. Ergo, it is science! Pity the name's been taken.

could prove this proposition to be wrong by observing a black swan makes it falsifiable and therefore a proper scientific matter. It is not the truth or untruth of the proposition that is important, only the fact that the truth or untruth could be determined by observation.

The problem here is that the proposition "all gods speak Aramaic" is equally falsifiable, given that the theoretical observation of a mono-lingual Greek-speaking god would suffice to falsify the proposition. This would therefore make divine linguistics a legitimate matter of science, the current difficulty of observing gods notwithstanding. And however impossible it might seem to credit, divine linguistics has indeed been an object of serious contemplation throughout history by some of Mankind's greatest minds, including Dante and Leibniz.[7] Now, Popper would presumably describe this as "naïve falsification" and place "Swans, Color" in the category approved by so-phisticated methodological falsification and "Linguistics, Divine" in the category not approved by it. But this merely expands the falsifiability test into a haphazard, technology-driven definition that dives headlong into tautology, defining science as whatever scientists believe science to be at the moment, or worse, whatever scientists are doing.[8]

This is dangerous ground, for it hoists science and scientists upon the paradoxical horns of their own Euthyphro dilemma, which if applied in the same manner that it is applied to God and morality, would force one to conclude that science does not exist. But given the masses of empirical evidence that testify to the material existence of both science and scientists, I assert that the more reasonable conclusion is that a) science does exist, and b) the Council of Thirty had a pretty good point.[9] In any event, the falsifiability definition is nebulous enough to be pretty useless.

If Richard Dawkins is less than forthcoming despite his volubility,

---

[7] Eco, Umberto. *The Search for the Perfect Language*. London: 1995. I interviewed Dr. Eco not long after the publication of his book dealing with this quixotic pursuit. It's by no means easy sledding, but it's intriguing to see how aspects of his work in semiotics has enriched his fiction.

[8] There is a school of thought that descends from Thomas Kuhn, author of *The Structure of Scientific Revolutions*, and asserts that science is best defined as "whatever scientists do." However, in this case, scientists might as well be bears.

[9] The Thirty Tyrants were a dictatorial oligarchy that ruled Athens for about a year after the Athenians lost the Peloponnesian War. Sentencing Socrates to death was only one of their many crimes but in addition to being their most notorious misdeed, it is perhaps their most defensible one.

we are fortunate to discover that one of his comrades in evolution-ary biology, P. Z. Myers, is distinctly more helpful. In addition to his duties as a professor of biology, Dr. Myers runs one of the Internet's more popular science blogs, Pharyngula.[10] When I posed the question to him, "What is science?" he responded with not one, but three definitions, all of them quite useful:

1. *Science is a changing and growing collection of knowledge, char-acterized by transparency (all methods are documented, and the lineage of ideas can be traced) and testability (prior work can be repeated or its results evaluated). It is an edifice of information that contains all of the details of its construction.*

2. *Science is what scientists do. We have institutions that train people and employ them in the business of generating new knowledge and we have procedures like the bestowal of degrees and ranks that cer-tify one's membership in the hallowed ranks of science.*

3. *Science is a process. It is a method for exploring the natural world by making observations, drawing inferences, and testing those in-ferences with further experimentation and observation. It isn't so much the data generated as it is a way of thinking critically about the universe and our own interpretations of it.*[11]

What we understand as science consists of three separate and dis-tinct aspects, a dynamic body of knowledge (scientage), a process (scientody), and a profession (scientistry). This three-in-one works together in a unified manner that should be recognizable to the suf-ficiently educated, wherein the body of knowledge reigns supreme, the process offers the only way to the body of knowledge, and those who blaspheme against the profession will not be forgiven. And, as this analogy suggests, it is the process that is the significant aspect insofar as humanity is concerned.

This tripartite distinction makes it precisely clear just what Richard

---

[10] My choice of Dr. Myers to provide this definition is not entirely random. In addition to launching the occasional barb my way, he is acquainted with Dr. Dawkins, who recently penned the following in honor of Myers's fiftieth birthday: "*All around the World Wide Web, the wingnuts get the crepys, As the faith-heads take a drubbing from our era's Samuel Pepys, That sceptical observer of the scene about the wyers, At Pharyngula, the singular redoubt of P Z Myers.*"

[11] Dr. P. Z. Myers, Pharyngula, 7 March 2007. http://scienceblogs.com/pharyngula/2007/03/what_is_science.php.

Dawkins is so enamored with, as when he sings the praise of rapturous wonders and poetic inspirations, he is not referring to science as a profession,[12] but rather science as a body of knowledge. Whereas when he describes it as hard and challenging, fun, and motivated by a sense of wonder, he is making reference to science as process.

It should be equally obvious that it is this second definition, or science as process, which is described by the *Oxford English Dictionary*. Therefore, that is the definition we shall henceforth use throughout the course of this book. But before proceeding, it is intriguing to at least consider the possibility that it is not the threat to science as process that so offends scientists, but rather the potential threat to science as profession that has whipped some scientists into an angry lather.

After all, scientists understand better than most how their bread gets buttered, and no one, not even the most dedicated idealist, is ever pleased with the possibility of that butter being taken away. It seems unlikely, however, that the passion of Richard Dawkins and the fervent militancy of Sam Harris in defense of science can be tied to any such fears. This would make little sense, since neither Sam Harris nor Christopher Hitchens are even scientists, Daniel C. Dennett has tenure, and the success of Richard Dawkins's many books has surely put him well beyond any petty pecuniary concerns. And regarding any potential fears for the profession as a whole, not even the most die-hard Young Earth Creationist or Intelligent Design advocate is calling for a ban on carbon dating or experiments in evolutionary biology, let alone mass defundings of public science programs and corporate-sponsored research.

Nor can their concerns be realistically tied to any fears for science as a body of knowledge, the occasional rhetorical sally aside. The protest of a biology textbook or a nineteenth-century novel notwithstanding, no one on either side of the debate is advocating the willful destruction or even reduction of the knowledge base. As for the process, the very existence of the Intelligent Design movement is a testimony to a respect for scientific methodology and an attempt to make use of it for marketing purposes, not a desire to destroy it.

---

[12] Unless, of course, Dr. Dawkins is one of those masochistic individuals who truly enjoys faculty meetings and filling out paperwork. But we shall grant him the benefit of the doubt.

But if religion poses no real threat to science in any of its forms, upon what is this vehement hostility toward religion on the part of science's self-appointed defenders based? What is the reason for all the shouting?

SCIENCE VS. RELIGION

The idea that science and religion are regarded as being inherently in conflict with one another is a very well-accepted idea these days, but this was not always the case. Some of history's greatest scientists are known to have been men of great Christian faith, while even some of those who weren't, such as Leonardo da Vinci, were on amiable enough terms with the Church to work for it and produced their masterworks based on its religious themes. Ironically, the famous institution where Richard Dawkins is currently employed was once a place where every Fellow of the University was expected to be an ordained priest until Sir Isaac Newton broke the mold at Cambridge with the permission of King Charles II.

As Dawkins himself admits, the overwhelming majority of scientists throughout centuries in which the scientific process was developed were religious, or at least claimed to be:

> Newton did indeed claim to be religious. So did almost everybody until— significantly I think—the nineteenth century, when there was less social and judicial pressure than in earlier centuries to profess religion, and more scientific support for abandoning it.[13]

What's significant about this statement is the way it contradicts the notion that the Catholic Church had been dogmatically opposing science, as evidenced by its notorious trial of Galileo Galilei, all throughout the Dark Ages and the Renaissance and well into the eighteenth century. Indeed, most people today are under the vague impression that the very reason for the Dark Ages' grim nomenclature stems from a puritanical, power-hungry, monolithic Church's iron-fisted repression of science and human liberty, a totalitarian religious oppression that was finally shaken off by the bold freethinkers of the Enlightenment.

---

[13] Dawkins, *The God Delusion*, 98.

But as medievalists such as Umberto Eco[14] and numerous historians have explained in copious detail,[15] this simply is not true. The Dark Ages were no more dark than the Church was undivided.

The negative view of the medieval period has a long and interesting history. Edward Gibbon, the author of the classic *The History of the Decline and Fall of the Roman Empire* famously describes them as "priest-ridden, superstitious, dark times." Of course, it can be reasonably suggested that anyone who is fascinated enough with the Roman Empire to write a million and a half words in six volumes about it, and is blindly prejudiced enough to blame its ultimate collapse on a religion that did not become commonplace until centuries after Juvenal was satirizing the mad decadence of imperial Roman society, is perhaps unlikely to be the most accurate guide in these matters.[16]

What is fascinating is that this modern misconception of medieval times is at least partly based upon the romantic perspective of a fourteenth-century Italian poet, Francesco Petrarca, a Christian humanist better known in English as Petrarch, who is considered to have created the very concept of the Dark Ages. Scholars assert that it was Petrarch who reversed the classic Christian metaphor of pagan darkness giving way to the Light of the World and eventually came to view his own time as a dark age following a lost golden antiquity. This reversed metaphor was picked up by medieval writers such as Giovanni Boccaccio, then again by anti-religious Enlightenment intellectuals such as Denis Diderot, Louis de Jaucourt, Voltaire, and Jean-Jacques Rousseau, who established the reversed tradition that persists today.

---

[14] "*The view that the Middle Ages were puritanical, in the sense of rejecting the sensuous world, ignores the documentation of the period and shows basic misunderstanding of the medieval mentality.*" Umberto Eco, *Art and Beauty in the Middle Ages*, (New Haven, 1986), 5.

[15] In his review of the new *Cambridge History of Christianity*, Philip Jenkins notes: "*The idea of a diversity of doctrines and Christologies in ancient Christianity . . . demands to be noted because of the common impression that 'the Middle Ages'—roughly, the era from 500 to 1500—the story of Christianity was that of a monolithic church that brooked no variations in doctrine. Apart from the obvious fact of the Eastern Orthodox churches, such a vision ignores the range of separate churches operating in Western and Central Europe during the later Middle Ages, including the Bohemian Hussites and Bosnian Dualists, not to mention the various national bodies adhering to one or another pope or antipope. And that takes no account of the millions of African and Asian Christians who knew nothing of Europe, still less of Rome.*" Jenkins, Philip. "Downward, Outward, Later": *Books & Culture*, September/October 2006.

[16] This flaw does not significantly detract from Gibbon's immense achievement in writing this classic historical work, in my opinion. I side with Lord Byron and Winston Churchill against Coleridge and Ruskin in rather liking his bombastic literary style.

Theodore Mommsen, whose essay on Petrarch was recently selected as one of the thirteen most important critical essays on the Italian
Renaissance, makes a convincing case of how it was Petrarch's fixa-
tion on Rome's past glories and his awe of its grandiose ruins that led
him to conclude, mostly on the basis of his nationalistic contempt
for Germanic domination of what had once been an Italian empire,
that he lived in an age of *tenebrae*, or darkness:

> *From these passages it is clear that Petrarch discarded the whole history*
> *of the Roman Empire during late Antiquity and the Middle Ages because*
> *within that age, every where in the [W]estern world, had come into pow-*
> *er "barbarous" nations which brought even Rome and the Romans under*
> *their domination. Because Petrarch could think of this whole develop-*
> *ment only with a feeling of scornful grief, he consistently consigned it to*
> *oblivion in all his writings. In his letters time and again he conjures up*
> *the great shades of Antiquity but scarcely ever does he refer to a mediae-*
> *val name.*[17]

It is ironic that the lamentations of an Italian Christian for the lost
greatness of his nation, a fate for which Christianity could not possibly
bear any significant responsibility,[18] should be so twisted as to take on an
anti-Christian religious implication instead of the obvious anti-German
nationalistic one. And while it is true that three of the barbarian kings
who sacked Rome from 410 to 546 A.D. were Christians, it must be noted that not only had the empire already been divided by this time, but
the capital of the Western Roman Empire had been moved first to Milan,
then Ravenna, by the emperor Honorius.[19]

It is not within the scope of this book to consider why many Enlightenment intellectuals were opposed to Christianity in general and
the Church in particular, it is enough to simply note that this was the

---

[17] Theodore E. Mommsen, "Petrarch's Conception of the Dark Ages." *Speculum*, Vol. 17, No. 2. (Apr. 1942), 236.

[18] It is even more ironic to note that at the same time Gibbon was blaming Christianity for the loss of Imperial Roman martial spirit, his Christian fellow countrymen were occupied with construct-ing an empire on which the sun never set. For a substantially more detailed case against Gibbon's theory, see John Bagnell Bury's *History of the Later Roman Empire* or Bryan Ward Perkins's *The Fall of Rome and the End of Civilization*.

[19] Another obvious blow to Gibbon's theory. Apparently the Visigoths, Vandals, and Ostrogoths were rather less militarily incapacitated by their Christianity than were the Romans.

case. In his Lectures on Modern European Intellectual History,[20] the historian Stephen Kreis, author of *The History Guide*, summarizes the Enlightenment figures thusly:

> *In the final analysis, the philosophes differed widely. To speak of them as a movement is to label them a school of thought. However, what united them all was their common experience of shedding their inherited Christian beliefs with the aid of classical thinkers, specifically Roman, and for the sake of modern philosophy. They were agreed that Christianity was a supernatural religion. It was wrong. It was unreasonable. It was the infamous. Écrasez l'infâme! shouted Voltaire. "Wipe it out! Wipe out the infamous!" Only science, with its predictable results, was the way to truth, moral improvement and happiness.*

This was particularly true of the French Encyclopédistes, and the influence of their landmark *Encyclopédie*[21] paved the way for modern rationalism and the French Revolution, as well as firmly fixed the notion of the irrationality, superstition, and tyranny of the previous millennium in the public consciousness. By waging a fierce intellectual war against Religion in the name of Reason and by defining the two concepts in inherent opposition to each other, it was the *philosophes* who were responsible for weakening that pre-nineteenth-century social and judicial pressure to which Richard Dawkins referred.

It is fitting, therefore, that in his Petrarch essay Mommsen should make use of encyclopedia definitions from 1883 and 1929 to trace the evolution of the term "Dark Ages" from "a period of intellectual depression in the history of Europe from...the fifth century to the revival of learning about the beginning of the fifteenth" to "the contrast, once so fashionable, between the ages of darkness and the ages of light have no more truth in it than have the idealistic fancies which underlie attempts at mediaeval revivalism."[22] Although historians rejected this idea of intellectual depression and religious oppression more than seventy years ago, it is apparent that this

---

[20] http://www.historyguide.org.

[21] *"Gracing the title page of Diderot's compendium in the first edition was a drawing of Lucifer, symbol of light and rebellion, standing beside the masonic symbols of square and compass. The Enlightenment mirrored the Christian religion. Reason became its revelation, nature its god."* Goeringer, Conrad. "The Enlightenment, Freemasonry and The Illuminati" at http://www.atheists.org.

[22] Mommsen, 226.

rejection has not yet managed to dislodge the commonplace belief in the fundamental rivalry between Religion and Reason established nearly 300 years ago by the passionate rational materialists of the Enlightenment.

RESURRECTING THE MYTH

Thomas Riggins, in the Marxist journal *Political Affairs*, notes that many Enlightenment intellectuals were not opposed to religion in itself, but rather to religion being used by "dictatorial religious elements using religion for their own selfish purposes." In a variant on this theme, I suggest that the New Atheists are not actually particularly interested in defending science in itself, but are deeply afraid of science reaching a friendly *rapprochement* with religion.

Since we have already established that the opposition of Dawkins, Dennett, and Harris to religion does not stem from any rational fears for science as a body of knowledge, a profession, or a process, and that there was no significant historical enmity between science and religion, it is apparent that the New Atheists' stated desire to destroy religion must stem from another source. And given the way in which their opposition to religion so closely resembles that of their rationalist antecedents, it is reasonable to suggest that they are not so much interested in defending science as they are in advocating an outdated, nineteenth-century meme.

The evidence fits the hypothesis. As will be demonstrated subsequently in no little detail, Richard Dawkins's grasp of history is not so much outdated as nonexistent. As for his adherence to the Enlightenment rather than science, he makes as many references to Denis Diderot in *The God Delusion* as he does to Sir Isaac Newton.[23] But even if Dawkins can't quite make up his mind as to the proper way to categorize the beliefs[24] of the man he rightly describes as "the great encyclopedist of the Enlightenment," there can be no question of his allegiance to Diderot's ideals, as in 2006 he informed *The Sunday Times* that he was setting up a charity to "divert donations from the hands of 'missionaries' and church-based charities because

---

[23] Dawkins, *The God Delusion*, 18, 84.
[24] He first defines Diderot as a Deist, which he describes as watered-down theism, then "atheistic."

'the enlightenment is under threat. So is reason. So is truth. So is science.'"[25]

Science, you'll note, actually comes in fourth, not first as you might have erroneously guessed. Dawkins thus reveals that it is not science in itself that he is defending so vociferously, but rather his Enlightenment ideals. It appears to be the possibility of "the subversion of science" to serve the interests of Christian values instead of those of its nineteenth-century competitor that has stimulated him to such feverish activity. This may also explain why Dawkins is so strangely unconcerned with other religions, including Islam, which would otherwise appear to pose a far greater threat to both science and the West.

It is even easier to establish Daniel C. Dennett's belief in precisely the same ideals, as Dennett not only directly equates science with the Enlightenment,[26] but also states that his "view of science is very much an enlightenment view."[27] And he sounds an unexpectedly Petrarchian strain by referring to the Enlightenment as a ruined antiquity, to which he has dedicated himself to rebuilding:

> Several hundred years ago at the triumph of the Enlightenment, which you and I both admire and wish to restore, many wise, well-informed people were very sure that now that we had science and enlightenment upon us, religion would soon die out. They were colossally wrong.[28]

It is important to note Dennett's distinction between science "and" enlightenment; while the two are allies, they are manifestly not one and the same. And one very much hopes that when Dennett speaks of wishing to restore 200-year-old triumphs, he is not referring to *la Terreur*.[29]

Sam Harris is known to be motivated by the same ideals as well, as Chris Lehman of *Reason* recognized[30] when he noted Harris's "litany

---

[25] "Godless Dawkins Challenges Schools." *The Sunday Times*, 19 Nov. 2006.

[26] Dennett, Daniel C. *Breaking the Spell*. New York: Allen Lane, 2006. 47.

[27] Blume, Harvey. "Interview with Daniel Dennett." *The Atlantic*.

[28] Wilson, E. O. "E. O. Wilson + Daniel Dennett:" *Seed Magazine*, 31 Oct. 2006.

[29] The French Revolutionary Reign of Terror, which took place from 19 Fructidor I to 9 Thermidor II. Or, as those benighted religious folk insist on counting it, September 5, 1793, to July 27, 1794 Anno Domini.

[30] Lehman, Chris. "Among the Non-Believers: the Tedium of Dogmatic Atheism:" *Reason*, Jan. 2005.

of Enlightenment-era objections to medieval models of piety" in his review of *The End of Faith*. It must be confessed that Harris doesn't refer directly to the Enlightenment himself in either of his books, but then, given his demonstration in them of his near-complete ignorance of religious, military, European, and world history, it is possible that he has never heard of Diderot, the Encyclopédistes, or the *philosophes* despite his regurgitation of their philosophy.

Dawkins, Dennett, and Harris, with academic credentials and standing as public intellectuals, represent the highest of the High Church atheists. But their dedication to science as a primary vehicle for their Enlightened faith is shared by even the humblest of the rationalists, as is their missionary zeal. Consider the way in which one unknown science blogger describes herself in vintage Petrarchian terms: "a self-proclaimed 'atheistic evolutionist missionary' who thinks of herself as a voice of rationality in a dark, gloomy world."[31] Dennett is far from the only one who considers the triumph of the Enlightenment to be far from complete.

Despite how it is commonly portrayed by the New Atheists, the rationalist war on religion cannot properly be described as a war between science and religion; it is more akin to a tug-of-war between rationalists and religionists over the way in which science is to be henceforth used and the purposes to which science is ultimately harnessed.

If religion and science were as fundamentally incompatible as the New Atheists assert, then it would seem more than a little strange that the magazine *Nature*, which bills itself as "the international weekly journal of science," would concur with *Science* magazine in reporting that one of the places where science is growing fastest is Iran,[32] a country not exactly famous for its militant atheism or general disdain for religion. The supposed incompatibility between religion and science can't be all that great if it is necessary to threaten the

---

[31] Scientia Natura: Evolution and Rationality, http://scientianatura.blogspot.com/.

[32] *"Iran's share of global scientific output rose from 0.0003% in 1970 to 0.29% in 2003, with much of the growth occurring since the early 1990s, according to a study earlier this year in the journal* Scientometrics." *Science* 1 July 2005. 36–37. It's interesting to see that their scientific output has increased by a factor of nearly 1,000 since the science-hating mullahs took power. Because the Islamic Republic represents only 1 percent of the world's population, this is a respectable showing; the People's Republic of China's share of global scientific output was only 1.38 percent despite accounting for 20.13 percent of the global population.

Islamic Republic with air strikes and invasion in order to prevent its scientists from performing research in unapproved areas.

And while it is indisputable that there are fewer scientists today who are openly religious than there were 200 years ago, they do exist. Dawkins admits the fact, but deals with this dichotomy by suspecting "that most of the more recent ones are religious only in the Einsteinian sense," before pronouncing himself baffled by the genuine religious faith on the part of those individuals with whom he has had personal contact. I suggest that it would be more rational for Dawkins to assume that scientists who dare to openly assert their faith today are most likely religious in the conventional sense of the word, particularly given the way they can expect to be viewed with "baffled amusement" by their colleagues. It's worth noting that this supposition would also have the benefit of being supported rather than contradicted by Dawkins's own anecdotal experience.

Despite this decrease in the number of religious scientists over the last two centuries, the great crime of Christianity against science is still generally considered to have been the Catholic Church putting Galileo Galilei, the father of modern physics, on trial for heresy. It is usually forgotten, however, that the ban on publication of Galileo's *Dialogue Concerning the Two Chief World Systems* was only nominal and that his *Discourses and Mathematical Demonstrations Relating to Two New Sciences* was published without incident in the Christian Netherlands in 1638, five years after the trial.[33]

It is particularly ironic, and perhaps even unfair, that Christians today are condemned for Pope Urban VIII's belief in the geocentric system formulated by the pagan Greek astrologer, Ptolemy, while the heliocentric system that provides the basis for this condemnation is named for Nicolaus Copernicus, the Catholic cleric who formulated the modern heliocentric theory in *On the Revolutions of the Celestial Spheres*. Copernicus's masterwork, which is considered to be a defining moment in the history of science, was published in 1543, a scant

---

[33] It is perhaps not entirely unreasonable to suggest that part of the reason the Pope had it in for Galileo was that in his book, the great scientist unwisely chose to ascribe the Pope's own words to a character defending the Ptolemic system named Simplicius. And considering that Galileo didn't even manage to get himself excommunicated despite his public baiting of the Pope, a feat achieved by dozens of princes, kings, and Holy Roman Emperors, it's clear that his dangerous Copernican ideas were never regarded as posing a dire threat to the Church, the modern mythology notwithstanding.

eighty-nine years before Galileo's supposed overturning of geocentric Christian dogma. Furthermore, if one considers the fact that the
Catholic Church reconsidered the issue and authorized the publication of Galileo's works in 1741, it seems a bit obsessive to continue
to hold the Pope's abuse of his office against Southern Baptists and
Methodists 375 years after the fact.

There is also genuine cause for doubting whether Enlightenment
atheism and science can honestly be considered as fundamentally compatible as religion and science have been for centuries. It is
worth noting that it was neither Christians nor Muslims but revolutionary atheists inspired by Enlightenment ideals who beheaded the
man known today as the father of modern chemistry, Antoine-Lau-
rent de Lavoisier, in 1794, declaring "*La République n'a pas besoin de
savants ni de chimistes; le cours de la justice ne peut être suspendu.*"[34]

---

[34] "*The Republic has no need of scientists or chemists; the course of justice cannot be suspended.*" Jean-
Baptist Coffinhall, President of the Revolutionary Tribunal.

III

THE CASE
AGAINST SCIENCE

Our technical advances in the art of war have finally rendered our religious differences—and hence our religious beliefs—antithetical to our survival. We can no longer ignore the fact that billions of our neighbors believe in the metaphysics of martyrdom, or in the literal truth of the book of Revelation, or any of the other fantastical notions that have lurked in the minds of the faithful for millennia—because our neighbors are now armed with chemical, biological, and nuclear weapons. There is no doubt that these developments mark the terminal phase of our credulity. Words like "God" and "Allah" must go the way of "Apollo" and "Baal," or they will unmake our world.

—SAM HARRIS, *The End of Faith*

A S RICHARD DAWKINS DEMONSTRATES in his ode to science, *Unweaving the Rainbow*, the New Atheists harbor nearly as great a love for science as they do a hatred for religion. Like the science fetishists who regard science as a basis for dictating human behavior, atheists like to posit that Man has evolved to a point where he is ready to move beyond religion. This has been their constant theme for more

43

than 100 years, but as Daniel C. Dennett points out, the evidence is mounting that this simply isn't going to happen. A more interesting and arguably more relevant question that none of the New Atheists dare to ask is whether science, having produced some genuinely positive results as well as some truly nightmarish evils over the course of the last century, has outlived its usefulness to Mankind. Man has survived millennia of religious faith, but if the prophets of over-population and global warming are correct, he may not survive a mere four centuries of science.

In spite of his scientific pretensions, Sam Harris is a mere science fetishist.[1] His book, *The End of Faith*, is a profoundly non-scientific expression of hope wrapped up in an emotional plea. This is why many militant atheists find it so stirring and why more rational non-believers find it uncompelling. It is not, as some optimistic infidels would have it, a prediction, much less a coherent case leading to a logical conclusion—it's just another expression of faith in Enlightenment utopianism. And as Harris's brave words about an absence of doubt indicate, it is an expression of surprisingly blind faith, lacking both common sense and evidence.

The five major religions of the world, in order of their appearance on the scene, are Hinduism, traditional Chinese folk religion, Buddhism, Christianity, and Islam. These five religions have approximately 4.85 billion adherents, representing an estimated 71.3 percent of the world's population in 2007, and they have been around for a collective 11,600 years. During the vast majority of those 116 centuries, the world has not been in any danger of extinction from weapons of any kind, nor has the human race been in serious danger of dying out from pollution, global warming, overpopulation, or anything else. Despite 116 centuries filled with hundreds, if not thousands, of diverse religions, all competing for mindshare, resources, and dominance, the species has not merely survived, it has thrived.

There is no aspect of Hindu teaching that has produced a means of potentially extinguishing Mankind. The occasional eleventh-century

---

[1] Harris's training is in philosophy, although in a 2006 debate with Dennis Prager he announced that he is "firmly grounded in the life sciences" and his continuing education requires him to "actually understand recent developments in biology."

rampages by the *Sohei* of Mount Hiei[2] notwithstanding, Buddhism provides no method of destroying the planet, while Christians have been waiting patiently for the world to end for nearly 2,000 years now without doing much to immanentize the eschaton except for occasionally footing the bill for Jews making aliyah.[3] Islam, for all the danger it supposedly presents, has not produced a significant military technology since Damascene steel was developed in the twelfth century and even that is of nebulous connection to the religion itself.

Modern science has only been around for the last 350 years, if we date the scientific method back to the man known as the Father of Science, Galileo Galilei. One could push that date back considerably, if one wished, to Aristotle and Archimedes, or forward to Newton and the Age of Enlightenment, but regardless, the dire threat to Mankind described by Harris only dates back to the middle of the twentieth century. In the last sixty years, science has produced a veritable witches' brew of potential dangers to the human race, ranging from atom-shattering explosive devices to lethal genetic modifications, designer diseases, large quantities of radioactive waste and even, supposedly, the accidental production of mini black holes and strangelets through particle collider experiments.[4]

So, in only 3 percent of the time that religion has been on the scene, science has managed to produce multiple threats to continued human existence. Moreover, the quantity and lethal quality of those threats appear to be accelerating, as the bulk of them have appeared in the most recent sixth of the scientific era. It is not the purpose of this chapter to examine whether religion exacerbates or alleviates these scientific threats—that appraisal must wait for a later chapter. Harris's extinction equation, which states that $S+F=\text{☠}$, is not inherently wrong. But his conclusion is, because it is Science, not Faith, that is the factor in the equation that presents a deadly danger to Mankind.

This is true of both the military and non-military threats to humanity.

---

[2] The warrior monks of Heian Japan. The emperor Shirakawa said of them: *"There are three things that even I cannot control: the waters of the Kamo river, the roll of the dice, and the monks of the mountain."*

[3] Pilgrimage to Israel.

[4] I personally find it difficult to believe that the good Swiss scientists at CERN are running any serious risks of blowing up the planet. I spoke with the people in the TH-PH department and they assured me that they would do their very best to keep any inadvertent black holes from getting out of hand.

While the jury is still out on the precise nature of the threat caused by global warming,[5] there can be no doubt that the scientific method is at least in part responsible for it, along with the threats supposedly posed by overpopulation, pollution, and genetic engineering. Religion simply cannot be held accountable for any of those things, not even overpopulation.[6] What could be more absurd than to claim that the Bahá'í are in some way responsible for any damage to humanity caused by CERN's Large Hadron Collider? Not even the most militant New Atheist would dare to set himself up for public ridicule that way. And yet, making religious faith the significant variable in the Extinction Equation is no less ludicrous.

However, the guilt of scientody does not mean that the profession of science can be held entirely blameless. The fact that it was the method that made the development of these threats possible does not indicate that their development via the method was inevitable. It was scientists who freely made the choice to develop these theories and, in many cases, the weapons, sometimes in innocence, like Alfred Nobel[7] being stunned to learn that his blasting cap and smokeless explosives would cause him to be remembered as "the merchant of death," and sometimes in full cognizance of their moral culpability, as in the case of Albert Einstein's[8] 1939 letter to President Roosevelt written in the hopes of encouraging F.D.R. to build an atomic bomb.

It is not the combination of religion and science, then, but rather the combination of scientists and the scientific method that has created this panoply of mortal dangers to Mankind.

---

[5] I note that I am a global warming skeptic myself. Greenland is still colder now than it was when Norse settlers were raising crops there in the eleventh century. So I don't see why a return to those temperatures should present a problem. Of course, when you grew up waiting for the school bus in forty below zero wind chills, global warming just doesn't sound all that ominous.

[6] Yes, religious people breed faster than the non-religious. But they breed slower now than they were when overpopulation was not a problem; to the extent overpopulation is a genuine threat to Mankind, it is a threat entirely created by the use of the scientific method in extending average lifespans and lowering death rates.

[7] "My dynamite will sooner lead to peace than a thousand world conventions. As soon as men will find that in one instant whole armies can be destroyed, they surely will abide by golden peace." One finds that great scientists seldom turn out to be particularly accurate prophets.

[8] "I made one mistake in my life when I signed that letter to President Roosevelt advocating that the atomic bomb should be built." Albert Einstein, letter to Linus Pauling. Unfortunately for Einstein's conscience, the opening of the Eastern Front and the failure of Operation Barbarossa ultimately rendered the theoretical threat of a Nazi bomb nonexistent two months and eight days before the first test of an atomic bomb on July 16, 1945.

THE GOOD, THE BAD, AND THE SCIENTIFIC

Questioning science in this manner invariably leads to one of five responses,[9] often rather heated.

1) The first response is an *ad hominem* one insisting the individual is only questioning the inherent munificence of science because he is stupid, anti-science, or incapable of understanding science. Like most *ad hominem* responses, this one is invalid because it doesn't even begin to dispute the issues raised. Neither the level of my intelligence nor my personal opinion about science is a factor in the question of whether some aspect of science is responsible for posing a threat to humanity. One need not understand a human being or the operation of the human body to comprehend that a particular individual is guilty of committing murder after witnessing the act.

2) The second response is to wonder how it is possible to live in the modern world, make use of modern technology, and still harbor any doubts that the benefits of science are worth whatever their costs might happen to be. After all, we have electricity, computers, television, X-rays, automobiles, antibiotics, vaccines, and many other valuable things thanks to science. Science has increased our lifespan, it has significantly increased the average individual's chance of surviving childbirth and childhood, and it has made those longer lives considerably more comfortable.

I do not dispute any of this. But I do note that this is a fundamentally illogical response, since if humanity is in danger of being wiped out by the weapons that science has also produced, then there will not be anyone to continue enjoying those scientific benefits. It does not matter how many wonderful contributions to humanity have been produced thanks to science, because wiping them all out is the equivalent of multiplying their sum by zero. One could certainly argue that the threat to humanity from science is not really all that dire, but then it would be necessary to admit that religious faith poses no threat to humanity, either, thus demonstrating Harris's thesis to be entirely bankrupt.

---

[9] These responses are not strawmen. All of them are specific responses I have either received via e-mail or read on Web sites responding to my columns and blog posts. In each of the five responses related, I am summarizing a series of similar responses.

3) The third is to argue that science cannot be held responsible for the evils it enables because to do so is to confuse facilitation with prescription. It is claimed that although science made the atomic bomb possible and scientists designed, tested, and built the bombs, it does not follow that science is responsible for the horrors of Hiroshima and Nagasaki. A variant on this is to argue that because the evils are not performed specifically "in the name of science" or in the interest of a scientific agenda, they cannot be blamed on science.

There are three errors inherent in this third response. The first is that causal factors do not depend upon motive. No reasonable individual would accept the argument that cigarettes don't cause lung cancer because no one smokes "in the name of Marlboro" or in the interest of a cigarette agenda. The distinction between motive and method may be significant in a court of law, but is largely irrelevant when considering if a particular problem exists and how it can be best resolved. The second error is that the presence of the danger is solely due to the existence of these dangerous weapons and technologies; while blame for any decision to actually use them should rightly fall upon the various politicians and government leaders who make those decisions based on a variety of reasons, blame for their existence can only lie with their creators.

The third error is that numerous evils have historically been committed, justified, and utilized by scientists "in the name of science," as demonstrated by the infamous Tuskegee syphilis experiments, the attempts of hypothermia researchers at the University of Minnesota and Victory University to use Nazi data obtained at Dachau, and the *Atlas of Topographical and Applied Human Anatomy*, which was produced with the bodies of 1,377 executed criminals sent to Professor Eduard Pernkopf at the University of Vienna by the Gestapo.[10] Although the defenders of science inevitably claim that unpleasantries such as Nazi science, racist science, and the 64,000 forced ster-

---

[10] While some scientists have argued that it would not have made sense for Pernkopf to use the emaciated bodies of Jewish concentration camp victims for his anatomical drawings, a 1998 report by the University of Vienna commission charged with investigating the affair admitted that at least eight of the victims were of Jewish origin. More to the point, because the crimes of the Gestapo were not limited to murdering Jews, it is likely that none of the 1,377 cadavers were obtained by legitimate means. This should have been obvious, since some of the victims were children.

ilizations done at the behest of American eugenicists should not be blamed on science because it is today considered "bad science," it is worth noting that religious individuals who commit acts in complete contradiction of their religious tenets are never absolved of responsibility for their crimes on the basis of their "bad theology." The fact that Richard Dawkins and other atheists have publicly called to reconsider the legitimacy of eugenics also serves to demonstrate that the historical evils of eugenics are properly blamed on science and scientists.

4) The fourth response is to claim that it is unfair to blame science for the actions of some scientists. Of course, it must then be equally unfair to blame religion for the action of some religious individuals. And it is spectacularly unfair to blame the adherents of one religion for the actions of a completely different religion, especially when those adherents are being actively persecuted by the members of that other religion. It is wildly irrational to argue that a religious moderate is somehow responsible for the actions of religious extremists he does not know and has never met, but that one scientist cannot be blamed for the actions of another scientist, not even one who belongs to the same professional organization or university and with whom he presumably has some influence. Also, one must always be careful to distinguish between the three aspects of science. Whether one is holding a particular scientist or the scientific method itself accountable for a particular scientific misdeed, this does not necessarily impute any blame to other scientists.

5) The fifth and final response is to declare that knowledge, regardless of its risks, is always better than ignorance. As Dr. P. Z. Myers puts it: "That's a deeply cynical view that Day has—that ignorance is better than knowledge, because awareness hurts and technological progress brings great risks. I guess I must be more optimistic than a weird Christian nihilist, because I think it's better to aspire to a better world than to give up and slide back into some benighted religious illusion."

But I am not arguing that ignorance is better than knowledge, I am merely pointing out that the evidence suggests that in some circumstances, ignorance may be preferable to knowledge, especially partial knowledge imperfectly understood and enthusiastically embraced too soon. I'm not eager to return humanity to a Stone Age state—an ironic accusation given Albert Einstein's assertion that the Fourth World War would be fought with stones and clubs, thanks in part to his scientific legacy—I am actually a classic early adopter.[11] But just as it is now considered bad science, if not an atrocity, to have sterilized thousands of American citizens against their will, it is not hard to imagine that there is likely a non-zero amount of scientific activity today that will be considered equally mistaken, perhaps even equally atrocious, in the future.

Only a complete fool would argue that all risks are inherently worth taking, or that all knowledge is inherently worth pursuing. Is the mapping of the human genome worth risking the possibility that some individuals will be denied insurance for diseases they are genetically bound to develop? I think so. Is it worth risking the development of genetic weapons coded to kill all individuals possessing a certain genetic marker? I'm not so sure about that, and there is certainly a case to be made that it isn't, especially by those who happen to belong to a group likely to be targeted by such an insidious invention. The argument that all risks are worth taking and all knowledge is worth pursuing is not only foolish, it is an argument that is based on neither evidence nor reason, only blind secular faith. Technological progress offers no guarantees of a better world, no matter how strong one's optimistic aspirations or beliefs in Man's inevitable progress toward a self-made paradise on Earth might be.

As for the better world of today, there are three obvious flaws in the assumptions that credit all of it to science. The first is the impact of science on human life expectancy.[12] Life in the pre-scientific era was not always as short as we commonly imagine it to have been. While life expectancy has risen dramatically in the last century, from forty-seven to seventy-seven in the United States, for the first two-thirds of the scientific era, life expectancy was comparable to that of ancient

---

[11] One of my friends commented a few years ago that my idea of a threesome was to take a Dana and a Treo to bed. Hot stuff!

[12] There is a quality of life argument that could be made as well, but as it could legitimately be made either way, I shall avoid discussing it. I'll simply note that I personally prefer to avoid the Big Room with the green carpet and the bright light as much as possible.

Rome for those who were not slaves.[13] Anyone familiar with Roman history is well aware that the average life expectancy of twenty-eight years that is commonly cited is misleading; the comparison of life expectancies between one society that practices population control through infanticide, which is factored into the mortality rates, and one that practices it through abortion, which is not, is not a reasonable one.[14] And since both infanticide and slavery were ended by predominantly Christian imperatives, it is improper to inherently credit all evidence of longer human lifespans to science.

The second flaw is that advocates for science in all its aspects habitually make use of a different measure depending on whether they wish to credit science for a technological innovation or to deflect blame from it. Consider the previous reference to vaccinations, for example. While vaccines, like massive ordnance air blast bombs, were discovered and developed by scientists making use of the scientific method, scientists no more provide shots to children than they drop bombs on unsuspecting civilian populations.[15] Politicians make the decisions regarding the way vaccines are to be funded and used while doctors and nurses administer them, just as politicians decide if bombs are to be utilized and air force pilots deliver them to their targets. One can either argue that science is responsible in both cases based on the involvement of scientage and scientody or that science is not responsible in either case based on the absence of scientistry, but what one cannot logically do is to conclude that science is responsible in the one case and not the other.

The third flaw is that capitalism and individual freedom arguably

---

[13] The life tables of Domitius Ulpianus used to capitalize annuities for imperial pensions indicate an average expected Roman lifespan of around fifty-five years. Other sources indicate average lifespans of 58.6 years for the rural clergy compared to only 17.5 years for urban slaves. Living within the confines of Rome itself reduced life expectancy for both professionals and slaves by 12 and 32 percent respectively. W. M. S. Russell, and Claire Russell, "The History of the Human Life Span," *The Journal of Postgraduate General Practice* (1976): 571–588.

[14] If the 1.287 million abortions performed in the United States in 2003 were considered Roman-style infanticides for the sake of a more accurate comparison and factored in with the 4,089,950 live births that year, the average American life expectancy at birth would be reduced by nearly two decades, from seventy-eight to fifty-nine. Science appears to be giving us about a decade in addition to allowing humanity to live in huge urban communities without dying like flies.

[15] The notable exception being the atomic bomb dropped on Hiroshima. Navy Captain William Parsons was a Manhattan Project scientist and acted as the *Enola Gay*'s bomb commander and weaponeer. Science can be held responsible for the dropping of the atomic bomb in literally every way.

play a greater role in technological advancement than all three aspects of science combined. Despite devoting double the percentage of its national expenditures to science than did the United States or any other country in the West,[16] the technologically retarded state of the scientifically enamored[17] former Soviet Union demonstrates that the link between science and technological progress is far more tenuous than is usually considered to be the case.

Because there is no hard line between pure science and applied science aside from the professional distinction between the research scientist and the applications development engineer, it can be difficult to ascertain precisely what responsibility should be assigned to science and the scientist for any given technological innovation. This is especially true when one takes into account the major role that economics and entrepreneurialism also play in technological development; the most prolific and successful inventors are seldom scientists and often are not even engineers. Regardless, it is important to keep in mind that whatever amount of responsibility deserves to be assigned to science, it applies to innovations that are harmful to humanity as well as those that are beneficial.

Two famous scientific Richards are in accord on this subject:

It is that scientific knowledge enables us to do all kinds of things and to make all kinds of things. Of course if we make good things, it is not only to the credit of science; it is also to the credit of the moral choice which led us to good work. Scientific knowledge is an enabling power to do either good or bad—but it does not carry instructions on how to use it.

—RICHARD FEYNMAN

People certainly blame science for nuclear weapons and similar horrors. It's been said before but needs to be said again: if you want to do evil, science provides the most powerful weapons to do evil; but equally, if you

---

[16] *"Certainly the U.S.A. spends about three times as much in absolute figures ($24 billion in 1967, of which $15 billion were for government research and development), but because of the great difference in scientific costs in the two countries, it is thought possible that the Kremlin gets about three times as much research per ruble as does Washington. If this calculation is approximately correct, then the U.S.S.R. is now spending almost as much in real terms as the U.S.A., although Moscow's effort is mounted from a much smaller economic base."* "Recent Developments in Soviet Science and Technology," *Current History*. November, 1968.

[17] *"Communist society can be built only on the summits of science and engineering."* V. I. Lenin.

want to do good, science puts into your hands the most powerful tools to do so. The trick is to want the right things, then science will provide you with the most effective methods of achieving them.[18]

—RICHARD DAWKINS

THE PHONY WAR: SCIENCE VERSUS RELIGION

The Party cannot be neutral toward Religion because Religion is something opposite to Science.

—JOSEPH STALIN

When considering the suggested conflict between science and religion, the first and most important is: Which science? In the previous chapter, a distinction was made between three aspects of science: scientage, scientistry, and scientody. Of those three aspects, which one can be most reasonably said to pose the greatest threat to humanity? And the second question is, if one or more aspects of science do pose a genuine danger to Mankind, then what should we do about it?

These questions are not rhetorical, even though they may strike the reader as being more outlandish than the calls for an end to faith to which this book is a response. If one troubles to consider the situation through the broad lens of history, two facts immediately become apparent:

- There are a lot more religious people than scientists.
- Religion has never been stamped out anywhere despite a number of vigorous efforts that lasted for decades. Science and technological development, on the other hand, have been successfully brought to a halt on several occasions in the past.

Science is not inevitable. Japan was closed to outside contact from 1639 to 1853, and although the Edo Shogunate kept its eye on developments in *rangaku*, or "Dutch learning," through the international trade permitted at a single port located near Nagasaki, Japanese

---

[18] Dawkins, Richard. "Science, Delusion and the Appetite for Wonder." Richard Dimbleby Lecture, BBC1 Television, 12 Nov. 1996.

society did not suffer greatly from its relative backwardness. It certainly suffered far more from its subsequent post-Meiji attempts to catch up to the West, which ended in the second atomic bomb being dropped, ironically enough, on Nagasaki. China, too, successfully arrested its scientific advancement around 1450, transforming itself from the world leader into a distinctly backward nation over a period of 500 years.[19] In short, the end of science is a much more practical goal for humanity than the end of faith.

I hope the reader will note that this book is not named *The End of Science* for a very good reason; I am not anti-science or even anti-scientist, nor am I arguing that the elimination of all science is a moral imperative for humanity. I am merely following the logic of Sam Harris's extinction equation to its proper logical conclusion, which is that if the world truly is in imminent danger, the only reasonable answer is for humanity to put an end to science.

But which science? While the body of knowledge certainly contains the danger, since atoms are not given to accidentally colliding and it is difficult to smash one without knowing exactly how to do it, the mere knowledge cannot be said to be the cause of the danger. Scientage in itself is static—it is its relationship with scientody and scientists that makes it dynamic. Knowledge does not give birth to itself. Athena may have appeared on the scene fully armored, but she still had to spring from the brow of Zeus.

The method of science, on the other hand, is directly tied to both the theoretical basis for the threats to Mankind as well as the specific applications of the various scientific theories required to develop them into lethal weapons. Hypothesis, experiment, and observation all play integral parts in both the research and engineering aspects of the weapons development process. Without scientody, these threats to the human race simply would not exist; there is a direct causal relationship between the scientific method and the existence of those things that are, in Harris's words, "antithetical to our survival."

But not all the New Atheists are convinced of an immediate danger to Mankind and they don't even present an entirely united front

---

[19] It's worth noting that Jared Diamond places the blame for China's backwardness on its political unity, which suggests some very negative implications for the fate of science in a globally governed world.

regarding the inherent opposition of religion and science. It is interesting to note that it is the least scientific individual who is the most certain that the two are bound to eternal conflict. Christopher Hitchens asserts that "all attempts to reconcile faith with science and reason are consigned to failure and ridicule."[20] Sam Harris has created the aforementioned extinction equation, of course, and adds that "the maintenance of religious dogma *always* comes at the expense of science."[21] Richard Dawkins is more temperate, but nevertheless admits that he is hostile to religion because "it actively debauches the scientific enterprise...subverts science and saps the intellect."[22] It is only the philosopher, Daniel Dennett, who argues that the two can conceivably coexist, which is the basis for his call to make "a concerned effort to achieve a mutual agreement under which religion— all religion—becomes a proper object of scientific study."

What is curious, however, is that once again the primary atheist argument presented is an unscientific and epistemological one that fails to provide any relevant evidence in support of the assertion. I found this curious, as surely this bitter centuries-old conflict must have left some recent signs of the vicious hostilities between the two warring camps. And yet, when I contemplated the matter, it occurred to me that the three most often cited crimes of religion against science are the Catholic Church's persecution of Galileo, the occasional school board battle over teaching evolution in the public schools, and the Christian opposition to the federal funding of research using stem cells taken from human embryos. As one might expect, all three of these issues are brought up in one of the New Atheist books.

And yet, these are not serious issues. Taken in their entirety, they barely amount to mild smack-talk between unarmed border guards from two neighboring countries caught up in a dispute over agricultural subsidies. To argue that these three things are in any way indicative of an implacable and incorrigible hostility is obviously absurd. Galileo was not attacked because he defended the Copernican theory that had been published eighty years before, but because he was foolish enough to both disobey and publicly caricature his former supporter,

---

[20] Hitchens, Christopher. *god is not Great*. New York: Twelve Books, 2007. 64–65.

[21] Harris, *Letter to a Christian Nation*, 63.

[22] Dawkins, *The God Delusion*, 284.

Pope Urban VIII, in a book that had been granted both papal permission and Inquisitorial authorization. Evolutionary theory is not only taught in the public schools, its teaching is largely unquestioned and unchallenged, a few high-profile cases of stickers on textbooks notwithstanding.

As for the stem cell controversy, it is looking increasingly likely as if there simply isn't one. Opposition to federal funding is not inherently religious, moreover, federal funding is not science and should never be confused with it. Unless scientists are being jailed and put on trial by church authorities for pursuing this morally suspect research, it is a huge exaggeration to claim that the controversy is an example of religion inhibiting science in any way. However desirable it may be, science has no inherent right to the public purse.

More importantly, after a decade of stem cell research, no scientist has successfully created a stem cell line using cloned human embryos.[23] But a Japanese researcher at Kyoto University, Shinya Yamanaka, has recently declared that neither human eggs nor human embryos are necessary, since his team has learned how to modify skin cells so that they can be transformed into any type of cell, thus creating a functional technique that provides an easier means of obtaining genetic matches and has the benefit of not engendering either ethical or religious opposition.[24]

If this Japanese technique proves successful in humans, one can't help but wonder if the next edition of *Letter to a Christian Nation* will omit the five-page screed—one-eighteenth of the entire book—hysterically condemning American Christians for their "obscene" opposition to the unnecessary destruction of unborn human children. Harris certainly might wish to revisit his declaration that resistance to embryonic stem cell research is uninformed; it looks as if science would have been poorly served if the Kyoto researchers had accepted the "fact" about the necessity of destroying three-day-old human embryos.[25]

This hoisting of Harris on his own scientific petard tends to highlight

---

[23] "Will a Disruptive Technology Mothball Therapeutic Cloning?" *TCS Daily*. 19 June 2007.

[24] "Simple Switch Turns Cells Embryonic:" *Nature*. 6 June 2007.

[25] Actually, this isn't necessary, either. *"Biologists have developed a technique for establishing colonies of human embryonic stem cells from an early human embryo without destroying it."* The New York Times. 24 Aug. 2006.

the problem of placing too much trust in science, given the constantly changing nature of the body of knowledge.[26] But stem cells are only a single issue, and since it seemed possible that I might have missed a skirmish or two in this ongoing intellectual struggle, I posed the question of what tangible sins Christianity had committed against science to the readers of my blog,[27] and, arguably more usefully, to the readers of the hitherto mentioned science blog Pharyngula. This was the most comprehensive list,[28] which covered pretty much everything brought up by anyone else:

1. Galileo's trial. (1633 A.D.)
2. The demonization of mathematics during the Dark Ages. (476 to 1000 A.D.)
3. The persecution of alchemists during the Middle Ages. (476 to 1485 A.D.)
4. The execution of Michael Servetus. (1553 A.D.)
5. Opposition to the theory of evolution.
6. The destruction of libraries and the burning of books during the fourth and fifth centuries.
7. The ban on the works of René Descartes. (1663 A.D.)
8. The imprisonment of Roger Bacon. (1277 A.D.)
9. The condemnation of Francis Bacon.[29] (1621 A.D.)
10. The destruction of Islamic manuscripts by Cardinal Ximenes. (1499 A.D.)
11. The execution of Giordano Bruno. (1600 A.D.)
12. The execution of Lucilio Vanini. (1619 A.D.)
13. The murder of Hypatia. (415 A.D.)
14. The recantation of the Comte de Buffon. (1753 A.D.)[30]

---

[26] One could reasonably draw the conclusion that scientists lounging in laboratories testing hypotheses is no basis for a system of ethics.

[27] The Ilk of Vox Popoli aren't without their strengths, but they do tend to be rather more useful when it comes to questions like "9mm or .45?" and "What's the best way to get rid of a dead body?" Feel free to stop by, but whatever you do, don't ask about anything to do with the Civil War, or as some prefer to call it, Round One. http://voxday.blogspot.com.

[28] This list was compiled by a Pharyngula reader named Daedelus.

[29] This is an interesting inclusion, as the indebted Bacon was briefly jailed after being charged with twenty-three counts of bribery.

[30] Georges-Louis Leclerc published the first volume of his thirty-six-volume Natural History in 1749, and the Catholic Church forced him to add a ten-paragraph recantation in 1753. This did not prevent him from publishing the additional volumes, including "The Epochs of Nature" in which

15. St. Paul's rants against the "wisdom of the wise" in Corinthians. (First century A.D.)
16. The Byzantine emperor Justinian's closing of Plato's Academy in Athens.[31] (529 A.D.)
17. The ecclesiastical monopoly upon lay education.
18. Martin Luther's attacks upon reason. (1517 A.D.)
19. Rejection of modern medicine by the Jehovah's Witnesses and other sects.
20. The excommunication of Johannes Kepler by the Catholic Church. (1612 A.D.)

Now, one can't help but note that the most recent of these terrible sins against science took place more than 250 years ago, in 1753, except for the three that still apply today. This is not evidence of an ongoing war, it is merely a collection of historical grudges, most of them remarkably petty. By this standard, Christians would be justified in continuing to hold the Jews liable for the historical crime of murdering their Lord and Savior.[32] Furthermore, five of these seven individual victims of Christian persecution were themselves Christians. No wonder the Unholy Trinity found it difficult to come up with anything more specific than the spurious example of stem cell research.

The idea that religion is the enemy of science is a remarkably silly one when examined in scientific terms. Consider that Christian nation and the hostility to science that it supposedly harbors due to its extraordinary religiosity. And yet the United States of America accounts for more than one-third of the global scientific output despite representing only 4.5 percent of the global population. The scientific overperformance of religious America is a factor of 7.89, representing

---

he estimated the age of the Earth to be 75,000 in 1778. He survived his conflict with the Church; his son, on the other hand, was guillotined by the French Revolutionaries.

[31] This is false, as the Academy was apparently closed by the philosophers themselves, and only for one year. Despite the emperor's effort to reduce the influence of Hellenism, the Academy continued to operate for several decades afterward.

[32] Hey, it's not only in the New Testament. The great Jewish scribe Maimonides was pretty pleased to claim responsibility for killing Jesus Christ. *"Jesus of Nazareth interpreted the Torah and its precepts in such a fashion as to lead to their total annulment. The sages, of blessed memory, having become aware of his plans before his reputation spread among our people, meted out fitting punishment to him."* I still don't see how it makes much sense to hold it against them, though; my philosophy is that if a guy comes back from the dead, no harm no foul applies.

28.7 percent more scientific output per capita than the most atheistic nation in Europe, France.[33]

Ironically, it is easy to provide an example of scientistry sinning against both the scientific method and the body of knowledge much more recent than most of religion's supposed crimes. For example, Ernest Duchesne was a French military doctor who discovered the medical benefits of mold and submitted his doctoral thesis showing the result of his experiments with the therapeutic qualities of bacteria-killing molds to the Institut Pasteur, which ignored it because he was only twenty-three and had no standing in the scientific community. It would take another thirty-two years before Alexander Fleming discovered the antibiotic qualities of penicillin. As historian Daniel Boorstin notes in *Cleopatra's Nose*, the chief lesson of the history of science is that it is not ignorance that menaces scientific advancement, but rather the illusion of knowledge.

While the scientific method may lead invariably to a more accurate understanding of the material world, the same is not true of the scientists who pursue it. The profession of science is growing increasingly authoritarian and political, as can be seen by the treatment of those who fail to fall in line with the scientific consensus on subjects where the evidence is far from settled, such as global warming. This poses a real danger to the credibility of all three aspects of science, which is particularly ill-timed in light of the very real danger that science presently poses to humanity. After all, it would be far easier to eliminate a few hundred thousand scientists, even a few million scientists, than 4.85 billion religious adherents.

Religion does not threaten science so much as science threatens itself. By combining increasingly authoritarian arrogance with an encroachment upon intellectual spheres they are manifestly unprepared to invade, scientists and their thoughtless science fetishist followers risk starting a genuine war they cannot possibly hope to win.

---

[33] Braun, Tibor, Wolfgang Glänzel, and András Schubert. "A Global Snapshot of Scientific Trends," *The UNESCO Courier*, May 1999.

IV

THE RELIGION
OF REASON

Reason has always existed, but not always in a reasonable form.[1]

—KARL MARX

ATHEISTS OFTEN EXPRESS ANGER and bewilderment at the low esteem in which they are collectively held by the rest of the world. This is a matter of particular frustration for the New Atheists, as they lament the Gallup poll[2] in which it was determined that Americans would rather vote for a toothless, illiterate, homosexual Afro-Hispanic crack whore with a peg leg than a well-qualified atheist with executive hair. That's a slight exaggeration, perhaps, but it is interesting to note that three years after the publication of the first

---

[1] Karl Marx and Arnold Ruge, Letters from the Deutsch-Französische Jahrbücher. September 1843.

[2] In the most recent poll on the subject, a *Newsweek* poll from March 31, 2007, only 29 percent of the respondents said they were willing to vote for an atheist. Amazingly, it appears that telling people how evil and stupid they are may not be the best way of convincing them to see things your way.

New Atheist screed, the expressed willingness of Americans to vote for an atheist has declined considerably.[3]

And yet, a strong majority of those same respondents, 68 percent, believe it is possible for someone to be a moral person and an atheist. At first glance, this might appear to be an irrational dichotomy, but upon reflection it makes sense. Politicians are not ordinary people, they are extraordinarily ambitious individuals who possess an active desire to seek power over the lives of others. Think about how obnoxious the kids who ran for student council president at your school were—that's the larval form of the national politician. Most Americans wisely distrust politicians on principle; after all, the country was founded upon the basic principle of limiting the power of those who have been successful in obtaining office.

Regardless of what one thinks of a politician's religion, the mere fact that he has one offers the voter essential information about where his moral and ethical lines are theoretically drawn. This doesn't mean that he is actually bound by them in any way, but at least the voter has some idea of where his limits should be. The voter has only to call upon his personal knowledge of the religion's tenets, to read the religion's holy book, or to ask an acquaintance who happens to share the politician's faith to obtain a basic understanding of what the religious politician's ideas of right and wrong are and what policies he is likely to pursue.

In the case of the atheist politician, however, the voter not only has no information, he has no easy means of obtaining that information. As I pointed out in the first chapter, it is atheists who are quick to assure us that there are absolutely no similarities between atheists, that the mere absence of god-belief in an individual is not information from which any reasonable inferences can be drawn. This is an erroneous assertion, as there is no shortage of evidence to the contrary, but there is a grain of truth to it that applies in this situation.

Anyone can behave according to any moral system without needing to subscribe to the beliefs from which that system is derived.

---

[3] "In a recent *Newsweek* poll, Americans said they believed in God by a margin of 92 to 6—only 2 percent answered 'don't know'—and only 37 percent said they'd be willing to vote for an atheist for president. (That's down from 49 percent in a 1999 Gallup poll—which also found that more Americans would vote for a homosexual than an atheist.)" *Newsweek*, 11 Sep. 2006. The 2007 Gallup poll also showed a decline, although only to 45 percent.

One doesn't have to be an Orthodox Jew to keep kosher, just as one doesn't need to be a Christian to believe that committing adultery is wrong. Most atheists abide by the morality of the culture that they inhabit, not because they have taken the effort to reason from first principles and miraculously reached conclusions that bear a remarkable similarity to the moral system of those around them, but because lacking any moral system of their own, they parasitically latch on to the system of their societal host.

That's a negative way of describing what is essentially a good thing, and it's why atheists in Christian cultures behave according to an individual morality that has more in common with the surrounding Christians than with Hindu atheists or Islamic atheists with whom they theoretically have more in common. In practice, this tends to work out as the dominant local moral system minus the proscribed behavior in which the individual really wants to engage, which is usually something involving sex or money. But this positive moral parasitism can never be confused with the possession of an independent system of morality,[4] so the problem is that a voter has no idea which specific aspects of the dominant moral system have been rejected by the atheist politician.

While the atheist next door is likely to limit his rejection to the specific aspects that proscribe premarital fornication or gluttony and indulge himself in the sort of everyday moral failure to which even the most devout Christians are susceptible, history demonstrates that the ambitious atheist who seeks political power is significantly more likely to reject the moral proscription on things such as slaughtering large numbers of people who stand in the way of establishing a godless utopia.[5] The peg-legged crack whore, on the other hand, only wants to shift agricultural subsidies from cereal crops to coca plants and poppies and install disco balls in the White House.[6]

This is why the philosopher John Locke reached the conclusion

---

[4] While Dawkins, Dennett, and Harris all recognize this, Hitchens doesn't understand the concept at all. His constant stumbling over this issue in his debate with Douglas Wilson was amusing at first, but by the end it was getting painful.

[5] What's strikingly weird about many of these individuals is what moral proscriptions they retain, as if at random.

[6] With the slogan "Party to the People," of course. Now, where is this crack whore and when can I vote for him?

that atheists could be tolerated in civil society, so long as they were not permitted to hold positions of political authority. Locke, who died in 1704, never lived to see just how astute his observation was; tens of millions of lives in dozens of nations would have been saved had his wisdom been heeded.[7]

> *Promises, covenants, and oaths, which are the bonds of human society, can have no hold upon an atheist. The taking away of God, though but even in thought, dissolves all; besides also, those that by their atheism under-mine and destroy all religion, can have no pretence of religion whereupon to challenge the privilege of a toleration. As for other practical opinions, though not absolutely free from all error, yet if they do not tend to estab-lish domination over others, or civil impunity to the church in which they are taught, there can be no reason why they should not be tolerated.*
>
> —JOHN LOCKE, "Letter Concerning Toleration," 1689

So, while atheists indubitably possess morals, it is the inability to know which specific morals they personally subscribe to and which they reject that renders them rightly suspect. The problem is root-ed in the fact that no atheist possesses a universally applicable mo-rality, since one cannot be derived from either his atheism or from science. However, this does not mean that the New Atheists do not subscribe to a specific moral system that makes the same sort of uni-versal claims as the moralities derived from religion, for they do, and it is not a new morality, but one that has been around for centuries.

LEIBNIZIANS AND NEWTONIANS

> *You are saying it should be the goal of all Natural Philosophers to restore peace and harmony to the world of men. This I cannot dispute.*
>
> —NEAL STEPHENSON, *Quicksilver*

It was this quote from *Quicksilver*, the first novel in Neal Stephen-son's excellent Baroque Cycle, that caused me to contemplate the way in which the clash between the New Atheists and evangelical Chris-tians can be usefully viewed as a continuation of the fundamental

---

[7] See chapter XIII, *The Red Hand of Atheism.*

dichotomy between the worldviews of Gottfried Leibniz and Sir Isaac Newton as described by Stephenson.[8] The most important difference between the two geniuses was not the theoretical basis of one's calculus and the geometric basis of the other's, but rather Leibniz's belief in the secular improvability of Man and Newton's skepticism regarding the same.

It's interesting to note that this basic difference may have even informed their different approaches to developing the calculus, as Newton's approach, like the Christian's view of Man, is a combination of religious faith and empirical observation, whereas both the Leibnizian and New Atheist[9] approaches are primarily based on reason. The fictional Leibniz saw Natural Philosophy as having a practical moral application. All the disgusting dog-torturing and corpse-carving in which the Natural Philosophers engaged was seen as being ultimately justified in order to bring about world peace through human means. The fictional Newton, on the other hand, saw Natural Philosophy primarily as a means of discovering the mechanics of God's Creation, hence his eventual loss of interest in it and subsequent turn to alchemy as a means of seeking an essence that transcends the material.

The New Atheists are Leibnizians, not literally, because Stephenson's Leibniz character sees no conflict between his Natural Philosophy and his belief in God,[10] but in an analogical sense. Based solely on their theoretical reasoning, the New Atheists declare that it should be the goal of all scientists, indeed, all rational thinkers, to bring peace and harmony to the world of men. They don't declare this in a succinct or straightforward manner, they don't even lay out their case in a coherent manner, but this is the only conclusion that can rationally be derived from their cumulative premises, logic, and stated goals. It is unclear why none of them are able to come out and state this clearly, but there are a number of possible explanations.

---

[8] I leave it to the reader to decide how historically accurate Stephenson's fictional portrayal of these worldviews are.

[9] Or New Natural Philosophy, as would arguably be a more accurate description of the movement.

[10] Technically, Daniel Waterhouse represents the atheists, but the analogy stands either way. And, of course, Leibniz's calculus was ultimately upheld by the evidence and, as shall be seen throughout this book, the same is seldom true of the New Atheist theories.

The first is a question of intellectual competence. They simply may not understand the correct way to articulate their argument. This is entirely possible with Harris and Hitchens, who are impressively incoherent thinkers at the best of times, but it isn't credible in the case of Dawkins or Dennett. Dawkins, at least, clearly understands the difference between his enthusiasm for science and his advocacy of an alternative secular morality,[11] even if he does not provide a concise description of precisely what that morality is or the basis of its claim on anyone's behavior.

The second possibility is that they genuinely believe science leads ineluctably toward certain moral conclusions. Although the careless reader could be convinced of this by a judicious selection of quotes, both Dawkins and Dennett specifically deny this to be possible and even Harris only dares to base his moral appeals on reason, not science. Hitchens, meanwhile, is almost completely indifferent to getting either the science or the theology straight. (He's just a journalist after all—he's not expected to make sense.)

The third and most likely explanation is that the New Atheists are pulling a deceptive bait-and-switch for marketing purposes. All four authors state outright that their books are works of atheistic evangelism, meant to either convince the Low Church atheist to publicly identify with the High Church or to convert a theistic reader by destroying his faith. Three of the four books are marketed as quasi-scientific works and are filled with a panoply of references to science and concepts that sound vaguely scientific, although Daniel Dennett's *Breaking the Spell* is the only one that actually utilizes a recognizably scientific approach or makes any use of the scientific method; unsurprisingly, Dennett is also the only New Atheist who presents the reader with a reasonable hypothesis worthy of consideration instead of a philosophical conclusion meant to be accepted at face value.

The division between science[12] and the moral and philosophical purposes toward which scientists ultimately direct the scientific method was always inevitable. Richard Feynman understood this, pointing out that scientific knowledge provides the ability to do good

---

[11] See chapter VIII.

[12] In the sense of scientage and scientody.

or evil, and that using it to do good is not only to the credit of science, but to the credit of the moral choice that led to the good work as well. And like Daniel Dennett, Feynman regretted that Man's accomplishments had fallen far short of what had been believed possible at the beginning of the Age of Reason.

> *Why can't we conquer ourselves? Because we find that even great forces and abilities do not seem to carry with them clear instructions on how to use them. As an example, the great accumulation of understanding as to how the physical world behaves only convinces one that this behavior seems to have a kind of meaninglessness. The sciences do not directly teach good or bad.*
>
> —RICHARD FEYNMAN

But Feynman's response to this division was a commendably scientific one that is profoundly different from the moral philosophy advocated by Dawkins, Harris, and Hitchens. Feynman believed that it was the responsibility of scientists to proclaim the value of intellectual freedom, to support open discussion and criticism, and to welcome doubt, not suppress it. He declared that demanding this freedom for all future generations was a fundamental scientific duty.[13] He was far more dedicated to protecting science as an effective means than he was to using it to advocate any specific ends.

The New Atheists harbor no similar dedication to open discussion, let alone criticism. To them, science is but a means to a specific end, something to be prostituted in order to sell the secularist Enlightenment morality that they see in competition with the Christian faith. Having already sold out science, they reject any sense of scientific responsibility and thus will tolerate no skepticism, let alone outright opposition. Dawkins is the worst offender—his prickly reaction to criticism is not to address it, not to discuss it, but to disdainfully dismiss it, unread. When Douglas Wilson[14] published his response to *Letter to a Christian Nation*, Dawkins lost no time in labeling him "Sam's Flea." According to Dawkins, arguably the most visible

---

[13] Feynman, Richard. *What Do You Care What Other People Think? Further Adventures of a Curious Character*. New York: 1985.

[14] The same Douglas Wilson who handed Christopher Hitchens his head in their 2007 debate. I haven't read the book, in fact, I haven't read any of the books criticizing Dawkins, either.

representative of science today, any published criticism of him and his fellow militants can only be driven by the desire for book sales.[15]

Feynman wept.

The key to understanding the New Atheism is that it is not based on science. The New Atheists have no commitment to scientage or scientody when either aspect of science happens to stand in the way of the secular morality they are selling with a scientific sheen. While their attacks are theoretically directed against all religions, they betray their focus for the main object of their hatred in both their language and the examples they choose. For all that he was supposedly inspired to write *The End of Faith* by the jihadist 9/11 attacks, Sam Harris will never write *Letter to an Islamic Nation* and Christopher Hitchens expends more of his bilious vitriol on one dead Catholic nun than he does attacking the entire Hindu pantheon worshipped by one billion individuals around the world.

So what, specifically, is this morality? Because it is never described in its entirety, it is necessary for us to piece it together from the hints sprinkled throughout the atheist canon. We know that Christianity stands in its way, courtesy of Bertrand Russell, who declares that the Christian religion is the principal enemy of moral progress in the world. And we know that it is in opposition to even the most moderate forms of religious faith, thanks to Sam Harris.

> My biggest criticism of religious moderation…is that it represents precisely the sort of thinking that will prevent a fully reasonable and nondenominational spirituality from ever emerging in our world.[16]

However, Harris never gets around to describing his proposed morality due to a tendency to meander into oxymoronic dicussions of his New Age, neo-Buddhist rational spirituality. For a system of morals and ethics, Harris offers nothing more concrete than half-baked utilitarianism in declaring that morality is merely a recipe for maximizing

---

[15] "Fleas" and "parasites" are Dawkins's favored means of referring to his critics. On March 4, 2007, at http://www.richarddawkins.net, Dawkins posted an entry entitled "Was there ever a dog that praised his fleas?" in reference to the "three new parasitic books released in response to *The God Delusion*." If the supercilious old fart ever wants to see who the bigger dog is, I'll be delighted to throw down with him. Oxford Union or the Octagon, it's all the same to me.

[16] Harris, Sam and Andrew Sullivan. "Is Religion 'Built Upon Lies'?" Beliefnet, 2 Feb. 2007.

happiness and minimizing suffering.[17] Hitchens is a bit more help-ful, as *god is not Great* builds up to a final chapter that informs us that there is a definite need for a New Enlightenment, and in the pro-cess asserts that the following things are positively immoral: present-ing a false picture of the world to the innocent and credulous,[18] the doctrine of blood sacrifice, the doctrine of atonement, the doctrine of eternal reward or punishment, and the imposition of impossible tasks. Other moral evils that go beyond this list of doctrinal thought crimes include frightening children, exploitation, suicide bombings, opposition to birth control, circumcision (male and female), ban-ning and censoring books, and silencing dissenters.

Regarding the basic moral structure of this new and shinier En-lightenment, Hitchens is, like Marx describing the long-awaited Worker's Paradise, more than a little vague. After 282 pages of fu-rious anti-religious foreplay, the climax is disappointing indeed, amounting to only a single paragraph of seven sentences.[19] But we are informed that the New Enlightenment will be based on the idea that the proper study of Mankind is man and woman. Literature and poetry will replace sacred texts, and most importantly, the sexual life will be divorced from fear, disease, and tyranny, all on the sole con-dition "that we banish all religions from the discourse" by knowing "the enemy" and fighting it. Sadly, it appears there are no seventy-two virgins in store.

Despite his grand eloquence and enlightened posturing, Hitchens is almost indistinguishable from a conventional Low Church atheist, who is content to dwell as a moral parasite on traditional Christian morality except when he wants to get laid without feeling guilty or catching a venereal disease.

Both Richard Dawkins and Daniel Dennett, on the other hand, are not looking for a New Enlightenment as they are still pledged to the old one. While it's absolutely true that atheism is not a religion, most High Church atheists subscribe to a specific denomination of the En-lightenment faith known as humanism.[20] In *The God Delusion* Dawkins

---

[17] Although he is to be commended for saying in a sentence what takes Michel Onfray seven vol-umes.

[18] The reader may wish to remember this charge in light of some of the subsequent chapters.

[19] Hitchens, *god is not Great*, 283.

[20] "*Humanism is a progressive philosophy of life that, without supernaturalism, affirms our ability and*

describes his belief in humanism, "the ethical system that often goes with atheism," and testified to his faith that "the broad direction of history is toward enlightenment"[21] in an interview with Salon. Although he's much more famous for his atheism, his humanism is no secret—the American Humanist Association named him the 1996 Humanist of the Year, while in 2004, it was Daniel Dennett's turn to be so honored.[22] Richard Dawkins is also a public signer of the third Humanist Manifesto, which summarizes the principle articles of the humanist faith thusly:

1. Knowledge of the world is derived by observation, experimentation, and rational analysis.
2. Humans are an integral part of nature, the result of unguided evolutionary change.
3. Ethical values are derived from human need and interest as tested by experience.
4. Life's fulfillment emerges from individual participation in the service of humane ideals.
5. Humans are social by nature and find meaning in relationships.
6. Working to benefit society maximizes individual happiness.

Specifically what those humane ideals and ethical values might be is not explained, although we are informed that Dawkins and company "aspire to this vision with the informed conviction that humanity has the ability to progress toward its highest ideals." This is all very scientific, of course, because we are assured that the humanist conviction—which is of course not to be confused with "faith"—is informed. But it is evidence that even the world's most militant atheists find that belief in a universally applicable morality is something to preserve, so that when they find the theistic foundations of Christian morality incredible, they don't give up, they seek a substitute instead. In *The God Delusion*, Dawkins suggests substituting the following for four

---

responsibility to lead ethical lives of personal fulfillment that aspire to the greater good of humanity." http://www.humanism.org.uk.

[21] Gordy Slack, "The Atheist." Salon. 30 April, 2005.

[22] I'll be astounded if Sam Harris or Christopher Hitchens doesn't pick one up in 2008, 2009 at the latest.

of the Ten Commandments, although he doesn't indicate which he'd leave out, his hatred for God combined with his marital history suggests that he has numbers One, Three, Four, and Seven in mind.

- Enjoy your own sex life.
- Do not discriminate or oppress on the basis of sex, race, or species.[23]
- Do not indoctrinate your children.[24]
- Value the future.[25]

The British Humanist Association, which Dawkins serves as an honorary vice president, provides some additional detail on humanist tenets in its ten-question quiz[26] meant to help one determine whether one happens to be a humanist or not. According to the BHA, the following answers indicate that one is either a humanist already or is very close to humanist thinking:

1. There is no evidence that any god exists, so I'll assume that there isn't one.
2. When I die, I will live on in people's memories or because of the work I have done or through my children.
3. The scientific explanations for how the universe began are the best ones available—no gods were involved.
4. The theory that life on Earth evolved gradually over billions of years is true—here is plenty of evidence from fossils showing that this is how it happened.
5. When I look at a beautiful view I think that we ought to do everything possible to protect this for future generations.
6. I can tell right from wrong by thinking hard about the probable consequences of actions and their effects on other people.
7. It's best to be honest because I'm happier and feel better about myself if I'm honest.
8. Other people matter and should be treated with respect because

---

[23] Discrimination based on looks is okay. That's just evolution in action.

[24] Except for teaching evolution to school children. That's a moral imperative.

[25] Even though this life is all you've got and you won't be there to see it.

[26] http://www.humanism.org.uk/site/cms/contentviewarticle.asp?article=1208 on 25 June 2007.

we will all be happier if we treat each other well.

9. Animals should be treated with respect because they can suffer, too.

10. The most important thing in life is to increase the general happiness and welfare of humanity.

As it turns out, Harris's morality of happiness is ultimately humanist in origin. From these examples, the educated reader should be able to see that the religion of reason is little more than a memetic chimera crossing the Summer of Love with Darwinism and scientific socialism: be happy, be nice, be Green, to each according to his needs, individuals exist for the purpose of serving the common good, human progress toward an earthly paradise is inevitable, all shined up with a thin veneer of science. It's no wonder Christopher Hitchens is seeking a New Enlightenment, he only recently disavowed his secular faith in the old one.[27]

RESURRECTING THE RED HAND OF REASON

The Marxist worldview has a relationship to the Enlightenment. I think that's impossible to doubt.

—CHRISTOPHER HITCHENS

The original Enlightenment led directly to the French Revolution, and only 349 days after the *citoyens sans-culottes* established the French Republic, the bloody Reign of Terror began. On 20 Brumaire An II,[28] the cathedral of Notre Dame was renamed the Temple of Reason and a dancer named Mademoiselle Maillard was enthroned upon the altar as Reason's goddess. Like a lethal virus transmitted from corpse to living carrier, Enlightenment ideals survived the collapse of the First Republic and were preserved by utopian socialists such

---

[27] "*I no longer would have positively replied, 'I am a socialist'. . . . There is no longer a general socialist critique of capitalism—certainly not the sort of critique that proposes an alternative or a replacement. There just is not and one has to face the fact, and it seems to me further that it's very unlikely, though not impossible, that it will again be the case in the future. Though I don't think that the contradictions, as we used to say, of the system, are by any means all resolved.*" "Free Radical:" *Reason.* Nov. 2001.

[28] Otherwise known as Anno Domini November 10, 1793.

as de Rouvroy, Fourier, and Cabet. De Rouvroy, who died in 1825, anticipated the Actually Not So New Atheists by nearly two centuries in arguing that a new religion purged of divisive Christian dogma, with scientists serving as priests, was required for the good of society. Twenty-three years after de Rouvroy's death, Marx and Engels put a scientific spin on their socialism, which inspired the Russian Revolution of 1919 and all the humane joys inherent in seventy years of Communist rule.

Although the fall of the Soviet Union in 1989 briefly left the enlightened humanists of the world without a state to call their own, that was soon remedied by the 1992 Treaty of Maastricht, which established the European Union[29] as a political entity dedicated to Enlightenment ideals[30] and from which all reference to Europe's historic Christian heritage has been carefully excised.[31] While the European Convention on Human Rights has not yet been ratified by the European Union because the EU is not yet a recognized state, the Convention serves as a good measure of Enlightenment morality in action since it has been ratified by all the EU's member states and is considered to be the basis for the EU's own Charter of Fundamental Rights.[32]

The Convention is a cornucopia of Enlightenment rights, including the right to life, the prohibition of slavery, the right to liberty and security, the right to freedom of expression, and so forth. Unfortunately, these rights come with strict caveats that leave holes in these theoretical protections large enough to drive a truck through... or an overcrowded train rattling along the tracks pointing toward a gulag. Nor do they come as unalienable rights endowed by a creator, they

---

[29] "If you go through all the structures and features of this emerging European monster you will notice that it more and more resembles the Soviet Union. Of course, it is a milder version of the Soviet Union." Vladimir Bukovsky. "Former Soviet Dissident Warns For EU Dictatorship." Brussels Journal. 27 Feb. 2006.

[30] According to Valéry Giscard d'Estaing, the former French president who presided over the Convention on the Future of the European Union at which the EU Constitution was created, "the philosophy of the Age of the Enlightenment and the contributions of rational and scientific thought define the European identity." "Is Turkey 'Enlightened' Enough to Join the EU?" The Globalist. 10 Dec. 2004.

[31] Cullinan, John. "Godless in Brussels." National Review Online, 16 June 2003.

[32] The Charter of Fundamental Rights is an expansion of the rights delineated in the Convention and includes such additions as right to good administration, workers social rights, personal data protection, and bio-ethics. At the time of writing, the Charter had not yet been formally incorporated into European Union treaty law.

are merely notional rights granted by the forty-seven signatory governments that belong to the Council of Europe, subject to the political and legal processes of those governments. Some of the limitations are even articulated in the explication of the rights themselves, while Article 17 ominously prohibits what it terms "the abuse of rights" granted in the Convention.[33]

> *"Freedom to manifest one's religion or beliefs shall be subject only to such limitations as are prescribed by law and are necessary in a democratic society...."* (Article 9) *"The exercise of these freedoms [of expression], since it carries with it duties and responsibilities, may be subject to such formalities, conditions, restrictions or penalties as are prescribed by law and are necessary in a democratic society...."* (Article 10) Similar caveats restrict the rights granted in articles 5, 6, 8 and 11.

The multiple references to the need for a democratic society to limit human rights is particularly ironic, as for all its democratic pretensions, European integration has been pushed inexorably forward without the democratic consent of many of Europe's peoples. Every significant step in the integration process has been the result of negotiations between the bureaucratic and political elites, and when the people have been given the opportunity to express their opinion democratically and rejected the results of these negotiations, they have either been forced to vote until they get it right, as was the case in Denmark and Ireland,[34] or simply ignored and overrun with semantic games.[35]

---

[33] A Canadian journalist named David Warren warns: *"The most frightening proposal is the one least appreciated: to create a European 'charter of fundamental rights' that will accomplish the precise opposite of what it claims. It will swing the iron claw of 'progressive thought' through the soft flesh of human variety, enterprise, and freedom, on an unprecedented scale....It is time people realized that 'human rights codes' are a weapon employed by the state to suppress disapproved behavior by the individual. They cannot be wielded by the individual against the state, as independent civil and criminal courts could be."* Warren, David. "Constituting EU," 23 June 2007.

[34] The Irish people voted against the Treaty of Nice in June 2001. After a year of intense government lobbying, they ratified it in October 2002. This followed the Danish example, in which the Danish people voted down the Treaty of Maastricht in June 1992 and then approved it in a May 1993 referendum. Of course, neither the Irish nor the Danish people have been given an opportunity to change their minds again. The Swiss people have rejected the EU twice already, but few doubt that they will have to do so a third time.

[35] German Chancellor Andrea Merkel was as shamelessly deceptive as any previous German Reichskanzler in repackaging the rejected European Constitution as a "treaty," thereby attempting to bypass any need to respect the will of the French, Dutch, and British people who oppose it. If the

The president of the European Union, Jean-Claude Juncker, answered with commendable, if anti-democratic, honesty when asked about the French vote on the EU constitution: "If it's a Yes, we will say 'on we go', and if it's a No we will say 'we continue.'"[36] And after the signing of the "treaty" to allow the governments of the nations who voted the constitution down to proceed with its adoption without the consent of the people, the president of the European Commission, José Manuel Barroso, declared, "We are unique in the history of Mankind.... Now what we have is the first non-imperial empire. We have twenty-seven countries that fully decided to work together and to pool their sovereignty."[37]

Perhaps because he is a recent apostate from Marxism, Christopher Hitchens alone among the New Atheists appears to see the creeping authoritarianism inherent in the religion of reason. When asked why so many individuals with theoretically anti-authoritarian beliefs somehow end up supporting authoritarian government actions, he explained that this was because of the way in which temporary expedients considered necessary for the achievement of a primary goal are easily transformed into dogma[38] that cannot be questioned lest the attainment of the goal be jeopardized. This is the very rational reason that the historical religion of reason so quickly produced massive violence and why its revival is very likely to lead to the same result. If the desired end cannot be reached without resorting to an ugly means, then either the end must be abandoned or the ugly means must be adopted. Therefore, while a decision to engage in mass slaughter can be an irrational one, it clearly cannot be considered inherently irrational. The process can be entirely based on reason, from utopian start to bloody finish. The problem is not in the logic or its absence, but rather in the basic premises that the logic serves.

This is why the humanist vagaries regarding their moral premises are so troubling, and it also explains why atheists in positions of power

---

history of the former European Coal and Steel Community is any guide, this anti-democratic power grab will be successful.

[36] "Keep up the pressure for a No vote, Left warned." *The Telegraph*. 26 May, 2005.

[37] "Call For Vote on Europe Empire," *The Times*, 11 July 2007.

[38] *"If you make your priority—let's call it the 1930s—the end of massive unemployment, which was then defined as one of the leading problems, there seemed no way to do it except by a program of public works.... And then temporary expedients become dogma very quickly—especially if they seem to work."* "Free Radical:" *Reason*.

have been inordinately disposed to commit mass murder in service to their ideals. History shows that it is easy enough for Christians to violate their fairly explicit moral strictures, and it is even easier for humanists to ignore their own nebulous moralities in self-righteous, rational pursuit of their ultimately irrational goals. As evidence of this, I note that while the European Union has not even formally adopted the European Convention on Human Rights yet, some of its member-states are already exploiting the aforementioned caveats to violate the right to respect for private and family life, the freedom of thought, conscience and religion, and the freedom of expression.[39]

After Belgian police beat up two leading Flemish politicians protesting pro-immigration policies in Brussels on September 11, 2007, the secretary general of the Council of Europe was inspired to announce: "The freedom of expression and freedom of assembly are indeed preconditions for democracy, but they should not be regarded as a license to offend." Free speech is permitted by the enlightened eurofascists, as long as one doesn't actually say anything they deem unacceptable.

Das Europa über alles
Über alles im Erdteil.
Einigkeit und Gewaltherrschaft
Für die neue Erleuchtung....

So, what is the ultimate goal of the religion of reason? And is it a rational one? Sam Harris's description of the result of this inevitable humanist progress is precisely the same as the end prophesied by the humanist and New Atheist icon[40] Bertrand Russell eighty-four years ago.[41] It is not the end of faith that is the ultimate goal, this is merely a

---

[39] Unsurprisingly, it is Germany that is the worst offender, jailing parents and seizing children under a 1938 Nazi anti-home schooling law that is still in effect, and imprisoning people for expressing their doubts about the official version of the Holocaust. It's a pity they didn't keep the snappy uniforms and give up the totalitarianism instead.

[40] Dawkins quotes or refers to Russell even more often than he does to his fellow New Atheists. Harris has eight references to him in his index, Hitchens five.

[41] "*I believe that, owing to men's folly, a world-government will only be established by force, and therefore be at first cruel and despotic. But I believe that it is necessary for the preservation of a scientific civilization, and that, if once realized, it will gradually give rise to the other conditions of a tolerable existence.*" Bertrand Russell. "Icarus, or, the Future of Science," 1924. Russell also called for the United States to use its nuclear monopoly to institute an international authority ruling the world

necessary prerequisite to the economic, cultural, and moral integration required for establishing the world government that the devotees of Reason hope will bring a permanent end to war.

But world government and a subsequent end to war is not a rational goal given the way it flies in the face of everything we know about human history and human nature, to say nothing of the grim results of past monopolies on legal violence. While Harris attempts to argue that the humanist dream is feasible based on the historical example of slavery, his argument requires ignoring the inability of modern society to bring an end to the sex slavery and human-trafficking that persist today in even the most civilized Western nations. The terrible tragedy of the New Atheists is that they are laboring to lay the foundation for yet another reprisal of the very horrors they think to permanently prevent in the name of Reason. Voltaire may have been correct to write that "those who can make you believe absurdities can make you commit atrocities," but a more meaningfully rational statement would be to say: If you commit atrocities, then you believe absurdities.

And the undeniable fact is that the absurdity most often believed by those who have committed Man's greatest atrocities is that there is no God.

---

in peaceful hegemony in his 1945 essay "The Bomb and Civilization."

V

SAM TZU AND
THE ART OF WAR

The rule with regard to contentious ground is that those in possession have the advantage over the other side. If a position of this kind is secured first by the enemy, beware of attacking him. Lure him away by pretending to flee—show your banners and sound your drums—make a dash for other places that he cannot afford to lose. . . .

—Sun Tzu Hsu Lu, Pi I-hsun

I N THE HISTORICAL INTRODUCTION to his famous military treatise, the Chinese general Sun Tzu advised the wise general to lure his opponent from ground where the opponent holds a strong position in the hopes of being able to attack him in a weaker one. It is interesting to see that Sam Harris and Richard Dawkins both make inadvertent use of this tactic with their mutual assertion that religious faith bears responsibility for enabling the making of war even when it is not, in itself, a primary cause of conflict. It is also ironic, given their near total ignorance of military history and the art of war.

On a superficial level, the assertion appears to make a good deal of sense. It is certainly reasonable to postulate that the religious individual who believes in some form of life continuing beyond death would be more willing to take the chances with his life that war demands than would the non-religious individual. The religious soldier is only risking a part of his existence, a rather small and unimportant part in the case of the Christian soldier who confidently expects eternal life awaiting him in the New Jerusalem. The *shaheed* finds courage in the prospect of seventy-two virgins and the delights of paradise. The pagan Norse warrior fearlessly anticipated endless feasting and battle in Valhalla; his only terror was an ignominious death in bed, far from the battlefields haunted by the Choosers of the Slain.

Even the Hindu soldier risks nothing but a single turn of the wheel, whereas the atheist stakes the totality of his existence. There is, then, an economic argument to be made in logical support of this claim of religious war-enabling, since the perceived cost of war is obviously much greater for the atheist than for the theist.[1]

There is etymological support for this notion as well. According to the Online Etymology Dictionary, the word "fanatic" is derived from the following source:

> c.1525, "insane person," from L. fanaticus "mad, enthusiastic, inspired by a god," originally, "pertaining to a temple," from fanum "temple," related to festus "festive" (see feast). Current sense of "extremely zealous," especially in religion, is first attested 1647. The noun is from 1650, originally in religious sense, of Nonconformists.[2]

For who can today hear the term "religious fanatic" and not immediately think of the suicide bombers of the Islamic jihad, who have struck terror into hearts around the globe? Nor are the modern jihadists the first religious fanatics to be inspired to deeds of astounding horror, as witnessed by Raymond of Aguilers's account of slaughter-maddened Christian knights riding through blood up to their knees after the fall of Jerusalem in the First Crusade, or the more recent example of the Basij Mostazafan, an Iranian teen militia famous

---

[1] One wonders if atheists would be so swift to embrace this logic if they understood it could be used to assert an atheistic inclination toward cowardice just as easily as it supports a hypothetical theistic inclination for war-mongering.

[2] Speaking of etymology, it is no small irony that such a famous Nonconformist as Richard Dawkins should be known by a phrase originally coined to describe clergy of the Church of England.

for voluntarily clearing minefields with their own bodies during the Iran-Iraq War.

And yet, even in these examples, one can see the first visible cracks in the argument. The First Crusade was a long time ago, it has been more than a thousand years since the massacre at Solomon's Temple took place. In that millennia, many wars have been fought, very few of which have involved unarmed youth militias inspired by insane devotion to a god. Moreover, from a military perspective, suicide attacks are a negligible tactic.[3] They are not intended to win battles, much less wars, and even if one goes as far back as the Japanese kamikazes of World War II, one will not find a single battle that is recorded as having been won by suicide tactics, with or without the presumed benefit of religious fanaticism.

Even so, Sam Harris insists that religion is a uniquely dangerous source of the intersocietal tensions that produce wars:

Religion raises the stakes of human conflict much higher than tribalism, racism, or politics ever can, as it is the only form of in-group/out-group thinking that casts the differences between people in terms of eternal rewards and punishments. One of the enduring pathologies of human culture is the tendency to raise children to fear and demonize other human beings on the basis of religious faith. Consequently, faith inspires violence in at least two ways. First, people often kill other human beings because they believe that the [C]reator of the universe wants them to do it.[4]

There are four errors in these four sentences. (1) Harris implies a direct connection between the commission of individual crime and mass inter-group conflict, however, he never bothers to explain just what this connection might happen to be. And while I shall address both forms of lethal violence, I note that it is simply not credible to suggest that the same motivation guides the killer who rapes and murders a stranger and the national leader who orders his troops to

---

[3] Suicide bombings and terror in general are not military tactics, but political ones. The reason terrorism is usually directed against civilian targets rather than military ones is not because the military targets are more difficult to reach, but because attacks on them are ineffective given the primary goal of influencing the political psychology of the situation. The bombing of the Italian Carabinieri base at Nasiriyah on 12 November, 2003 and the Madrid train attacks of 11 March, 2004 are good examples of this.

[4] Harris, *Letter to a Christian Nation*, 80.

defend against a military invasion by an enemy.

(2) It is impossible to raise the stakes of human conflict any higher than the total eradication of the opposing out-group. Due to the possibility of religious conversion present in most religions, it can be reasonably argued that religious conflict actually offers a less intractable form of conflict than that created by tribalism or racism; the release of Fox News journalists Steve Centanni and Olag Wiig after their coerced "conversion" to Islam is only one of the many examples of this. Whereas one cannot so easily change one's skin color or one's tribe, and one need merely cite the murderous deeds of the pagan Genghis Khan or the atheist Saloth Sar to prove that non-religious motivations are sufficient to raise the stakes to the highest level.

And while bringing children up to fear and demonize others may be a pathology of human culture, there is no shortage of evidence demonstrating that this is done more often, and to greater effect, for reasons other than that of religious faith (3). It is no coincidence, after all, that public schooling is one of the ten pillars of the Communist Manifesto, that Germany's National Socialist regime passed a compulsory school attendance law in 1938, and that the infamous Hung Wei Ping who launched the bloody Cultural Revolution in 1966 that killed 400,000 people[5] in only two years were children in junior high school[6] who had been raised from birth as atheists.

It is true, of course, that people have been known to kill other human beings because they believe that the Creator of the universe wants them to do it. The Bible is replete with such examples, and there are a few pitiful specimens of humanity spending the rest of their lives in lunatic asylums[7] for this very reason. (4) But Harris's use of the word "often" is more than a little questionable here, given how much more often people are known to murder other human beings for reasons unrelated to religion.

Harris frequently points out the extreme religiosity of American

---

[5] Agence France Presse, 3 Feb. 1979.

[6] "*The first Red Guards appeared on 29 May. They were from the middle school, aged about twelve to fourteen. . . . Soon they were joined by children from younger and older age-groups, by students and, most important, by members of the CCP Youth Leagues. . . .*" Johnson, Paul. *Modern Times.* New York: HarperCollins Publishers, 1991. 556.

[7] One hopes, anyhow.

society compared to the rest of the world, which therefore makes the United States an ideal subject of investigation on this particular point. Fortunately, the FBI not only keeps track of how many murders take place in the United States in its Uniform Crime Reports every year, but also records who committed them, how they were committed, against whom they were committed, and why.

In 2005, there were 16,692 American murders.[8] Of these, precisely six[9] were attributed to hate crimes, a definition that encompasses all racial, religious,[10] sexual orientation, ethnic, and disability motivations for criminal actions. Of the other 10,283 murders for which the motivations have been determined, none were attributed to anything that could conceivably be related to a belief in a deity's desire to see a particular individual dead. Instead, the two most frequent motivations were arguments (36.7 percent) and felony offenses such as robbery and narcotic drug laws (21 percent).[11]

Unless the vast majority of arguments that end with one interlocutor murdering the other are inspired by erudite debates between individuals belonging to divergent schools of soteriological thought,[12] it is obvious that Harris is wildly incorrect about the frequency with which religious faith inspires murderous actions. Even if we were to categorize every murderer who successfully pleads a "not guilty by reason of insanity"[13] defense among the religious faithful—a dubious proposition at best—this would only add an additional forty-one murders to the total that could conceivably be blamed on religion.

Since the maximum number of potential victims of religious faith

---

[8] Federal Bureau of Investigations, *Crime in the United States*. 2005.

[9] Federal Bureau of Investigations, *Hate Crime Statistics*. 2005. Table 2.

[10] There were 848 anti-Jewish hate crimes in 2005. One hundred and twenty-eight offenses were anti-Islamic, ninety-three were anti-Other Religion, fifty-eight were anti-Catholic, fifty-seven were anti-Protestant, thirty-nine were anti-multiple religions, and only four were anti-Atheism/Agnostism. When Dawkins wrote that "*the status of atheists in America today is on a par with that of homosexuals fifty years ago,*" he was apparently unaware that there were 1,017 anti-homosexual hate crimes in the same year as those four offenses.

[11] Federal Bureau of Investigations, *Supplementary Homicide Report*. 2005. Expanded Homicide Data Table 11.

[12] Or one could simply say "people that have different ideas about salvation." But I wouldn't want anyone to be embarrassed by thinking he or she's reading a book written by someone who isn't, like, college-educated and everything.

[13] "*This is the reality of the insanity defense in America: difficult to plead, seldom used and almost never successful.*" The Crime Library. It is estimated that 0.25 percent of all murder defendants successfully plead "not guilty by reason of insanity."

is six percent of the number of American bicyclists killed annually, and only six-tenths of 1 percent of those killed by doctors with poor writing skills,[14] I wonder if we can look forward to a future book from Mr. Harris decrying the moral evil of the bicycle accompanied by a call for mandatory calligraphy classes for all medical professionals.

KILL THY NEIGHBOR

If he is unsuccessful in demonstrating that the religious are unusually inclined to commit lethal hate crimes, Harris appears to find somewhat more promising ground on which to do battle with his concluding notion, wherein he blames intercommunal conflict on religion.

> *Second, far greater numbers of people fall into conflict with one another because they define their moral community on the basis of their religious affiliation: Muslims side with other Muslims, Protestants with Protestants, Catholics with Catholics. These conflicts are not always explicitly religious. But the bigotry and hatred that divide one community from another are often the products of their religious identities. Conflicts that seem driven entirely by terrestrial concerns, therefore, are often deeply rooted in religion. The fighting that has plagued Palestine (Jews vs. Muslims), the Balkans (Orthodox Serbians vs. Catholic Croatians; Orthodox Serbians vs. Bosnian and Albanian Muslims), Northern Ireland (Protestants vs. Catholics), Kashmir (Muslims vs. Hindus), Sudan (Muslims vs. Christians and animists), Nigeria (Muslims vs. Christians), Ethiopia and Eritrea (Muslims vs. Christians), Ivory Coast (Muslims vs. Christians), Sri Lanka (Sinhalese Buddhists vs. Tamil Hindus), Philippines (Muslims vs. Christians), Iran and Iraq (Shiite vs. Sunni Muslims), and the Caucasus (Orthodox Russians vs. Chechen Muslims; Muslim Azerbaijanis vs. Catholic and Orthodox Armenians) are merely a few, recent cases in point.*

This long list might appear to be persuasive, were it not for the fact that the list of potential examples to the contrary is considerably longer, to say nothing of the fact that nearly every example given

---

[14] According to the Bicycle Helmet Safety Institute, 784 bicyclists died in 2005. The National Academy of Sciences' Institute of Medicine published a study in July 2006 stating that prescription errors caused by poor handwriting kill 7,000 Americans every year.

here includes Muslims. To Sam Harris, all religions might be equally mythical and therefore the same, but it is hard to fail to notice that it is not the Jains, Mormons, Hindus, or Christians who are actively stirring up violence all over the world. In fact, Harris even left out a few relevant examples, such as East Timor, while mistakenly assigning religious motivations to at least four of the conflicts mentioned.

1. The conflict in Palestine is primarily ethnic, not religious. Atheist Jews, who represent 22.9 percent[15] of the Israeli population, are targeted by their Arab enemies as readily as the ultra-Orthodox. (Another 21 percent call themselves secular and do not practice any religion, but nevertheless profess to believe in God.) Moreover, the violence in Palestine began with the secular Zionists attacking the Christian British.

2. The conflict in Northern Ireland is primarily ethnic and political, not religious, being a holdover from the British colonial establishment of the Ulster Plantation in 1609. Indicative of this is the fact that more people were killed in the intra-nationalist Irish Civil War of 1922–23, which pitted Catholic against Catholic, than the 3,523 deaths resulting from the thirty-two years of the modern inter-denominational troubles.

3. Although foreign Muslims have come to the aid of their co-religionists in the Chechen war, the cause has absolutely nothing to do with any religious conflict between the Chechen Muslims and the Orthodox Russians, but the fact that Chechnya has been seeking independence from Russia since it was forcibly annexed in 1870 by Tsar Alexander II. While the Chechens tried, and failed, to take advantage of the collapse of the tsarist empire in 1917, they have been marginally more successful in the more recent set of wars for independence they have waged following the collapse of the Soviet Union.

4. In Sri Lanka, the political divide is linguistic, not religious. Tamil-speaking Hindus and Christians are allied against Sinhalese-speaking Buddhists and Muslims. The government's main rival, the revolutionary Liberation Tigers of Tamil Eelam, are secular Marxists seeking political independence for a Tamil-

---

[15] Shmuel Neeman Institute for Advanced Study in Science and Technology, Haifa.

speaking state. The LTTE's own Internet FAQ settles the matter conclusively, stating in no uncertain terms that the Tamil Tigers is not a religious organization.[16]

To list the many historical counterexamples that disprove Harris's contention would require a book of its own, but a short list of territorial conflicts between co-religionists would have to include the Roman wars of the Italian peninsula, the Renaissance wars of the Italian city-states, the wars of the Greek city-states, the wars of the petty German principalities, the eleven Russo-Swedish wars, the English War of the Roses; in short, nearly the entire history of European warfare.[17] It is simply not true that most conflicts that "seem entirely driven by territorial concerns" are "often deeply rooted in religion." They almost never are.

For as Jared Diamond, the author of the award-winning *Guns, Germs, and Steel*, informs us, territorial conflicts are predominantly rooted in geography, not religion. To suggest otherwise would be to eviscerate his explanation for how Europe's technological development managed to leapfrog that of China during the fifteenth century, as it was European political disunity created by geography that prevented the centralized stasis that left a backward-looking China mired in the past.

> *Hence the real problem in understanding China's loss of political and technological preeminence to Europe is to understand China's chronic unity and Europe's chronic disunity. The answer is again suggested by maps. Europe has a highly indented coastline, with five large peninsulas that approach islands in their isolation, and all of which evolved independent languages, ethnic groups, and governments....Europe is carved up into independent linguistic, ethnic, and political units by high mountains (the Alps, Pyrenees, Carpathians, and Norwegian border mountains), while China's mountains east of the Tibetan plateau are much less formidable*

---

[16] *"Is the LTTE a religious organization? No. Most members of the LTTE are Hindus, however there are many members who are Christian. The LTTE does not have religious motivation for fighting against the government of Sri Lanka. The theoretician for the LTTE and one of the founding members is Anton Balasingham, who is a Christian."* http://www.tamiltigers.net, 2006.

[17] I shall concede the Thirty Years' War and the eight French Huguenot wars, and, in an ecumenical spirit of generosity, exclude the Peasants' War and the English civil wars from my list of counterexamples.

barriers....Unlike China, Europe has many small core areas, none big enough to dominate the others for long, and each the center of chronically independent states.[18]

In a continent with only four religions or religious denominations of note in 1400,[19] Europe was divided into more than 1,000 independent political states.[20] This number was reduced by half only 117 years later, at the start of the Protestant Reformation. And while there was certainly an amount of violent inter-denominational Christian conflict during the Reformation and Counter-Reformation, it is difficult to imagine that even with the increase in the amount of potential religious conflict, more wars took place than occurred during the century leading up to it, wherein half the political entities disappeared, swallowed up by their larger, more powerful neighbors.

Indeed, the contrast between the largely peaceful spread of Christianity throughout the continent of Europe with the violent migratory invasions that wracked it from 300 to 700 A.D. as the Goths, Vandals, and Franks moved westward, later followed by the Slavs, Alans, Avars, Bulgars, Hungarians, Pechenegs, and Tatars, underlines the fundamental absence of historical support for Harris's assertion.

IN-OUT ENMITY

But while the points raised by Harris on religion and the art of war are obvious and easily dismissed, Richard Dawkins is rather more subtle. Having wisely refrained from directly suggesting a causal relationship between religion and warfare (and in fact, as was previously demonstrated, he actually contradicts Harris on that very point[21]), he nevertheless cannot stop himself from slyly implying in numerous places throughout *The God Delusion* that this "divisive force" is nevertheless somehow responsible for the fact that wars take place, mostly due to the way in which it supplies labels for "in-group/out-group enmity and vendetta," which aren't necessarily worse than

---

[18] Diamond, Jared. *Guns, Germs, and Steel.* New York: W. W. Norton & Company, 1999. 413.

[19] Catholic Christianity, Orthodox Christianity, Judaism, and Islam. Martin Luther posted his 95 Theses in 1517.

[20] Diamond, 413.

[21] Dawkins, *The God Delusion*, 259.

other labels such as language and skin color, but are "often available when others are not."

The problem with this is that in-group/out-group[22] enmity has next to nothing to do with either waging or inspiring war. Most endo-exo rivalries stem from basic territorialism and the will to power, not rival group identities; the champions of reason have it backward. Consider the rival groups we currently identify as "French" and "German." As recently as 814, they were a single ethnic group known as "the Franks." While the French national identity was forged early on, thanks in part to the open geography of France, there was no German nation as such, instead there was only the multiplicity of principalities known collectively and inaccurately as the Holy Roman Empire, which over time came to be dominated by the Austrian Hapsburg dynasty in the south and the Kingdom of Prussia in the north.

It was not until after the Napoleonic wars and the Franco-Prussian wars that anything resembling what we would recognize today as being "Germany" came into existence, in 1871. By 1941, Germany had invaded France twice, conquered it once, and been defeated twice by France's allies. France was estimated to have lost 1.4 million dead in the Great War, plus another 520,000 killed in round two.

Is it more reasonable, then, to assume that any latent French hostility toward Germans stems from an out-group identity that didn't even exist for most of French history, or from a simple and understandable distaste for being invaded and slaughtered by a group of distant cousins with a proven historical predilection for doing so?

CRUSADER OR CONSCRIPT?

The Crusades have long been the *sine qua non* of the atheist case against religion on the grounds of its causal relationship with war. And it would be foolish to insist that any war conceived by a monk, blessed by a Pope, marked by the sign of the Cross, inspired by the battle cry *Deus le volt*,[23] and fought against a rival religion in order to

---

[22] There's that phrase again. I don't know why Harris and Dawkins are so fond of it. Reading these gentlemen one after another is disturbingly like being forced to watch atheist bukkake.

[23] God wills it!

reclaim a holy site did not have anything to do with religion.

Still, it must be noted that the consensus among modern historians is that religion was not anywhere nearly as central to the Crusades as is customarily thought to be the case. Sir Charles Oman points out various times when, following the Crusaders' establishment of the four principalities of Outremer, alliances between Christian kingdoms and Muslim emirates flowed freely across religious lines; indeed, without the vicious internecine Muslim rivalries that existed at the time, the First Crusade would never have succeeded in taking Jerusalem nor would the Crusader lands carved out of Muslim territory have survived for nearly 200 years.[24]

While Oman sees religion as only one of the "many complicated impulses" that led the European nations to invade the Levant, John Julius Norwich goes so far as to write of the First Crusade: "The entire Crusade was now revealed as having been nothing more than a monstrous exercise in hypocrisy, in which the religious motive had been used merely as the thinnest of disguises for unashamed imperialism."[25]

Nevertheless, if we set aside the historians' pedantic insistence on detail for the moment and concede that the Crusades are quite reasonably considered to be the classic example of a religious war by the average individual, we may find them to be a very useful model in demonstrating how a religious war comes about, how religion can be used to inspire individuals to commit violence at the behest of religious leaders, and the impact such a religious motivation makes on behavior of the individuals so inspired. For by conceding the point, the Crusades thus provide us with a means of dividing the religious aspects of war-making from those aspects that have little or nothing to do with religion.

The salient features of the First Crusade that are relevant for considering the question of religious inspiration are the following:

---

[24] Oman, Sir Charles. *378–1278 A.D.* Vol. 1 of *A History of the Art of War in the Middle Ages*. London: Cornell University Press, 1991. 233.

[25] Norwich, John Julius. *The Middle Sea: A History of the Mediterranean*. London: Pimlico, 2006. 119.

1. It was publicly advocated by religious leaders.
2. Its appeal transcended national and political boundaries.
3. Large numbers of civilians voluntarily took part.
4. Individuals with neither military nor organizational authority held prominent leadership roles.[26]
5. Professional soldiers volunteered to fight without demanding wages up front.

With the exception of the first great wave of Islamic expansion, very few wars in history can be described by any of these five features, let alone all of them. And it is this last aspect that is particularly intriguing, for while it was unnecessary to pay many of the civilians and the soldiers who volunteered to take the Crusader's Cross, nearly every military leader before or since has found it to be an absolute requirement.

Livy informs us that the Romans found it necessary to begin paying wages to their knights as early as 405 B.C. as a result of the Siege of Veii, although the plebs' complaints[27] about the need to pay a war tax in addition to being forced to serve in the military levy required for the four simultaneous wars in which Rome was engaged at the time make it clear that the infantry was being paid wages long before then. In the later Republican and Imperial eras, conscription was seldom required except in the event of civil war, although the standard legionary pay was 112.5 denarii per year (later doubled by Julius Caesar), which was almost twice the sixty-eight denarii it is calculated that was required for a family of four to live for a year.

Put in modern terms, this would equate to roughly $32,471.71 in 2005 dollars. Considering that this was the annual salary of the lowest-ranking legionaries and that centurions drew annual wages equivalent to $520,000,[28] it is not hard to understand why Rome had

---

[26] A French priest named Peter the Hermit led an "army" of 100,000 men, women, and children that outnumbered the nobles' Crusade led by Raymond of Toulouse, Bohemond, Godfrey, and Robert of Flanders. The fact that the nobles hailed from Northern France, Southern France, England, and Italy demonstrates the transnational appeal of the First Crusade. Of course, the Third Crusade demonstrated even broader appeal, featuring the King of England, the King of France, and the Holy Roman Emperor.

[27] Livius, Titus. Vol. 1 of *The History of Rome*. 5.10.

[28] That was actually on the low end! Under Domitian, centurions were paid between 5,000 and 20,000 denarii per year, which were sixteen to sixty-six times more than the 300 denarii annually paid to legionaries.

no need to play upon the religious sentiments of prospective recruits in order to convince them to join the army.

Now, if it were true, as the New Atheists suggest, that religious faith is a source of military fervor, it logically follows that the militaries of avowedly religious countries would rely less heavily on conscription than do the militaries in secular countries. However, an examination of the world's militaries[29] reveals that even in Muslim countries, there is no correlation between religious fervor and a low rate of forced military service. The high rate of conscripts in the Islamic Republic of Iran is particularly worthy of note here, in light of Western fears of the warlike nature of its bellicose and theocratic government.

Nation	Dominant Religion	Conscripts	Military Forces	Volunteers
United States of America	Christian	zero	1,427,000	100 percent
Republic of India	Hindu	zero	1,325,000	100 percent
People's Republic of China	Atheist	1,275,000	2,840,000	55.1 percent
Republic of Turkey	Islam	295,000	514,850	42.7 percent
Islamic Republic of Iran	Islam	320,000	450,000	28.9 percent

It is also perhaps worth noting that the world's five largest militaries, those belonging to China, the United States, India, North Korea, and Russia, are controlled by two atheist governments, a country that was formally atheist until recently, and two legally secular governments.

THE SILENCE OF THE CLASSICS

But the most conclusive evidence against the idea that religion is a vital aspect of the art of war can be found in the collective writings of Man's greatest military strategists. Or rather, it cannot be found. One will scour the works of Sun Tzu, Julius Caesar, Vegetius, Maurice, Leo the Wise, and Clausewitz in vain for instructions on how to make use of the gods, the faith of the soldiers, or anything even remotely religious in their recommendations about how to best

---

[29] Institute for Strategic Studies, *Military Balance 1997/98*. London, 1997.

execute the art of war. If religion were an important element of war-making, one would expect to find a great deal of text commenting upon it. Instead, one finds that Sun Tzu devotes one of his thirteen chapters entirely to spies and fully half of another to instructions on starting fires.

Clausewitz dedicates entire chapters to military concepts such as friction, boldness, perseverance, and geometry, while Vegetius has sections dealing specifically with the importance of individualizing shields, what music is the most inspirational, and the proper way to combat elephants. The emperor Maurice, in his *Strategikon*, address-es heralds and trumpets as well as "Dealing with the Light-Haired Peoples" and "Hunting Wild Animals Without Serious Injury or Ac-cident," while Caesar is predominantly concerned with chronicling the astonishingly heroic martial deeds of a certain Gaius Julius.

Of all classical military strategists, Machiavelli alone sees suffi-cient benefit in making use of religion to mention it in passing, as in *The Art of War* he reminds Lorenzo di Filippo Strozzi of the way in which Sertorius assured his troops of a divine victory guaranteed by a talking deer, and how Charles VII of France found Joan of Arc to be of some utility in convincing his men that God was on their side. Machiavelli believed religion to be useful in much the same way that Richard Dawkins imagines it to be, as a means of instilling morale and military discipline into the soldiery.

However, there is a fundamental contradiction between the idea that the same religion that produces unruly militias full of fanatics like the Basij Mostazafan will simultaneously provide the basis for the rigid military discipline required by elite troops. Given that the penalty for breaking military discipline has been death by execution in nearly every military force in history regardless of its religious identity, from Sun Tzu's famous beheading of the King of Wu's favor-ite concubines to the U.S. Army's execution of Pvt. Eddie Slovik in 1945, it is clear that it is the very material fear of death at the hands of the military authorities, not religious faith, that provides the foun-dation for this discipline.

It is worth noting that Machiavelli is not only the lone classic strat-egist to see the military usefulness of religion, he is also the only one to have never held a combat command. His attempt to build a Florentine militia to replace the mercenary companies then ubiquitous in Italy was a failure, and the value of his military acumen can perhaps be best judged by the following anecdote from Bandello about the Florentine's famous visit to the mercenary camp of the condottiere Giovanni delle Bande Nere:[30]

> *The men were training and Giovanni mischievously invited his guest to try out on the ground some of the formations he had described in* The Art of War. *The author accepted with delight, and in the course of the next hour reduced the troops to a chaos of puzzled and perspiring humanity, whereupon Giovanni tactfully intervened, murmuring that it was a very hot day and past dinner-time, unraveled the tangle with a few decisive orders and quickly produced the disposition Machiavelli had been trying to achieve.*[31]

I believe that on the basis of the historical evidence, the reasonable reader will correctly conclude that both Machiavelli and Richard Dawkins can be safely ignored with regards to their speculations about the source of military discipline as well as the utility of religion in maintaining it.

However, I should note that when I mentioned this significant omission of all things religious from the great works of military strategy and tactics in a column last year, I received an e-mail complaining that Sun Tzu, at least, had made mention of "Heaven," and in fact had laid some degree of importance upon it. While this is true, as Sun Tzu lists Heaven as one of the five constant factors[32] of the art of war that must be taken into account when seeking to determine the conditions obtaining in the field, the general also goes on to explain in chapter I, section 7 that Heaven "signifies night and day, cold and heat, times and seasons." In this particular case, "Heaven" merely means the environmental setting in which the battle takes place.

This demonstrates the importance of actually reading the text

---

[30] Giovanni de' Medici, an Italian mercenary captain and father of the first Grand Duke of Florence. His company was known as "The Black Bands" due to the mourning markers worn on their insignia after the death of Pope Leo X.

[31] Tease, Geoffrey. *The Condottieri: Soldiers of Fortune.* New York, 1971. 339.

[32] The other four are Moral Law, Earth, The Commander, and Method and Discipline. I contend Moral Law is best translated as morale, as it is a vital stategical and tactical concern. Giles considers this possibility, but prefers "is in harmony with his subjects."

instead of merely running a word search on it or relying upon what one vaguely remembers seeing one evening on the History Channel.

However, it must be admitted that religion is not entirely without application in times of war. It is, after all, an extremely effective means of applying Sun Tzu's Moral Law in order to inspire those who are not a part of the soldiery during wartime, quite possibly the most effective means. More than 2,000 years ago, after Hannibal crushed the Roman army led by the consul Gaius Flaminius at Lake Trasimene, a fearful and despairing Rome turned to Fabius Maximus to save it from the brilliant Carthaginian and his army. To the modern reader, the first actions of Fabius after being named dictator might seem more than a little strange, but no doubt Sun Tzu would see the wisdom in them and agree with Plutarch's verdict:

> *After this, he made the best of beginnings, that is by turning his attention to religious matters, and he left the people in no doubt that their defeat had not been brought about by any cowardice on the part of their soldiers, but by their general's neglectful and contemptuous attitude towards religious observances.... By encouraging the people in this way to fix their thoughts upon religious matters, Fabius contrived to strengthen their confidence in the future.*[33]

For what is the purpose of religious faith, after all, but to provide hope in a time of despair? The faith of the Roman people was rewarded in the end, as Fabius patiently wore Hannibal down over a period of fifteen years until the Carthaginian was finally forced to withdraw from Italy. But the agnostic reader will no doubt be pleased to learn that despite his ready willingness to make use of the religious superstitions of the Romans, Fabius Maximus himself chose to place his own trust in rather more material forces.[34]

Still, providing the promise of light when all seems dark and preventing the civilian population from sinking into a slough of desperation is a far cry from whipping the god-addled masses into a blood-maddened frenzy of slaughter. While religion can play an important role in the lives of noncombatants during wartime, history

---

[33] Plutarch, *Makers of Rome*, Ian Scott-Kilvert translator (1965), 57–58.

[34] "*For his own part, however, he trusted entirely to his own efforts to win the victory, since he believed that the gods grant men success according to the courage and wisdom that they display. . . .*" Plutarch, 58.

and the written works of Man's greatest military minds clearly demonstrate that religious faith is not a tool in the blood-stained hands of those who practice the arts of war.

VI

THE WAR
DELUSION

Religion makes enemies instead of friends. That one word, "religion," covers all the horizon of memory with visions of war, of outrage, of persecution, of tyranny, and death.... Although they have been preaching universal love, the Christian nations are the warlike nations of the world.

—ROBERT GREEN INGERSOLL, "The Damage Religion Causes"

THUS BEGAN AN INFLUENTIAL nineteenth-century essay by Ingersoll, the famous American freethinker and atheist. While Ingersoll's assertion might be contested by modern atheists who deny that America was ever a Christian nation, and by sociologists who have conducted numerous polls confirming European post-Christianity, many people surely agree with his general sentiment that religion is the primary cause of war throughout the world.

Sam Harris agrees enthusiastically, or at least he appears to do so at first glance:

A glance at history, or at the pages of any newspaper, reveals that ideas which divide one group of human beings from another, only to unite them in slaughter, generally have their roots in religion. It seems that if our species ever eradicates itself through war, it will not be because it was written in the stars but because it was written in our books....

Because Harris is a careless writer, lurching from baseless assertion to errant conclusion with all the elegance of a drunken orangutan, it is always wise to examine his words closely. Most readers, scanning quickly over the paragraph, will conclude that Harris is stating that most martial slaughter has its roots in religion, and because of that, conclude that religion is a threat to eradicate humanity. But the fact that Harris attempts to condemn religion through implication instead of direct accusation is a clear indicator that Harris knows how weak his argument is, and the historical evidence proves that both his statement and his subsequent conclusion are incorrect.

Religion does not endanger our species because religious faith does not cause war.

Harris is far from the only atheist who makes a habit of incessantly implying or even outright stating that religion is the cause of most military conflict, and he is not the only one expressing the belief that if only there was no religion polluting the planet, Mankind might finally know an end to war. It could even be plausibly suggested that adherence to this notion is one of the Ten Commandments of the High Church atheist: Thou shalt believe that religion causes war.

The concept is articulated at the heart of John Lennon's atheist anthem, "Imagine":

Imagine there's no countries
It isn't hard to do
Nothing to kill or die for
And no religion too[1]

Lennon, of course, is here blaming nationalism in addition to religion, but since both Harris and Dawkins tell us that nationalism is a function of religious belief, we know that from the atheist's point of

---

[1] The end of the song reveals Lennon to have been a bit of an apotheosan.

view, the two are one and the same. Dawkins, for example, approvingly quotes a Spaniard who states that religion and nationalism operating in tandem "break all records for oppression and bloodshed." Ergo, without religion and its haphazard division of humanity into warring nations, there will be nothing to kill or die for and we can all live together in stoned and naked bliss.

However, it's more than a little risky to base one's basic concept of global geopolitics and world history on a folk song written by a college dropout who failed all of his O-levels.[2] I imagine few would consider it worthwhile to consult Britney Spears about the continual crisis in the Middle East; indeed, the mere fact of learning that one's understanding of the geostrategic situation is in accordance with a pop singer's, however successful, should serve to give one cause to reconsider the matter post-haste.

And yet Dawkins inadvertently reveals the illogic underlying this atheist dogma when he writes of how "thousands" of people have died "for loyalty to one religion against a scarcely distinguishable alternative."[3] But these thousands of deaths, however tragic, are a trivial number, a statistically insignificant fraction of the billions of human beings who have been killed for reasons wholly unrelated to religion; World War II alone accounted for an estimated 60 million deaths while Hulagu Khan slew around 130,000 in the 1258 sack of Baghdad.

A VERY SHORT MILITARY HISTORY OF THE UNITED STATES

The New Atheists are not very happy about the fact that the United States of America is the most religious nation in the Western world. This clearly annoys them, as they tend to dwell on the matter. But if the hypothesis that religion causes war is true, then we can safely assume that the U.S.A. must be a particularly warlike nation, and moreover, that it regularly goes to war for reasons associated with the strong religious faith of its people. In order to see if this

---

[2] The U.K. General Certificate of Education Ordinary-level examinations, as opposed to the GCE Advanced-levels. Lennon was a talented musician, but he was also the English equivalent of the kid who has to take the GED instead of the SAT. And then fails it.

[3] Dawkins, Richard. "What Use is Religion?" *Free Inquiry*, Volume 24, Number 5.

is indeed the case, I have constructed the table below, which consists of all the wars fought by the United States, the enemy against whom it was fought, the primary religious faith of the two sides, and the number of American deaths as a result of the military conflict.

War	Year	Enemy	Religious Faith	U.S. Deaths
Revolutionary War	1775–1783	England	Christian v. Christian	4,435
War of 1812	1812–1815	England	Christian v. Christian	2,260
First and Second Barbary Wars	1801–1815	The Barbary States	Christian v. Muslim	11
The Navajo Wars	1846–1866	Navajo and Apache	Christian v. Pagan	250
Mexican War	1846–1848	Mexico	Christian v. Christian	1,733
The Sioux Wars (3)	1854–1877	Sioux	Christian v. Pagan	500[*]
The Civil War	1861–1865	Confederate States	Christian v. Christian	214,938
The Apache Wars (2)	1871–1886	Apache	Christian v. Pagan	250
Spanish-American War	1898	Spain	Christian v. Christian	385
World War I	1917–1918	The Central Powers	Christian v. Christian & Muslim[**]	53,402
World War II	1941–1945	The Axis Powers	Chr. & Ath. v. Chr. & Pagan	291,557
The Korean Conflict	1950–1953	China	Christian v. Atheist	36,574
The Vietnam War	1954–1973	North Vietnam	Christian v. Atheist	58,209
The Invasion of Panama	1989–1990	Panama	Christian v. Christian	24
The Persian Gulf War	1990–1991	Iraq	Christian v. Muslim	529
The Global Struggle Against Violent Extremism[***]	2001–present	Afghanistan, the global jihad	Christian v. Muslim	3,302
The Iraq War	2003–present	Iraq	Christian v. Muslim	2,711

[*] Precisely how many U.S. fatalities occurred during the various Indian Wars is unknown, but they are generally estimated to be less than 1,000 in total. I have therefore distributed 1,000 deaths between the Navajo, Sioux, and Apache wars.

[**] The Ottoman Empire, today's Turkey, was one of the Central Powers.

[***] This has got to be one of the nominees in the "War, Dumbest Name Ever" category. Although its other name, The War on Terror, is right up there, too. But given how embarrassed they are about GSAVE, I insist on using it.

In 232 years, the United States of America has fought seventeen wars. That's about one new war every fourteen years it has existed, which isn't exactly peaceful, but also isn't anywhere nearly as aggressively martial as the pagan Roman Republic, which regularly launched simultaneous wars against as many as four different and unrelated foes in a single year, or the Assyrian king Shalmaneser III, whose Black Obelisk records his habit of regularly crossing the Euphrates and instigating twenty-three wars in the first twenty-three years of his reign.[4]

Of those seventeen wars, the only one that can properly be characterized as religious is the strangely named Global Struggle Against Violent Extremism, of which the invasion and subsequent occupation of Afghanistan has been an integral part. Due to the secular nature of Saddam Hussein's Ba'athist dictatorship, the fact that the current Iraqi War is technically a continuation of the Persian Gulf War, and the absence of a direct connection between Hussein and the 9/11 attacks, I deem the Iraq war to be a separate war to which it would be incorrect to assign a religious motivation, the various Muslim factions now battling for power in post-Hussein Iraq notwithstanding.

Looking at the list, it is clear that Christian America was as likely to make war against other Christian nations as it was to fight pagan Indian tribes, Muslim pirate nations, or atheist Communist regimes. It even allied with an atheist regime to fight two historically Christian nations. After perusing the list, it should be clear to even the most casual observer that the United States does not go to war for reasons associated with the particular religious faith of its people.

Over the centuries, 671,070 Americans have died fighting in its wars. Less than one-half of 1 percent of those deaths, or 3,302, can be reasonably blamed on religious faith. Over the course of U.S. history, that amounts to 14.2 American deaths per year attributable to religion-inspired war, and while every American death is lamentable, it should be noted that religious war is actually less lethal to Americans than their dogs, as they annually suffer 15.7 fatalities due to dog bites.[5] And yet, I rather doubt that Dawkins and Harris will soon be

---

[4] In the twenty-fourth year of his reign he must have finally gotten bored with the Euphrates, as he crossed the lower Zab instead and burned four cities belonging to King Yan'su of the Zimri.

[5] Jeffery J. Sacks, MD, MPH, Richard W. Sattin, MD, and Sandra E. Bonzo. "Dog Bite-Related Fatali-

publishing books entitled *The Dog Delusion* and *Letter to a Canine Nation* while angrily urging Americans to abandon their misguided attachment to Man's best friend.

WAR AND RELIGION

It would be foolish to insist that religion never causes war. The on-going occupations in Afghanistan and Iraq clearly bear some relation to religion, as does the nonsensically named War on Terror. In this age of Islamic jihadist revival, it is easy to see why a theory of religious causation holds some appeal for the historically ignorant. The recent conflicts in Sudan, Nigeria, East Timor, the Philippines, Kashmir, and Chechnya certainly have a strong Islamic element, and the thought of an army of the West swooping down on the Middle East cannot help but conjure up images of Raymond, Godfrey, and Bohemond before the walls of Jerusalem.

But much time has passed between the taking of Jerusalem in 1099 and the fall of Baghdad in 2003, and very little of it has been peaceful. Furthermore, Islam did not exist prior to the year 610, nor did Christianity prior to 33 A.D. And yet, ancient documents such as the Chronicles of the Assyrian Kings are filled with descriptions of what certainly appear to be matters of martial concern. For example, the Black Obelisk of Shalmaneser III records some of the bloody-minded Assyrian king's martial deeds:

> *In my 24th year, the lower Zab I crossed. The land of Khalimmur I passed through. To the land of Zimru I went down. Yan'su King of the Zimri from the face of my mighty weapons fled and to save his life ascended [the mountains]. The cities of 'Sikhisatakh, Bit-Tamul, Bit-Sacci, Bit-Sedi, his strong cities, I captured. His fighting men I slew. His spoil I carried away. The cities I threw down, dug up, [and] with fire burned. . . . The cities of Cua-cinda, Khazzanabi, Ermul, [and] Cin-ablila with the cities which were dependent on them I captured. Their fighting men I slew. Their spoil I carried away. The cities I threw down, dug up [and] burned with fire. An image of my Majesty in the country of Kharkhara I set up.*

ties From 1979 Through 1988." *Journal of American Medicine.* 11 (1989).

To cite a more recent example, historians record that all of Europe anticipated that Charles VIII of France, upon coming into his own in 1491 (he had been subject to an eight-year regency upon inheriting the crown at thirteen), would launch a military campaign because that was what was expected of young, energetic kings with armies. And within three years, Charles had invaded Italy and laid the groundwork for thirty years of war on the Lombard plain. This was not war caused by religion or even economics; it was simply war for war's sake.

But there is no point in arguing from anecdotal evidence. A more systematic review of the 489 wars listed in Wikipedia's list of military conflicts, from Julius Caesar's Gallic Wars to the 1969 Football War between Honduras and El Salvador, shows that only fifty-three of these wars—10.8 percent—can reasonably be described as having a religious aspect, even if one counts each of the ten Crusades separately.

Of course, Wikipedia is not an ideal foundation on which to base an argument, not if one wishes it to be taken seriously. I have no doubt that my contention that religion does not cause war in the overwhelming majority of circumstances would meet with more than a little skepticism were I content to rely on an open-access encyclopedia as the primary support for it. Still, it served as a reasonable starting point. I was not looking forward to the arduous task of sitting down amidst a mountainous pile of military histories and painstakingly assembling a more comprehensive list of wars, nor did I have much confidence that anyone would take it very seriously given my lack of academic standing, but I was fully prepared to do so since there didn't seem any other way to prove my hypothesis.

I had barely begun separating the teetering stacks of books dedicated to ancient and medieval warfare when Charles Phillips and Alan Axelrod fortuitously happened to publish their three-volume *Encyclopedia of Wars*,[6] a massive 1,502-page compendium compiled by nine reputable professors of history, including the director of the Centre of Military History and the former head of the Centre for Defence

---

[6] Phillips, Charles and Alan Axelrod. *Encyclopedia of Wars*. New York: Facts on File, 2005. It's a rather handsome set, and although the summaries of the various wars are necessarily brief, it makes for some fascinating reading.

Studies, of what amounts to a significant percentage of all the wars that have taken place throughout recorded human history.

America's seventeen previously mentioned wars account for less than 1 percent of the 1,763 wars chronicled in the encyclopedia. These 1,763 wars cannot be considered entirely comprehensive—for example, Shalmaneser III's thirty-four campaigns against various Syrian kingdoms are included in the single entry entitled "Assyrian Wars (c. 1032–c. 746 B.C.)." If one considers that Shalmaneser, despite his martial success, managed to conquer less territory than his father, Ashurnasirpal II, did, we should probably note that what is counted here as a single war could cover as many as 250 separate Assyrian conflicts. But we shall leave that for the compilers of a future military encyclopedia that will surely require another volume or ten, as the current encyclopedia contains more wars than anyone but a military expert has ever heard of. In any event, the very large size of the sample set definitely provides enough detail for the purpose of determining what percentage of Man's wars are caused by his diverse religious faiths with some degree of accuracy.

At the risk of providing significantly more ammunition to those who argue that religion causes war and invariably cite 1) The Crusades, 2) The Wars of Religion, and 3) The Thirty Years' War, here is a list of all the wars that the authors of the *Encyclopedia of Wars* saw fit to categorize as religious wars for one reason or another:

Albigensian Crusade, Almohad Conquest of Muslim Spain, Anglo-Scottish War (1559–1560), Arab Conquest of Carthage, Aragonese-Castilian War, Aragonese-French War (1209–1213), First Bearnese Revolt, Second Bearnese Revolt, Third Bearnese Revolt, First Bishop's War, Second Bishop's War, Raids of the Black Hundreds, Bohemian Civil War (1465–1471), Bohemian Palatine War, War in Bosnia, Brabant Revolution, Byzantine-Muslim War (633–642), Byzantine-Muslim War (645–656), Byzantine-Muslim War (688–679), Byzantine-Muslim War (698–718), Byzantine-Muslim War (739), Byzantine-Muslim War (741–752), Byzantine-Muslim War (778–783), Byzantine-Muslim War (797–798), Byzantine-Muslim War (803–809), Byzantine-Muslim War (830–841), Byzantine-Muslim War (851–863), Byzantine-Muslim War (871–885), Byzantine-Muslim War (960–976), Byzantine-Muslim War (995–999), Camisards' Rebellion, Castilian Conquest of Toledo, Charlemagne's Inva-

sion of Northern Spain, Charlemagne's War against the Saxons, Count's
War, Covenanters' Rebellion (1666), Covenanters' Rebellion (1679), Cov-
enanters' Rebellion (1685), Crimean War, First Crusade, Second Crusade,
Third Crusade, Fourth Crusade,[7] Fifth Crusade, Sixth Crusade, Seventh
Crusade, Eighth Crusade, Ninth Crusade, Crusader-Turkish Wars (1100–
1146), Crusader-Turkish Wars (1272–1291), Danish-Estonian War, German Civil War (1077–1106), Ghost Dance Uprising, Siege of Granada,
First Iconoclastic War, Second Iconoclastic War, India-Pakistan Partition
War, Irish Tithe War, Javanese invasion of Malacca, Great Java War, Kap-
pel Wars, Khurramite's Revolt, Lebanese Civil War, Wars of the Lombard
League, Luccan-Florentine War, Holy Wars of the Mad Mullah, Maryland's Religious War, Mecca-Medina War, Mexican Insurrections, War of
the Monks, Mountain Meadows Massacre, Revolt of Muqanna, Crusade
of Nicopolis, Padri War, Paulician War, Persian Civil War (1500–1503),
Portuguese-Moroccan War (1458–1471), Portuguese-Moroccan War
(1578), Portuguese-Omani Wars in East Africa, Rajput Rebellion against
Aurangzeb, Revolt in Ravenna, First War of Religion, Second War of Reli-
gion, Third War of Religion, Fourth War of Religion, Fifth War of Religion,
Sixth War of Religion, Eighth War of Religion,[8] Ninth War of Religion,
Roman-Persian War (421–422), Roman-Persian War (441), Russo Turk-
ish War (1877–1878), First Sacred War, Second Sacred War, Third Sacred
War, Saladin's Holy War, Schmalkaldic War, Scottish Uprising against
Mary of Guise, Serbo-Turkish War, Shimabara Revolt, War of the Son-
derbund, Spanish Christian-Muslim War (912–928), Spanish Christian-
Muslim War (977–997), Spanish Christian-Muslim War (1001–1031),
Spanish Christian-Muslim War (1172–1212), Spanish Christian-Muslim
War (1230–1248), Spanish Christian-Muslim War (1481–1492), Span-
ish Conquests in North Africa, Swedish War, Thirty Years' War, Transyl-
vania-Hapsburg War, Tukulor-French War, Turko-Persian Wars, United
States War on Terror, Vellore Mutiny, Vjayanagar Wars, First Villmergen
War, Second Villmergen War, Visigothic-Frankish War.

That is 123 wars in all, which sounds as if it would support the
case of the New Atheists, until one recalls that these 123 wars represent only 6.98 percent of all the wars recorded in the encyclopedia.

---

[7] Just being generous here. See chapter XII.

[8] Ironically, the Seventh War of Religion was not a religious war. The Encyclopedia of Wars has this
to say: "The Seventh War of Religion in 1580, also known as the 'Lovers' War' had little to do with hostilities between the Catholics and Protestants. Instead fighting was instigated by the actions of Margaret,
the promiscuous wife of Henry IV of Navarre."

However, it does show that skeptics would have been right to doubt my Wikipedia-based estimate, as I *overestimated* the amount of war attributable to religion by nearly 60 percent. It's also interesting to note that more than half of these religious wars, sixty-six in all, were waged by Islamic nations, which is rather more than might be statistically expected considering that the first war in which Islam was involved took place almost three millennia after the first war chronicled in the encyclopedia, Akkad's conquest of Sumer in 2325 B.C.

In light of this evidence, the fact that a specific religion is currently sparking a great deal of conflict around the globe cannot reasonably be used to indict all religious faith, especially when one considers that removing that single religion from the equation means that all of the other religious faiths combined only account for 3.23 percent of humanity's wars.

The historical evidence is conclusive. Religion is not a primary cause of war.

THE ONTOLOGICAL ARGUMENT FOR RELIGIOUS WAR

An ontological argument is one that depends solely on reason and intuition rather than observation or evidence. Its most famous application is an argument for the existence of God, first used by St. Anselm of Canterbury, and it states that because we can conceive of God, something of which nothing greater can be imagined, God must exist. René Descartes also made use of a variant of this argument, but it has never been an important part of Christian theology due to its rejection by Thomas Aquinas. Its fame is more due to its later resurrection and rejections by David Hume and Bertrand Russell.

Richard Dawkins describes the ontological argument for the existence of God to be an infantile one. He pronounces himself offended at the very idea that "such logomachist trickery" could be used to produce such grand conclusions.[9] And he's correct to reject it, in my opinion, as ontological arguments boil down to the idea that if something can be conceived, it therefore must exist. No supporting

---

[9] Dawkins, *The God Delusion*, 81.

evidence is necessary, mere reason and intuition suffice to prove the matter. Daniel Dennett scorns it as well, describing it as the logical equivalent of a carnival fun-house illusion.

It is curious, then, that Dawkins, like Sam Harris, so blithely subscribes to an ontological argument in support of the idea that religion is the implicit cause of war. While both men are too cautious to ever come right out and state that they believe religion is the direct and primary cause of war, most likely due to the fact that it is so easy to disprove such a belief, they nevertheless attempt to insinuate that this is the case by repeatedly associating religious faith with group violence and military conflict. For example, despite admitting that "wars...are seldom actually about theological disagreements," Dawkins makes nineteen specific connections between religion and war in *The God Delusion* while Harris does likewise on twenty-nine occasions[10] throughout *The End of Faith*.

They justify these accusations by insinuation on the basis of an argument concocted in order to attack religion as "one of the most pervasive causes of conflict in our world."[11] This is done by claiming that while religion is not the *explicit* cause of most wars, it is still responsible for the fact that those wars are taking place because religious faith is the reason there are two different sides in the first place. Of course, this is nothing more than an ontological argument based on their ability to imagine why war happens to exist in the first place, but both men try to conceal that fact by constructing a pair of shaky parallel arguments based on the idea that religion causes division.

Their arguments go like this:

1. Religion causes division between people.[12]

> *"Religion is undoubtedly a divisive force."*
>
> —DAWKINS

---

[10] To be fair to Harris, I must note that many of these twenty-nine references are to specific connections between Islam and war.

[11] Harris, *The End of Faith*, 27, 29.

[12] This is an ontological argument in itself. There is plenty of evidence that religion tends to *unite* people.

"The religious divisions in our world are self-evident."

—HARRIS

2. Religion provides the dominant label by which people are divided into groups.

"Without religion there would be no labels by which to decide whom to oppress and whom to avenge."[13]

—DAWKINS

"The only difference between these groups is what they believe about God."[14]

—HARRIS

3. Wars are fought between divided groups of people with different labels.

"Look carefully at any region of the world where you find intractable enmity and violence between rival groups. I cannot guarantee that you'll find religions as the dominant labels for in-groups and out-groups. But it's a very good bet."

—DAWKINS

"Religion is as much a living spring of violence today as it was at any time in the past."

—HARRIS

4. Therefore, religion is the implicit cause of war.

"The problem's name is God."[15]

—Dawkins

---

[13] Dawkins, *The God Delusion,* 259. Using this quote here might appear to be a little unfair, as Dawkins is only referring to the conflict in Northern Ireland, except that he is doing so as part of an example that he subsequently applies to *"any region of the world where you find intractable enmity and violence between rival groups."*

[14] Harris, *The End of Faith,* 27.

[15] Dawkins is quoting Salman Rushdie here, but he is doing so approvingly.

"Faith...the most prolific source of violence in our history."

—HARRIS

Quod istis erat demonstrandum.

Superficial thinkers who know very little history find this argument compelling because the statements flow nicely from one into the other, and because there is a certain amount of truth in each of the assertions that lead up to the final conclusion. It cannot be denied that religion HAS been known to divide friends and families as well as entire nations. Religion HAS provided a marker by which opposing groups identify each other. War IS fought between divided groups of people bearing different labels; it takes two to tangle. The problem is that merely stringing together three statements that are factually true in some circumstances does not always lead to a logical conclusion.

Consider the same argument, only this time substituting three similarly valid assertions.

1. Pelicans eat sardines.
2. Pelicans improve the sardine species through aiding natural selection.
3. Natural selection is the mechanism through which evolution occurs.
4. Therefore, pelicans are the implicit cause of evolution.

Now, I'm no evolutionary biologist, but I'm fairly certain that human evolution is not dependent upon pelicans. Or elephant evolution, penguin evolution, or even, for that matter, the intelligent machine evolution[16] that will lead us all into joyous mental union with Gaia in the next three decades. The fourth statement cannot be logically concluded from the preceding three assertions, no matter how much these great rationalist champions of reason would like to pretend it does.

This lack of a logical conclusion is not the implicit argument's

---

[16] Although if Charles Stross could work lobsters into the Singularity, I have no doubt that he could find a role for pelicans, too.

only flaw, because the first two assertions are demonstrably more false than true. For example, in *Breaking the Spell*, Daniel Dennett informs us that language is far older than any current religion or religion for which we possess historical evidence. If Dennett is correct, then it is obvious that the existence of diverse languages (and therefore different human groups) in the absence of different religions slashes the legs out from under this surreptitious attempt to blame the reality of war on religious faith by way of the back door.

Consider the division of the Franks, a single nation ruled by Charlemagne, as he is known today in France. Karl der Grosse, as Charlemagne is known in Germany, died in 814 A.D., whereupon Louis le Débonnaire (or if you prefer, Ludwig der Fromme) inherited the Kingdom of the Franks, which thanks to Charlemagne/Karl der Grosse's conquests, was now styled an empire. Louis/Ludwig had four sons and his ill-considered attempts to divide the empire between them led to four civil wars that finally came to an end with the Treaty of Verdun in 843. His eldest son, Lothar, received the Middle Frankish Kingdom, which is now Italy, the Netherlands, Alsace-Lorraine, Burgundy, and Provence, while his third son, Louis the German, inherited what is now, unsurprisingly, known as Germany, and his youngest son, Charles the Bald, ended up with the lands west of the Rhône, or France. (Pepin, Louis/Ludwig's second son, died before his father.)

When Lothar died in 855, he divided his kingdom into three more parts, one for each of his three sons, Louis II, Charles of Provence, and Lothar II. As one might expect, by 858 war had broken out, with Louis II allying with his uncle Louis the German against Lothar II and Charles the Bald. More wars were fought over the centuries, the Eastern and Western Franks grew more and more apart, until finally it reached the point where they spoke separate languages, possessed separate identities, and, in the end, adopted different forms of Christianity. But the division of the Franks into Germans and Frenchmen predates the division of Christendom into Catholics and Protestants by more than 675 years.

Religion obviously had no more to do with the division of the Franks than it did with the 1993 division of Czechoslovakia into Slovakia and the Czech Republic or last year's divorce between Serbia and Montenegro. It couldn't have, because there was no religious difference between the divided parties.

Regardless of whether one argues that religion is the explicit cause of war or the implicit one, the argument simply does not stand in the face of the historical evidence. History shows very clearly that the vast majority of divisions between different groups of people are not based on religious faith, and that religion is not the dominant label by which most distinct groups are identified. The New Atheist argument that religion is the implicit cause of war fails in every single way.

And it is more than ironic, it borders being completely bizarre that both Dawkins and Harris should insist on the absolute need for scientific evidence to prove God's existence while simultaneously basing the major part of their case against religious faith on arguments that are ontological, illogical, and empirically incorrect.

The historical evidence is conclusive. Religious faith very seldom causes war, either implicitly or explicitly. God is not the problem.

VII

THE END OF SAM HARRIS

If I could wave a magic wand and get rid of either rape or religion, I would not hesitate to get rid of religion.

—SAM HARRIS

S AM HARRIS IS A GRAVE EMBARRASSMENT to atheism, intellectuals, and the Stanford University philosophy department. The awarding of the 2005 PEN/Martha Albrand award for Nonfiction to *The End of Faith* bears more than a little resemblance to Columbia University's decision to give the 2001 Bancroft prize to Michael Bellesiles[1] for his alternate history novel, *Arming America*. Harris's basic thesis, which asserts that religious faith poses an imminent danger to humanity, is every bit as demonstrably incorrect as Bellesiles's argument ever was. If his arguments in support of that thesis are less intentionally fraudulent than those presented by Bellesiles, they are no less invalid.

---

[1] The Bancroft award was rightly rescinded the following year later for "scholarly misconduct" and Bellesiles resigned his position as a tenured professor of history at Emory University after a pair of university inquiries examined his research. Bellesiles was claiming that widespread gun ownership in America dates from the Civil War, not its founding.

Harris isn't attacking any specific religious faith, but all of them at once.[2] However, his definition of religious faith is as prone to bursts of punctuated mutation as are his multiple definitions of atheism quoted in the first chapter. His ignorance of the basic tenets of the faiths he targets most directly is astonishing, especially considering that he's not attacking obscure Iraqi Mandaeans or Bakongolese worshippers of Nzambi Mpungu, but the world's two most popular religions. For example, Harris repeatedly demonstrates an inability to distinguish between the relative significance of the Old Testament and the New Testament to Christians, while raising issues that have been debated by theologians and philosophers for nearly 2,000 years as if they were new and no one had ever thought of them before. Reading Harris, one would never know that the evidential problem of evil, or reconciling the idea of a benevolent God with the fact that evil exists, is considered to be one of the principle intellectual puzzles of Christianity and *has been for centuries*.[3]

To put into perspective how completely Harris ignores the active and ongoing intellectual debate that has continued within the Christian community since the Apostles Paul and Peter were arguing over whether Jewish Christians—about the only Christians at the time—were required to keep kosher, I note that my friend and pastor, Dr. Greg Boyd, published a book on the subject entitled *Satan & the Problem of Evil: Constructing a Trinitarian Warfare Theodicy*[4] in 2001. He then published *Is God to Blame?: Moving Beyond Pat Answers to the Problem of Evil* in 2003. His 1997 book, *God at War: The Bible & Spiritual Conflict* also went into the subject in some detail, while *Letters From a Skeptic: A Son Wrestles with His Father's Questions about Christianity*, published in 1995, provided a less arduous look at some of the same issues. And Dr. Boyd is far from the only theologian to examine the subject. In addition to the many other Christian authors who have also addressed it, you may

---

[2] Except Buddhism, naturally.

[3] "*The problem of vindicating an omnipotent and omniscient God in the face of evil (this is traditionally called the problem of theodicy) is insurmountable.*" Harris, *The End of Faith*, 173. And yet it's not insurmountable, but very easily solved, at least from a Christian perspective. It's interesting, though, that he considers free will to be an incoherency.

[4] And yes, it's about as light and fluffy a read as the title suggests. Start with *Letters From a Skeptic* if you're interested.

remember there was a very popular book entitled *Why Bad Things Happen to Good People* written by a rabbi, Harold Kushner, back in the early 1980s.

It's clear from both the nature of his arguments and the absence of any relevant references in his bibliography that Harris has never bothered to examine these specific and, in some cases, incredibly detailed responses to the old dichotomy; instead, he merely repeats it and prances away congratulating himself for having posed what he declares is an "insurmountable" conundrum. But how can he possibly know that, considering that he clearly hasn't even looked at most of the proposed answers? This behavior demonstrates Harris's intellectual immaturity as well as his irresponsible failure to do even the most rudimentary research into his chosen subject.

But perhaps that's not entirely fair. While Harris doesn't once cite minor Christian intellectual figures such as Tertullian, Ambrose, Jerome, Gregory the Great, Thomas Aquinas, John Calvin, John Wesley, G. K. Chesterton, or even C. S. Lewis, he does find it relevant to provide one reference to Tim LaHaye, thirteen references to Hitler, Himmler, and Hess, and six whole pages dedicated to Noam Chomsky. Because, after all, no one is more suited to explain the Christian faith quite so well as an elderly author of pop religious fantasies, a trio of dead Nazis, and a left-wing Jewish linguist.[5]

Harris is also shamelessly intellectually dishonest. Anyone planning to debate Sam Harris would do well to ensure that there is a moderator, preferably one with a shock collar, as Harris is one of those slippery characters who invariably attempts to avoid answering all questions posed to him while simultaneously accusing the other party of arguing in bad faith and failing to address his points. I haven't been pursuing a doctoral degree in neuroscience for the last twenty years or anything, but I seem to recall that "projection" is how psychologists describe that sort of behavior. It doesn't matter whom he's debating, Harris will invariably declare himself to be misrepresented and misunderstood, usually by his second response.

---

[5] In fairness to Harris, he has clearly at least paged through St. Augustine's *Confessions* and *City of God*. I merely note that Augustine is considered one of the FOUR Latin Fathers of the Church and that there has been the occasional book written about the Christian faith since 430 A.D. But seriously, how could anyone possibly write an entire book attacking the modern Christian faith without even glancing at *Mere Christianity*?

It seems to escape him that if he's so often misunderstood, the only solution is to express himself more clearly.

Finally, for an individual who claims to be passionately dedicated to reason and names one section of his book "The Necessity of Logical Coherence," Harris is an appallingly incoherent logician. He frequently fails to gather the relevant data required to prove his case, and on several occasions inadvertently presents evidence that demonstrates precisely the opposite of that which he is attempting to prove. His postulates are often only partially true, and even when the information on which he bases an argument is reliable, the conclusions he draws are seldom reasonable.

But there is no need to take my word for any of this. Unlike Sam Harris, I believe in offering substantial support for my assertions. One might even dare to call it an empirical approach. So, in the best spirit of scientific inquiry, here is the hypothesis: Sam Harris is an ignorant, incompetent, and intellectually dishonest individual who attacks religious faith because it stands in the way of his dream of the ultimate destruction of America. While this may sound more than a little extreme at the moment, allow me to present the evidence, and you, the reader, shall be the judge.

THE IGNORANT ATHEIST

In his two books, Harris commits dozens of easily demonstrable factual and logical errors. While detailing these errors in their fullness would fill a book in its own right, perhaps highlighting a few of the more obvious mistakes will suffice to illustrate the case.

1) **Factual error.** Harris begins *The End of Faith* by strongly implying that almost all suicide bombers are Muslim. *Jane's Intelligence Review* reports that the Liberation Tigers of Tamil Eelam, who are not Muslims but a Marxist liberation front that committed 168 of the 273 suicide bombings that took place between 1980 and 2000, have historically been the leading practitioners of suicide bombing.[6] Harris tries to cover up his

---

[6] Gunaratna, Rohan. "Suicide Terrorism, a Global Threat." *Jane's Intelligence Review*. 20 Oct. 2000. The Karum Puligal are known to have committed 244 suicide attacks prior to the 2001 ceasefire, invented both the suicide vest and the naval suicide attack, and are considered to be the world's most effective suicide strike force due to their discipline and lack of religious fanaticism.

blunder in the notes section of the paperback edition by claiming that to describe the Tigers as secular "is misleading" because they "are Hindus who undoubtedly believe many improbable things about the nature of life and death." But the Tamil Tigers themselves expressly claim secular status, a declaration supported by the fact that the recently deceased Anton Balasingham, the LTTE's chief political strategist and ideologue, was a Roman Catholic.[7] It's also worth noting that slain Tigers are buried rather than cremated according to Hindu ritual. More importantly, there is no definition of "secular" that precludes a belief in improbable things about the nature of life and death or anything else, including the Labor Theory of Value, String Theory, or multiple universes.

2) **Logical error**. In *Letter to a Christian Nation*, Sam Harris borrows from Stephen F. Roberts in challenging Christians with a variant of the One Less God argument.[8] He informs Christians that they reject Islam in "precisely the way" that Muslims reject Christianity, which is also the same reason he rejects all religions.[9] So, either Harris believes that the Christian God exists and is a powerful spirit of evil or he doesn't know what is almost literally the first thing about Christian theology. Christians WORSHIP the one Creator God, but they BELIEVE in the supernatural existence of many spiritual beings that are often worshipped and are legitimately described as gods. Harris has not read the Bible very closely if he is under the impression that Christians do not believe in "the god of this age," "the prince of this world," or any of the rulers, authorities, and powers mentioned in Ephesians 6:12.[10]

---

[7] Balasingham died of cancer in London on 14 December, 2006. A BBC editor described him as the only man within the organization who had any influence on Tiger leader Velupillai Prabhakaran and regretted his death as the only moderating element within the militant group.

[8] "*I contend we are both atheists, I just believe in one fewer god than you do. When you understand why you dismiss all the other possible gods, you will understand why I dismiss yours.*" This is probably the most ignorant argument for atheism in common use today, stating that Christians are ur-atheists who only believe in one more god than the atheist. It is the result of confusing belief with worship and taking the concept of monotheism too literally.

[9] I note that Christians do not reject Islam for the same reason Muslims reject Christianity. Christians do not believe that Mohammed was a prophet, whereas Muslims do not believe that Jesus Christ was the resurrected Son of God, the Word made flesh. There is a considerable difference there, especially since Muslims honor Jesus as a prophet.

[10] There's plenty of room for Christian debate on the essential difference between God and gods, but the relevant point here is that Christians believe in the literal existence of multiple supernatural beings that are worshipped by human beings. By every atheist standard, that's a god.

3) **Factual error**. Harris claims "religion has been the *explicit* cause of literally millions of deaths in the last ten years" in these places: Palestine, the Balkans, Northern Ireland, Kashmir, Sudan, Nigeria, Ethiopia and Eritrea, Sri Lanka, Indonesia, the Caucasus.[11] However, even if we accept his assertion that these conflicts are all religious in nature, the sum total of deaths in all these places since 1994 is most likely below 750,000. Palestine is often in the headlines, but there have only been about 7,500 deaths on both sides combined over the last ten years. In the Balkans, there were 96,495 deaths (most of which occurred before 2004), while fewer than 100 of the 3,225 deaths in Northern Ireland since 1969 occurred in the last decade. The Timor-Leste Commission for Reception, Truth, and Reconciliation reports that most of the 102,800 deaths in formerly Indonesian East Timor took place in the 1970s, and the estimated 150,000 fatalities in the 1998–2000 Ethiopian-Eritrean war pale in comparison with the 1.5 million deaths attributed to the "Red Terror" previously committed by Ethiopia's atheist Derg regime.

4) **Factual error**. Harris says that certainty about the next life is simply incompatible with tolerance in this one. But since Sam Harris is tolerated and allowed to live unmolested in a nation where 150 million people, by his account, possess such certainty, this is obviously wrong. The statement is particularly ironic given how he argues explicitly *against* tolerance for the religious faithful.[12] Given the evidence of Harris himself, it is certainty about the nonexistence of the next life that is incompatible with tolerance in this one.

5) **Factual error**. Harris claims that human standards of morality are what Christians use to establish God's goodness.[13] This is incorrect. Christians do not believe that God is subject to human morality.

---

[11] Harris says these are merely a few cases in point, but given that there haven't been enough explicitly religious-related killings in the entire world over the last decade to reach the smallest number that can qualify as literal millions, it's clear that he is simply making up these numbers. The emphasis on "explicit" is his.

[12] Harris has subsequently claimed that he only advocates "conversational intolerance." But it strikes me as supremely counterproductive for an already unpopular minority to try to win friends and influence people by behaving in an even more obnoxious manner than they do already. As to whether this is evidence of Harris's irrationality or merely his social autism, I shall leave it to the reader to decide.

[13] Harris, *Letter to a Christian Nation*, 55.

This should be obvious from considering the Ten Commandments. Is God prone to have another god before Himself? Does God have a neighbor whose wife He might covet? Who is God's father and how might He fail to honor him?

6) **Factual error.** Harris states that "questions about morality are questions about happiness and suffering."[14] They are not. Questions about morality concern what action is correct in light of the moral system to which the individual subscribes. Questions about Christian morality, the specific moral system Harris is addressing in *Letter to a Christian Nation*, are questions about what actions are deemed right in the eyes of God. In any case, morality should never be confused with a hedonic metric of happiness or suffering.

7) **Logical error.** Harris claims religious moderates are responsible for the actions of religious extremists. But no individual can possibly be held responsible for the actions of another individual over whom he has no authority or influence and has never even met.

8) **Logical error.** Harris asserts that competing religious doctrines have shattered the world into separate moral communities.[15] He also claims that the objective source of moral order is distinguishing between better and worse ways of seeking happiness.[16] However, he cites no evidence that Christians seek happiness any differently than Hindus, nor does he explain, precisely, how Jews seek happiness differently than Muslims. It's worth noting that Harris has probably caused greater human unhappiness with his books than his fellow atheist, Jeffrey Dahmer, ever did with his exotic diet, so by his own reckoning, Harris is less moral than Dahmer.

9) **Logical error.** Harris claims that religious prudery contributes daily to the surplus of human misery while bemoaning the existence of AIDS in Africa and other sexually transmitted diseases in the United States. But this widespread disease is the direct result of the sexual promiscuity that Christians condemn as immoral and which Harris

---

14 Ibid., 8.
15 Ibid., 79.
16 Ibid., 23.

praises as the pursuit of happiness. More to the point, scientific research shows that religious individuals are both happier[17] and more sexually satisfied[18] than non-religious individuals.

10) Factual error. Harris asserts that the entire civilized world now agrees that slavery is an abomination. Given that there are 700,000 slaves[19] being trafficked across international borders every year, this is a significant exaggeration. In September 2003, *National Geographic* reported that "there are more slaves today than were seized from Africa in four centuries of the trans-Atlantic slave trade." Obviously, more than a few people in the civilized world disagree.

11) Logical error. Harris says Muslims have "far fewer grievances" with Western imperialism than the rest of the world and that these grievances are "purely theological." As of this writing, the United States and twenty-one other countries have more than 225,000 troops occupying Afghanistan, Iraq, Kuwait, Qatar, Bahrain, and Saudi Arabia. Regardless of one's opinion about the wisdom of the ongoing occupations, one should be able to recognize that there's nothing theological about being aggrieved at the military occupation of your country.

12) Factual error. In *Letter to a Christian Nation*, Harris twice cites the high American rate of infant mortality in a disingenuous attempt to associate poor health and/or inferior medical science with the American rate of religious adherence, despite his subsequent claim that he isn't actually making any such argument. Regardless, he neglects to mention that this rate—the second highest in the developed world—is primarily due to the fact that the U.S.A. has the best neonatal care in the world, with the most neonatologists and neonatal intensive care beds per capita. Premature babies have a fighting chance to live in the United States; whereas in other developed coun-

---

[17] *"This kind of pattern is typical—religious involvement is associated with modest increases in happiness."* Nielsen, M. E. (2006) "Religion and Happiness." Retrieved 20 May 2007 from http://www.psywww.com/psyrelig/happy.htm.

[18] *"Previous research has produced mixed results. Davidson et al. (1995) reported that religious commitment (as measured by frequency of church attendance) did impact on "physiological" sexual satisfaction, but not "psychological" satisfaction. Davidson and Moore (1996) found no relationship between sexual satisfaction and religiosity among female undergraduates.... The three items related to religiosity, when considered together, did account for a small, but statistically significant amount of the variation in sexual satisfaction."* M. Young, G. Denny, T. Young, and R. Luquis. "Sexual Satisfaction in Married Women," *American Journal of Health Studies*, 2000.

[19] Trafficking in Persons Report, 2006.

tries, most live births below 3.3 pounds are not registered and never appear in their infant mortality statistics. Religious America's superior medical technology likewise accounts for the world's highest five-year cancer survival rate, which at 64.6 percent for all cancers is as much as 81 percent higher than some European countries and 22.5 percent higher than the acclaimed Dutch health care system. More importantly, while comparing American societal health to that of "the most atheist societies," Harris forgets that he has defined Buddhism as a form of atheism, therefore the societies to which religious America's health must be compared are not historically Christian countries like Norway, Iceland, Australia, Canada, Sweden, Switzerland, and Belgium, but rather heavily Buddhist countries such as Thailand, Cambodia, Myanmar, Bhutan, Sri Lanka, Laos, and Vietnam. The U.S.A.'s Human Development Index rank is 10, significantly better than the average rank of 114 for the seven "most atheist" countries, so both Harris's implied and explicit arguments fail based on his own measures and definitions.

THE INCOMPETENT ATHEIST

One of the most oft-cited passages in *Letter to a Christian Nation* is Harris's Red State-Blue State argument, in which he purports to prove that there is no correlation between Christian conservativism and social health. Richard Dawkins found the data to be "striking," so much so that he quotes the following paragraph from Harris's book in its entirety:

> While political party affiliation in the United States is not a perfect indicator of religiosity, it is no secret that the "red [Republican] states" are primarily red because of the overwhelming political influence of conservative Christians. If there were a strong correlation between Christian conservatism and social health, we might expect to see some sign of it in red-state America. We don't. Of the 25 cities with the lowest rates of violent crime, 62 percent are in "blue" [Democrat] states and 38 percent are in "red" [Republican] states. Of the twenty-five most dangerous cities, 76 percent are in red states, and 24 percent are in blue states. In fact, three of the five most dangerous cities in the U.S. are in the pious state of Texas. The twelve states with the highest rates of burglary are red. Twenty-four

of the twenty-nine states with the highest rates of theft are red. Of the twenty-two states with the highest rates of murder, seventeen are red.[20]

There are several layers of problems with this apparent proof of Christian immorality. The first is that political identity is a very poor substitute for religiosity. As the 2001 ARIS study showed, only 14.1 percent of Americans are adherents of one of the various churches of atheism. Since about half of eligible Americans bother to vote, the maximum potential number of godless blues in the country is 28.2 percent of the total, which would have accounted for 29.4 percent of John Kerry and Ralph Nader's combined 59,028,109 votes, if every atheist, agnostic, and non-believer in God had voted Democrat or Green in 2004.

But they didn't. In fact, the exit polls indicated that atheists were less likely to vote than the religious faithful, as only 10 percent of voters in the CNN exit polls described themselves as "no religion."[21] That godless 10 percent did lean heavily blue, as more than two-thirds voted for Kerry or Nader,[22] but a third went red without an imaginary friend providing them with instructions to vote for George W. Bush.

This means that out of a potential 17,338,916 godless voters in 2004, only 12,148,002 showed up to vote, of whom 8,260,641 can reasonably be described as blue. This leaves another 51,178,772 voters who are blue, but not godless. Setting aside the fact that Harris provides no evidence indicating that the 121.4 million Americans who voted committed all, or even any, of the violent crimes, burglaries, and thefts he mentions—there were another 80,451,439 eligible Americans who didn't vote, not including the 2,861,915 felons out on parole or probation who couldn't vote[23] and just might have committed a crime or two that year—it is absurd to credit all the supposedly law-abiding behavior of blue voters to the 16 percent of them

---

[20] Dawkins, *The God Delusion*, 229.

[21] Given Nader's success among the most highly educated voters, I would guess that High Church atheists voted more heavily than the norm, but their high level of participation was outweighed by the relative lack of participation by their more numerous Low Church counterparts. You may recall that the broad spectrum of atheism accounts for about 14 percent of the American population.

[22] Sixty-seven percent for Kerry, 1 percent for Nader, to be exact.

[23] McDonald, Michael, Ph.D. "2004 Voting-Age and Voting-Eligible Population Estimates and Voter Turnout." George Mason University. <http://elections.gmu.edu/Voter_Turnout_2004.htm>.

who lack religious faith.

If this isn't sufficient evidence of the foolishness of trying to equate Democratic votes with atheism, the ARIS 2001 survey reported a higher *percentage* of Democrats among Jews, Baptists, Catholics, Methodists, Pentecostals, Episcopalians, Buddhists, and Muslims than among the not religious, of whom only 30 percent reported a preference for the Democratic Party. (However, the not religious tend to describe themselves as political independents, not Republicans.)

So while the data may be striking, the argument based upon it can only be described as strikingly stupid. But just for kicks, let's pretend that it is not a measure so ridiculously inaccurate as to be completely useless. Let's imagine that Harris's metric really is relevant, that an American voter's 2004 presidential vote truly is indicative of his religious faith, or the lack thereof, and that statewide criminal statistics are a reasonable measure of an individual's predilection for immoral behavior.[24] This exercise in imagination is necessary, in fact, because only by accepting his measure at face value and examining it in detail can one fully grasp the true depth of Harris's exceptional incompetence.

Richard Dawkins may be excused for his ignorance of the American governmental structure since he is not an American, but rather a subject of Her Majesty, Queen Elizabeth the Second, by the Grace of God of the United Kingdom of Great Britain and Northern Ireland and of Her other Realms and Territories Queen, Head of the Commonwealth, Defender of the Faith, in right of the United Kingdom. But Sam Harris has no similar excuse for overlooking the fact that there is a unit of regional self-government below the state level, a useful little unit by which both electoral votes and criminal acts are recorded.

In other words, Sam Harris should have been looking at the electoral and criminal data by county, not by state.

Consider the red state of Florida. Its eleven blue counties account for 44 percent of the state's population, but more than 50 percent of its murders and 60 percent of its robberies.[25] The bluest county,

---

[24] This is a common statistical error known as the Ecological Fallacy. Harris appears to be particularly susceptible to it.

[25] Having spent several years living near Jacksonville, I can personally attest to the fact that most

Gadsden, voted for Kerry by a 70–30 margin and had the state's highest murder rate at 12.8 per 100,000, while the two reddest counties, Baker and Okaloosa, averaged a murder rate of 0.7 per 100,000 to go with their identical 78–22 margins for George Bush. And this was the case even though the population of the two red counties is more than four times that of blue Gadsden.

This tendency for blue counties to be home to higher crime rates is true in blue states as well. For example, the blue state of Maryland's five blue counties possessed an average murder rate of 13.22 per 100,000 residents, which is nearly fifteen times higher than the 0.89 murder rate in Maryland's nineteen red counties. And the District of Columbia, which voted 91 percent blue in 2004, also happened to possess the highest murder rate in the nation, which at 35.7 per 100,000 was nearly seven times the U.S. national average of 5.5.

Given that red counties have murder rates that tend to range from five to twenty times lower than blue counties, this is a pretty powerful sign that the "strong correlation between Christian conservatism and social health" that Harris claimed to be unable to find does, in fact, exist. But in case you're not convinced yet, consider the cities to which Harris refers and see what the red-blue divide reveals once one looks at the political orientation of the county in which those safe and dangerous cities are located instead of the state.

The first thing one notices is that Sam Harris can't even manage elementary school math. The percentage for the safest cities determined by state voting patterns is not 62 percent; seventeen blue state cities divided by twenty-five total cities equals 68 percent safe blue cities. (Apparently it's only division that gives him trouble because he does manage to subtract 62 from 100 successfully, which explains his incorrect percentage of 38 percent safe cities located in red states.)[26]

His math issues are minor. What is much more important is the way in which using the more accurate county data demonstrates that Harris's conclusions are precisely backward. Thirteen of the twenty-five safest

---

of Duval County's nominally red violent crime in fact takes place in its blue urban strongholds. So the blue responsibility for murders and robberies taking place in Florida is probably closer to 61 percent and 68 percent respectively.

[26] It's clearly a math problem, not a question of state identification or data from a previous year, because the only other mathematical possibilities are 64–36 and 60–40.

25 Safest and Most Dangerous Cities in 2005, with State and County Voting Percentages[*]

25 Safest Cities	State	County	25 Most Dangerous Cities	State	County
Newton, MA	Blue 62	Blue 76	Camden, NJ	Blue 53	Blue 63
Clarkstown, NY	Blue 60	Red 50	Detroit, MI	Blue 52	Blue 70
Amherst, NY	Blue 60	Blue 58	St. Louis, MO	Red 53	Blue 80
Mission Viejo, CA	Blue 55	Red 61	Flint, MI	Blue 52	Blue 61
Brick Township, NJ	Blue 53	Red 60	Richmond, VA[**]	Red 54	Blue 70
Troy, MI	Blue 52	Blue 51	Baltimore, MD	Blue 57	Blue 83
Thousand Oaks, CA	Blue 55	Red 52	Atlanta, GA	Red 59	Blue 59
Round Rock, TX	Red 62	Red 66	New Orleans, LA	Red 57	Blue 78
Lake Forest, CA	Blue 55	Red 61	Gary, IN	Red 60	Blue 61
Cary, NC	Red 56	Red 51	Birmingham, AL	Red 63	Red 54
Colonie, NY	Blue 60	Blue 63	Richmond, CA	Blue 55	Blue 63
Fargo, ND	Red 63	Red 60	Cleveland, OH	Red 51	Blue 67
Irvine, CA	Blue 55	Red 61	Washington, DC	Blue 91	Blue 91
Orem, UT	Red 73	Red 87	West Palm Beach, FL	Red 52	Blue 61
Dover Township, NJ	Blue 53	Red 57	Compton, CA	Blue 55	Blue 75
Warwick, RI	Blue 60	Blue 59	Memphis, TN	Red 57	Blue 58
Sunnyvale, CA	Blue 55	Blue 64	Dayton, OH	Red 51	Blue 51
Hamilton Township, NJ	Blue 53	Blue 62	San Bernardino, CA	Blue 55	Red 56
Parma, OH	Red 51	Blue 67	Springfield, MA	Blue 62	Blue 72
Canton Township, MI	Blue 52	Blue 70	Cincinnati, OH	Red 51	Red 53
Greece, NY	Blue 60	Blue 62	Oakland, CA	Blue 55	Blue 63
Simi Valley, CA	Blue 55	Red 52	Dallas, TX	Red 62	Red 51
Coral Springs, FL	Red 52	Blue 65	Newark, NJ	Blue 53	Blue 71
Port St. Lucie, FL	Red 52	Blue 52	Hartford, CT	Blue 56	Blue 84
Centennial, CO	Red 52	Red 51	Little Rock, AR	Red 54	Blue 56
	17 Blue	13 Red		13 Red	21 Blue

[*] Twelfth Annual America's Safest (and Most Dangerous) Cities. Morgan Quitno Press. This is the same source to which Harris refers in *Letter to a Christian Nation* on page 45, although unfortunately he does not specify the year. <http://www.morganquitno.com/cit06pop.htm#25.>. The rankings are based on FBI data for 2005 released on September 18, 2006.
[**] Don't confuse Richmond County with Richmond City if you're checking this out yourself. The city is much more populous than the county and is more than fifty-three miles away.

cities are situated in RED counties and twenty-one of the twenty-five most dangerous cities are located in BLUE counties. This provides precisely the information that Harris claimed to have sought in vain, it is definitive proof that the social health of Red America is significantly superior to that of Blue America *by Harris's own chosen measure*.[27]

By applying his metric to the state-wide voting instead of the more precise and relevant county, Harris exaggerates the number of safe blue cities by 20 percent and minimizes the number of dangerous blue cities by an astounding 70 percent! How Harris could possibly have made such a mistake is a mystery indeed, since the fact that a) crime rates are higher in urban areas, and b) Christian conservatives are usually denigrated as rednecks, not sophisticated big-city dwellers, should have alerted him to the probability that something was wrong with his calculations.

The question that remains to be answered is if Harris published these misleading conclusions through innocent incompetence or not. Was he being knowingly deceptive in attempting to blame religious red staters for the crimes committed by their godless blue county residents? While it's possible that he wasn't aware that the county data was readily available on CNN's Election 2004 site, there are troubling signs that his decision to use the misleading statewide data instead may have been intentional.

It is Harris's reference to the FBI's Uniform Crime Reports on page 95 of *The End of Faith* that shows he must have been aware that the statewide data was not the most accurate available, since he cannot have examined it without seeing that the FBI records crime by state *and by county* throughout the UCR. That's where I got the county data for Florida and Maryland myself. It's also worth noting that if Harris was primarily interested in examining the difference between red states and blue states, there was never any need to bring cities into the discussion at all, because Morgan Quitno also publishes a separate report on which states are the most and least dangerous. However, because a 63 percent red state, North Dakota, was named the safest in the nation, that particular report would not have served Harris's purpose in trying to prove that religious red staters commit

---

[27] I repeat: it's a stupid measure. But Harris chose it, which speaks volumes about both his incompetence and his ability to reason.

more crime than their supposedly godless blue state counterparts.

Perhaps Sam Harris has a good explanation for what appears to be either total incompetence or some very shady statistical shenanigans. If so, he would do well to provide it.

THE INTELLECTUALLY DISHONEST ATHEIST

By this point, it should be clear to the rational reader that Sam Harris cannot be trusted with statistics, or even to correctly calculate a tip. But because his many factual and logical errors, however suspicious, could merely indicate that he is careless, proving intellectual dishonesty requires evidence of a deliberate intent to deceive. Of course, intent isn't always easy to discern, let alone prove, as there must be at least some indication that the deceiver knows the truth that would weaken his argument but is electing to intentionally hide it.

Sometimes such deception is easy to detect. While talking about the spread of sexually transmitted diseases in *The End of Faith*, Harris cites a study showing that abstinence-pledged virgin teens were more likely to engage in oral and anal sex in an attempt to create the impression that those teens were more likely to contract an STD. What he neglected to mention was that while the study showed that 4.6 percent of the abstinence-pledged teens contracted an STD, this was 35 percent less than the 7 percent of non-pledged teens who also acquired one.[28]

When the deception is not so obvious, one way of detecting if someone is arguing in good faith or not is to see if his argument has been constructed as a tautology, or in other words, presented in the form "heads I win, tails you lose." Since a tautology cannot, by definition, be contradicted because it is universally true, presenting a tautology as if it were a legitimate matter for debate is inherently dishonest. One form of argument by tautology is known informally as the "No True Scotsman" argument, courtesy of a British philosopher named Antony Flew. It goes like this:

---

[28] Martin, Samuel. "A Two-Letter Word for Little Miss Pure: It Begins with N." *The Times*, 26 June, 2007.

ASSERTION: No Scotsman drinks Jack Daniels.

RESPONSE: But my uncle Angus is from Glasgow and he drinks Jack Daniels.

REBUTTAL: Then your uncle Angus is no true Scotsman![29]

Because the historical record of atheism is so bloody, so recent, and so well-known, Harris is forced to construct a No True Atheist argument in a preemptive attempt to ward off the inevitable response to his assertion that religious faith causes murder and genocide.

> ...the most monstrous crimes against humanity have been inspired by unjustified belief. This is nearly a truism. Genocidal projects tend not to reflect the rationality of their perpetrators simply because there are no good reasons to kill peaceful people indiscriminately....Consider the millions of people who were killed by Stalin and Mao: although these tyrants paid lip service to rationality, communism was little more than a political religion.[30]

In order to deflect attention from the obvious fact that Stalin and Mao, both undeniably atheists, killed tens of millions of people despite a complete lack of the religious faith that Harris claims is necessary to commit such monstrous acts, Harris constructs a No True Atheist argument.

HARRIS: Atheists don't kill people because they have no good reason to do so.

RESPONSE: Stalin and Mao were atheists and they killed millions of people.

HARRIS: Then Stalin and Mao were No True Atheists.

Of course, Harris doesn't come right out and present this argument directly, because even a militant atheist would laugh in his face.

---

[29] The actual No True Scotsman example is as follows: "*Imagine Hamish McDonald, a Scotsman, sitting down with his* Press and Journal *and seeing an article about how the 'Brighton Sex Maniac Strikes Again.' Hamish is shocked and declares that 'No Scotsman would do such a thing.' The next day he sits down to read his* Press and Journal *again and this time finds an article about an Aberdeen man whose brutal actions make the Brighton sex maniac seem almost gentlemanly. This fact shows that Hamish was wrong in his opinion but is he going to admit this? Not likely. This time he says, 'No true Scotsman would do such a thing.'*" Flew, Antony, *Thinking About Thinking—or do I sincerely want to be right?* London: Collins Fontana, 1975.

[30] Harris, *The End of Faith*, 79.

Instead, he uses several deceptive techniques to try to disguise the fact that he is defending his thesis with a No True Scotsman argument. Notice how much deceptive tap-dancing takes place in just this single paragraph.

- Harris surreptitiously substitutes "unjustified belief" for "religious faith." Now, "unjustified belief" is one of his many descriptions of religious faith, but obviously there are many unjustified beliefs that are not related to religious faith in any way.[31] The subset is not equal to the entire set, and since the two are not synonymous they cannot be exchanged in this manner; this is the logical fallacy known as the Undistributed Middle. Harris also implicitly swaps "an absence of rationality" for "religious faith," once more swapping the specific subset in favor of the broader set that includes it.

- Harris states there are no good reasons to kill people indiscriminately, just twenty-six pages after writing that "[s]ome propositions are so dangerous that it may even be ethical to kill people for believing them."[32] So it's okay to kill people who believe in dangerous propositions—Harris just wants to make sure that you kill them in a discriminating manner. Unfortunately, he does not inform us precisely which propositions justify execution in his mind, although given the context of the statement and the title of his book, it's apparent that he has intransigent religious belief in mind.

- Harris states that Stalin and Mao only paid lip service to rationality, but their murderous actions were perfectly rational given their goals. Stalin was seeking to destroy Ukrainian national identity, while Mao was trading agricultural products for the atomic weapons technology. It was his "Superpower Programme" that was the motivation behind the Great Leap Forward, sending food that the Chinese peasantry required to survive to Hungary, East Germany,

---

[31] Such as my aforementioned belief that the Minnesota Vikings will win the Super Bowl. Although I am reliably informed that this is more accurately described as a "forlorn hope."

[32] Harris, *The End of Faith*, 53. Harris's apologists invariably attempt to spin this as referring to self-defense, but if that were the case, Harris need not have even brought up the "dangerous propositions" in the first place. Harris is not talking about killing in self-defense when attacked, but rather killing on the basis of beliefs that he suspects could lead to future attacks due to the connection he draws between belief and behavior. To put it more plainly, Harris is making a case for lethal preemptory self-defense.

and the Soviet Union.[33] Considering that Mao had hundreds of millions of peasants who he didn't value and lacked the powerful weapons development capacity that he badly wanted, it was an entirely reasonable exchange, if a diabolical one.

• Harris claims that Communism was a religion. But however convenient and necessary to his argument this claim might be, it still isn't true. Communism is a political ideology, not a religion, and moreover, the Communisms of Lenin, Stalin, Mao, Pol Pot, Mengistu, and Kim Il-Sung all differed in the details. While each of the six dictators identified himself as communist, the only belief these mass murderers held completely in common was an atheism more militant than that of Harris himself.

Harris's attempt to gloss over this giant, gaping hole in his thesis was a complete failure, which is why he begrudgingly made a half-hearted stab at addressing it again in the afterword to the paperback edition of *The End of Faith*:

This is one of the most common criticisms I encounter. It is also the most depressing, as I anticipate and answer it early in the book (p. 79). While some of the most despicable political movements in human history have been explicitly irreligious, they were not especially rational.

This time, he tries to substitute "not especially rational" for "religious faith" and insinuates an *implicit* case because the *explicit* one didn't go over so well on the previous attempt. (You may recall that Harris tried the same trick in trying to blame religion for war.) Notice that his claim that Communism is a religion has now disappeared, although it isn't clear whether he is actually recanting his earlier position or simply does not consider Communism to be one of the most despicable political movements in human history.

Of course, the simplest explanation for this mystery of why so many people believe that citing the historical atheist predilection for mass murder is a devastating retort to the assertion that religious faith is dangerous for Mankind is because it *is* a devastating retort that demolishes the argument. The obvious explanation also hap-

---

[33] Chang, Jung and Jon Halliday. *Mao: The Unknown Story.* London: Anchor, 2007. 465.

pens to be the correct one. After all, if religious faith is the root cause of violence, then it should not be so easy—so trivially easy—to find so many historical examples of individuals who lacked religious faith and still managed to commit large-scale acts of lethal violence. While Harris may have anticipated the criticism and provided an answer, the only relevant point is that he did not provide a credible answer on either of his two attempts!

Harris's fellow atheist, Christopher Hitchens, serves as the final witness for the prosecution here as the lapsed Marxist doesn't hesitate to admit that Marxism—and therefore Communism—cannot be reasonably described as a religion, or even a faith:

> No, it's not a religion; it is defined as a non-belief in the supernatural and as a repudiation of anything [that] could be called a faith. Marxism's great mistake was it believed it had found material evidence for a past, a present and a future; and that material means alone could install it. You could say that that was a terrible idea, but you can't call it a religion.[34]

Still, Harris's repeated attempts to disguise the obvious flaw in his argument are useful in the way they reveal his habitual intellectual dishonesty. For now that we are familiar with his unscrupulous methodology and willingness to play semantic games, it is easy to demonstrate how Harris's entire case against religious faith is nothing but a thinly disguised tautology.

Early in *The End of Faith* Harris writes: "As a man believes, so he will act"[35] and he goes into some detail explaining how an individual's actions are dependent upon the beliefs he holds. "A belief is a lever that, once pulled, moves almost everything else in a person's life." In light of this, it is important to recall that Harris repeatedly defines atheism as being a lack of a belief,[36] primarily a lack of belief in the existence of God. This allows him to inoculate atheism against the historical crimes of known atheists and blame them on the religious faithful in the following manner:

---

[34] "An Evening with Christopher Hitchens," *FrontPage Magazine*. June 1, 2007.
[35] Harris, *The End of Faith*, 24.
[36] In addition to his many other definitions, of course.

1. Belief is required for action.
2. Atheism is a lack of belief.
3. Therefore, an individual's atheism cannot cause him to act in a harmful manner.
4. Belief is synonymous with faith.
5. Therefore, all negative actions stem from faith.

It's a truism! It is self-evident! Stalin, Mao, Pol Pot, etc., may have all been atheists, but because they are known to have taken action, they must have believed in something besides their atheism that caused them to act, therefore atheism cannot possibly be blamed for the actions of these so-called atheists.[37] Hallelujah, peace on Earth is in our grasp! Of course, the only way to achieve it is to somehow get rid of all those troublemaking believers...now how would one go about doing that?

And this is where Harris ceases to be an amusing figure blundering about taking incompetent and illogical potshots at religion and becomes something ominous, something malicious, in which the shadowy seed of the atheists whose monstrous crimes he disavows can be discerned. For if, as I have shown there is some reason to suspect, Harris is aware there are no rational grounds for his case against religious faith, then why is he making it? What is the point? What is his purpose in declaring faith itself to be an enemy?

Given his declarations that a diversity of religious beliefs cannot be tolerated, that every human being should not be free to believe whatever he wants, and that the killing of those who harbor intolerable beliefs can be ethically justified, the following statement betrays the evil root of his hatred for religion, for the U.S. Constitution, and for the very concept of America itself:

"We can say it even more simply: we need a world government.... The diversity of our religious beliefs constitutes a primary obstacle here."[38]

So you see, the atheist Sam Harris is a believer after all, a utopi-

---

[37] This is merely a sophisticated version of the "in the name of" fallacy.

[38] Harris, *The End of Faith*, 151. His words almost precisely mimic those of Kim Jong-il in justifying the concentration camps in which tens of thousands of North Koreans, many of them Christians, are currently being martyred.

an would-be philosopher-king cut out of the very same intellectual cloth as those who murdered more human beings in the twentieth century than every war, civil war, and criminal act[39] combined. And in a manner that Harris echoes most disturbingly with his defenses of torture and calls for forcibly imposed dictatorships, they did not commit their crimes in the name of their atheism, but rather in the name of building a new and better humanity to replace the old one.

---

[39] In 2004, I did some research on murder rates and global population growth that led me to conclude that around 11.9 million murders were committed by individual criminals in the twentieth century, which is 6.43 percent of the 185 million individuals murdered by their own governments from 1900 to 2000. If one adds the estimated 38.5 million victims of all the wars and civil wars during the century to that 11.9 million, the logical conclusion is that global government of the sort Harris advocates can be expected to be at least 3.7 times more deadly than the war, civil war, and crime it is supposed to resolve. Or, as it would be more accurate to say, replace.

VIII

DARWIN'S
JUDAS

Evolution isn't a cause of anything; it's an observation, a way of putting things in categories. Evolution says nothing about causes.

—SCOTT ADAMS, *God's Debris*

SCIENTISTS COME WITH A SELL-BY DATE. The mathematician G. H. Hardy declared that math is a young man's game, while Albert Einstein formulated the mass-energy equivalence at twenty-six and Sir Isaac Newton's famous *annus mirabilis*[1] occurred when he was only twenty-three. A California researcher has estimated that the mean age of a biologist's first noteworthy contribution to science takes place when he is 29.4 years old.[2] So, at sixty-six, three decades after publishing the

---

[1] In his "extraordinary year," which was more like eighteen months spanning 1665 and 1666, Newton laid the groundwork for his eponymous system of physics. This included calculus, optics, gravitation, and the laws of motion. I enjoyed my twenty-third year, unfortunately it revolved around a Porsche, a record deal, alcohol, and models. *Sic transit gloria mundi....*

[2] Dean K. Simonton of UC-Davis studied the contributions of nearly 2,000 famous scientists. He found that while biologists made their first historically noteworthy contribution at a mean age of 29.4 years, their contribution most often cited by historians and biographers occurred at a mean of forty years, six months. Of the eight scientific fields studied, mathematicians burned out the quickest at 27.3 and 38.8 years respectively. 24 May 2007. <http://sps.nus.edu.sg/~limchuwe/articles/youth.html>.

controversial bestseller *The Selfish Gene*, it's clear that Richard Dawkins is well past his scientific expiry, and his latest book, *The God Delusion*, offers copious evidence that Dawkins has become as careless as he is crotchety in his old age.

But this does not mean that either he or his recent works should be dismissed out of hand. His oft-acerbic literary persona notwithstanding, it is impossible to dislike anyone so utterly sound on the destructive academic drivel of postmodernism, still less a man who harbors such genuine appreciation for beauty and the arts. His writing style remains as approachable as ever, but what he no longer possesses is a firm grasp of the very Reason of which he believes himself a champion.

Even more strangely, the world's foremost spokesman for secular science, that method of advancing human knowledge based upon the primacy of empirical evidence, increasingly shows a tendency to ignore mountains of conclusive evidence in favor of mystical pronouncements about ontological possibilities. Whether this drift into what could reasonably be described as metascience is a function of Dawkins's boredom with science proper or merely an age-related disinclination for doing the required intellectual heavy-lifting is impossible to say, but it is readily apparent to anyone who has read a substantial portion of his published *ouvré*. The witty, meticulous, and inventive Dawkins of *The Selfish Gene* is simply not the clumsy, error-prone Dawkins of *The God Delusion*.

This is in part due to the fact that in his most recent book, Dawkins is not only operating outside of his area of professional expertise, he is actually pitting himself directly against it. Whereas he describes himself as a "passionate Darwinian" as an academic scientist, he calls himself "a passionate anti-Darwinian" with regards to the proper conduct of human affairs.[3] This naturally puts Dawkins in an untenable position, as he not only lacks both education and professional experience in the academic fields that relate to human conduct, such as history, philosophy, political science, literature, psychology, and theology, it also renders his book somewhat of a fraudulent bait-and-switch.

In *The God Delusion*, Richard Dawkins is using his reputation as a famous Darwinian scientist to sell a propagandistic vision that is

---

[3] Dawkins, Richard. *A Devil's Chaplain*. Boston, 2003. 10–11.

directly opposed to that very science as well as the religions it purports to attack. In fact, the entire book can be summarized as a version of the fallacious argument that Dawkins himself labels "The Argument from Admired Religious Scientists." It is the book's foundation in emotional anti-science that explains Dawkins's mysterious failure to make significant use of the important scientific tool known as evidence, as he prefers instead to rely on pure reason even when the relevant empirical evidence is readily available. Interestingly enough, this substitution of logic in the place of evidence is not new for Dawkins, as he confesses in the essay "Human Chauvinism and Evolutionary Progress" that whereas his longtime nemesis, Stephen Jay Gould, prefers to make an empirical case against the concept of evolutionary progress toward humanity, he would prefer to attack it on logical grounds.[4]

It is most unfortunate for Dawkins, then, that it is not at all difficult to demonstrate his logical incompetence with empirical evidence.

It is a real pity how most of Dawkins's critics have completely failed to notice the way in which Dawkins's abandonment of science has rendered him naked and vulnerable. While there have been a number of critical books written about Dawkins, including *The Dawkins Delusion*, *Dawkins' God* and *Letter to an Influential Atheist*, most of this criticism revolves around Dawkins's ignorance of Christian theology rather than his anti-science. It is true that the criticism is well-founded, as his dearth of knowledge on the subject is exceeded only by Sam Harris, but it is still mostly irrelevant regarding the question of God's existence as well as the substance of Dawkins's case against religion.[5]

For example, the citations of the fourteen arguments for the existence of God in *The God Delusion*, Thomas Aquinas's Five Proofs, the Ontological Argument, the Argument from Beauty, the Argument from Personal "Experience,"[6] the Argument from Scripture, the Argument

---

[4] Ibid., 208.

[5] It is important to note that Dawkins's case against religion differs subtly from Sam Harris's campaign against religious faith. While there is a substantial amount of overlap between the two atheists, Dawkins is far more focused on specific religions and their idiosyncracies, while Harris is attempting—however incompetently—to attack the very concept of faith itself.

[6] I find it amusing that Dawkins should see fit to put scare quotes questioning the very concept of

from Admired Religious Scientists,[7] Pascal's Wager, and the Bayesian Arguments, are as spurious as Dawkins believes the arguments themselves to be. They are tempting honey-traps in which the Dawkins critic is all too easily caught; because Dawkins is convinced that God almost certainly does not exist, attempting to engage him in a reasonable discussion of theological proofs is like trying to mathematically prove the speed of the Earth's rotation to someone who does not believe in numbers, and furthermore, is utterly convinced that the Earth is a disc mounted on the back of a very large turtle. Trying to debate the existence of God with Richard Dawkins is ultimately pointless, because for Dawkins, not even Jesus Christ's triumphant return in front of a crowd of tens of thousands would suffice to prove anything to him, not with his "familiarity with the brain and its powerful workings."[8]

Dawkins is not actually interested in genuinely considering the question of God's existence, as evidenced by his cursory perusal of a few of the less complicated arguments for the existence of God. His dismissal of the 3,020 pages of the *Summa Theologica* in less than three pages is no demonstration of surpassingly brilliant logic, it's merely waving a dead chicken over the keyboard in an attempt to deceive the ignorant into believing that the argument has been seriously considered and found wanting.[9] This is particularly egregious given that part of those three pages is devoted to a tangent that is entirely unrelated to the *quinquae viae*![10]

The only reason Dawkins even bothers to go through the motions is because without providing at least a nominal pretense at addressing a few of the many reasons religious people believe in God, not even his most mindless cheerleaders could find his case convincing.

---

personal experience, especially in light of his own tendency to instruct by sharing his own.

[7] His response to this is even more amusing, considering how he disproves this argument by constructing an Argument from Admired Atheist Scientists, as if the truth of God's existence is best determined by scientific democracy.

[8] Dawkins, *The God Delusion*, 92. It's always impressive how scientists can diagnose mass hallucination without ever speaking with a single eyewitness. A pity they're not as good at identifying cancer from a distance.

[9] For example, the third objection to Question 2, Article 1, "Whether the existence of God is self-evident" raises some interesting questions about whether scientific truth is more properly considered a false god or an aspect of God. Dawkins doesn't so much as mention the article or even the obviously pertinent Article 2, "Whether it can be demonstrated that God exists." The Five Proofs he dismisses so readily are from the third article.

[10] I address this childish tangent, which is related to the assumed contradiction between divine omnipotence and divine omniscience, in Chapter XV.

But he's knowingly setting fire to strawmen, for as he admits at the end of the three pages nominally dedicated to attacking Aquinas's Five Ways, the Argument from Design "is the only one still in regular use today." This causes the observant reader to wonder: If he's so terribly upset about why people believe in God today, then why is he attacking the reasons some people used to believe in God more than 700 years ago? And why does he expend more effort explaining that he is not attacking Einstein's metaphorical God than he does actually considering any of the many current beliefs of Christians, Muslims, Jews, and Hindus, let alone Jains, Sikhs, and Buddhists? It's strange, but *The God Delusion* features four times more references to Albert Einstein than to Allah, and devotes the same number of pages to discussing Adolf Hitler as it does to considering Jesus Christ.

While Dawkins incessantly complains about the lack of evidence for God, he never quite gets around to explaining precisely what proof, presumably scientific, would be sufficient for him. He poses no potentially falsifiable experiment that would suffice to prove or disprove God's existence nor does he even consider the question of whether any such experiment would conceivably be possible. But if rabbit fossils found in a Pre-Cambrian strata would suffice to disprove evolution, then surely a brilliant scientist like Richard Dawkins should easily be able to come up with a few propositions that would suffice to falsify a specific religion such as Christianity. I suggest a few possibilities:

- The elimination of the Jewish people would falsify both God's promise to Abraham and the eschatological events prophesied in the Book of Revelation.
- The discovery of Jesus Christ's crucified skeleton.
- The linguistic unification of humanity.
- An external recording of the history of the human race provided by aliens, as proposed by science fiction authors Arthur C. Clarke and James P. Hogan.
- The end of war and/or poverty.
- Functional immortality technology.

Dawkins is so unimaginative that he even regards the theoretical question about his response should he one day find himself confronting God as being "so preposterous that [he] can hardly grace it with a hypothetical answer."[11] And yet, he has no trouble whatsoever in believing seven impossible things on the basis of even scantier evidence.

ATHEISM'S RED QUEEN

Looking for art in science
Is a peculiar aspiration,
For there is little wonder
Once Man denies Creation.
And his reduction to mere numbers
O'er the passing of the years,
Leaves us with naught but the aesthetics
Of damned white coat pamphleteers.

(1) The Ontological Argument for Science-Inspired Art

In *Unweaving the Rainbow*, Dawkins writes: "By more general implication, science is poetry's killjoy, dry and cold, cheerless, overbearing and lacking in everything that a young Romantic might desire. To proclaim the opposite is one purpose of this book, and I shall here limit myself to the untestable speculation that Keats, like Yeats, might have been an even better poet if he had gone to science for some of his inspiration."

Of course, this speculation is as improbable as it is untestable, given the centuries of evidence demonstrating that science is totally incapable of providing the inspiration for passable poetry, much less the sort of great art that religion has reliably inspired for millennia. Forget Irish astronomical telescopes and D. H. Lawrence's hummingbirds, what could be more profoundly inspirational than the dystopian prospect of Man's suicidal annihilation by the deadly fruits of his own mind? And yet, in six decades of science's glorious Atomic Age, the only memorable pronouncement that comes to mind is J. Robert Oppenheimer's invocation of the ancient verses of the *Bhagavad Gita*!

---

[11] "Richard Dawkins: Beyond Belief." *The Guardian.* 10 Jan. 2006.

While one can, with some effort, envision Byronesque epics dedicated to the tortile beauties of the DNA helix or dolorous quatrains lamenting the darker aspects of apoptosis, it would require Oscar Wilde's proverbial heart of stone to do so with a straight face. Consider an actual example of science-inspired poetry: Edmund Halley's unforgettable "Ode on This Splended Ornament of Our Time and Our Nation, the Mathematico-Physical Treatise by the Eminent Isaac Newton":

> From this treatise we learn at last why silvery Phoebe moves at an unequal pace,
> Why, till now, she has refused to be bridled by the numbers of any astronomer,
> Why the nodes regress, and why the upper apsides move forward.
> We also learn the magnitude of the forces with which wandering Cynthia
> Impels the ebbing sea, while its weary waves leave the seaweed far behind
> And the sea bares the sands that sailors fear, and alternately beat high up
>   on the shores
> The things that so often vexed the minds of the ancient philosophers
> And fruitlessly disturb the schools with noisy debate
> We see right before our eyes, since mathematics drives away the cloud.

Great stuff, that scientific poesy! It's undeniably entertaining, in a sort of an Adamsian "Ode to the Lump of Green Putty I Found in My Armpit One Midsummer Morning" manner. Still, I daresay it's not on quite the same artistic level as Alexander Pope's rather more succinct and religious tribute to the very same gentleman:

> Nature and nature's laws lay hid in night;
> God said "Let Newton be" and all was light.

At Richard Dawkins's core is a band geek who is unable to accept the reality that marching tubas and embroidered uniforms will never impress the girls. For all its passionate and detailed explanations of water droplets and entirely new variants of suns, *Unweaving the Rainbow* ultimately amounts to little more than an unconvincing and repetitive refrain of "This one time, at band camp...." Still, Dawkins's belief in the artistic possibilities of science is rather sweet. It is, as I believe I have read somewhere before, the substance of things hoped for, the evidence of things not seen.[12]

---

[12] That would be the Apostle Paul's definition of faith.

It is also worth noting that Dawkins's insistence that science not only leaves room for poetry[13] but is more capable than religion of inspiring it, flies directly in the face of his claim to suspect any form of argument that reaches a significant conclusion "without feeding in a single piece of data from the real world."[14]

The inadequacy of science and other secular replacements for religion has not escaped the notice of one of the more enthusiastic champions of the arts, Camille Paglia, who despite her atheism insists that religion is an artistic necessity. She explains that whereas the first generation of secular artists, such as James Joyce, Igor Stravinsky, Pablo Picasso, and Marcel Proust, achieved greatness through their rebellion against religious tradition, it is their very success that has crippled their successors. She complains that "today, anything goes, and nothing lasts" before declaring that secular humanism has reached a dead end and that religion must be taught in every school.[15]

(2) Martial Victory Through Blind Obedience

Dawkins's stated belief that religion is a primary cause of war has already been dealt with and refuted in no little detail. But his similarly groundless belief that nations "whose infantrymen act on their own initiative rather than following orders will tend to lose wars" is worthy of highlighting for the way it will be met with a great deal of amusement by anyone familiar with USMC war fighting doctrine[16] or even general military history.

The Marine Corps' style of warfare requires intelligent leaders with a penchant for boldness and initiative down to the lowest levels.[17]

His theories about war's implicit causes notwithstanding, it's obvious that Dawkins hasn't paid any attention to developments in warfare over the last 150 years, because the Third Generation Warfare waged by the Kaiserheer, the Wehrmacht, and the U.S. Marines is

---

[13] Dawkins, *Unweaving the Rainbow*, 180. Sadly, there is no room for religion at the inn.

[14] Dawkins, *The God Delusion*, 82.

[15] Paglia, Camille. "Art Movies: R.I.P." Salon, 8 Aug. 2007.

[16] "In war games in the 19th Century, German junior officers were routinely given problems that could only be solved by disobeying orders....Initiative is more important than obedience." Lind, William. "Understanding Fourth Generation War."

[17] MCDP1: Warfighting. The United States Marine Corps.

designed around the very concept of personal initiative he claims to be martially ineffectual. Fourth Generation Warfare, which describes the decentralized war of the sort waged by the Viet Minh, the Mujahideen, or al-Qaeda doesn't even possess a central command structure capable of giving the orders that Dawkins believes are so vital to martial success. As for the relevant empirical evidence, it is almost unanimously contrary to Dawkins's theoretical assertion in light of how 4GW forces designed around independent low-level initiative have been extraordinarily successful, so much so that the martial theoretician who articulated the concept, William S. Lind, gloomily notes that "Almost everywhere, the state is losing."[18]

(3) Atheist Respect for Architecture

It's not hard to demonstrate that Richard Dawkins has been almost as successful in remaining as ignorant of world history as he has of warfare. He betrays an astonishing lack of knowledge about the Spanish Civil War or the atrocious acts of the previous century's most notorious atheists when he declares with great confidence:

> *I do not believe there is an atheist in the world who would bulldoze Mecca—or Chartres, York Minster or Notre Dame, the Shwe Dagon, the temples of Kyoto or, of course, the Buddhas of Bamiyan.*[19]

Mr. Mikhail Mashin, the director of the ZIL, has built a thriving business on the refutation of this particular Dawkinsian myth. Under Soviet rule, ZIL made cars, but the competition ZIL faced from Western automotive manufacturers after the fall of the Soviet Union forced the company to creatively explore other markets. ZIL now manufactures church bells because there is a booming business in church construction due to the fact that from 1917 to 1969, the atheist Soviets destroyed 41,000 of Russia's 48,000 churches, including Christ the Savior Cathedral, a Moscow landmark that was built to commemorate the defeat of Napoleon's invasion. This massive

---

[18] Lind, William. "Understanding Fourth Generation War." Most state militaries, like Dawkins, are stuck in 2GW, based on a centralized, hierarchic, order-dependent organization.

[19] Dawkins, *The God Delusion*, 249.

destruction of religious art and architecture was neither ideological nor political in nature, it was *The God Delusion* in action, a material atheist argument for the nonexistence of God.

> *During early Soviet times, thousands of churches, monasteries and convents across the country were destroyed by the Bolsheviks in their drive to cleanse the Soviet Union of religion.... Across the country, bells were pushed from their belfries and destroyed. Russian author Inna Simonova calls it the "aggressive atheism" that was practiced by the Bolsheviks to sway Russians. "They said, 'Look, you believe in God, and yet we've thrown these bells off the roof and nothing has happened,'" said Mrs. Simonova....[20]*

The empirical evidence simply blows away another of Richard Dawkins's ontological arguments. Dawkins isn't just wrong, he is spectacularly incorrect. In place of the 41,000 Soviet churches destroyed between 1917 and 1969 I could have as easily cited any of the many thousands of historical examples of similar behavior in atheist-run Spain, Poland, Romania, or East Germany to prove that not only are there many atheists in the world who have done exactly what Dawkins believes to be inconceivable, but that architectural devastation is far more likely to be committed by atheists than by the believers of all the various religions in the world combined.[21] Dawkins's mention of the "temples of Kyoto" is especially ironic,[22] considering the way in which atheists have been responsible for destroying 7,000 temples and monasteries in Tibet, 440 of the 500 Buddhist temples in North Korea, and 240 of the 700 Buddhist temples in Vietnam. The only reason that Mecca, York Minster, and Notre Dame survive today is that they are located in nations where atheists have not possessed control of the government for an extended period of time.

---

[20] "Saved by the Church Bell." *Cox News Service.* 25 April, 2004. The Commission for the Rehabilitation of the Victims of Political Repression reported in 1995 that a similar percentage of Jewish and Islamic buildings had also been destroyed.

[21] "*In the interest of recreating proletarian states, ruthless killings of the intelligentsia and peasants were combined with leveling indigenous and religious architecture to re-create a 'utopia on the ruins of the past.'*" Hayeem, Abe. "Destruction as Cultural Cleansing": *Building Design.* 3 Feb. 2006.

[22] "*The government from the province of Henan has in fact decreed that the historic sanctuary dedicated to Our Lady of Mount Carmel will be blown up with dynamite; a complete ban on Catholics organizing their annual pilgrimage; a complete ban on any religious gathering or function being celebrated in the area.*" AsiaNews. 21 June 2007.

(4) The Inherent Goodness of Humanity and Moral Gradients

Dawkins finds it hard to believe that people would become callous, selfish hedonists without God. Setting aside the fact that his most successful atheist counterpart, Michel Onfray, is arguing specifically for a philosophy of hedonism to replace Dawkins's own compromise with Christian morality, the evidence suggests that this is exactly what should be expected. Dawkins may even suspect as much, since he refers to himself as perhaps being naïve and a Pollyanna while relating a tale of the massive disorder that accompanied a strike by the Montreal police in 1969.

It has been established that Christians give three times more to charity[23] and are less criminal than the broad spectrum of atheists; experiments at the Economic Science Laboratory suggest that this might be because they believe that their actions are known to God. In variations on an envelope experiment designed to test random charity on the part of a subject who was given ten dollars as well as the opportunity to share it anonymously, the knowledge that the experimenter was watching increased the subject's likelihood of giving by 142 percent and the amount given by 146 percent.[24]

Furthermore, Dawkins erroneously states that behaving in a traditionally moral manner in the absence of policing is somehow "more moral" than the very same behavior when it is witnessed. This confuses action with intent and reveals a basic misunderstanding of the nature of Christian morality. It is an aspect of the common atheist fallacy that I describe as the Argument from Superior Morals in Chapter XIV.

(5) The Equation of Christian Theocracy with Islamic Fascism

Dawkins claims that the goal to have a Christian nation built on God's Law and the Ten Commandments "can only be called a Christian fascist state" and claims that it is "an almost exact mirror image" of an Islamic fascist state. This is preposterous on several levels.

---

[23] "*In 2000, religious people gave about three and a half times as much as secular people—$2,210 versus $642.*" Ben Gose, "Charity's Political Divide," *The Chronicle of Philanthropy*. 23 Nov. 2006.

[24] Landsburg, Steven. "Stuffing Envelopes": *Reason*, March 2001. The dollar difference increased from $1.08 to $2.66 if the subject thought the amount of his contribution would be known to the observer.

There have been hundreds of Christian kingdoms and principalities that incorporated the Ten Commandments and aspects of biblical law into the foundation of their legal systems, and a tiny fraction of them have been fascist. Dawkins himself lives in one such historically Christian nation; Queen Elizabeth II also happens to be the current Supreme Governor of the Church of England.

Fascism is not merely a word that means "scary," it is a specific historical ideology no less readily identifiable than Marxism or Communism. While there were avowedly fascist governments in the Christian nations of Italy and Austria, there is no such thing as Islamic fascism. Islamic fascism does not exist and it has never existed, either as a political ideology or a practical system of government. The concept is a meaningless term of propaganda used primarily by American neocons and third-rate political pundits seeking to stir up public support for the Global Struggle Against Violent Extremism during the lead-up to the Iraqi invasion; it is already falling out of the political discourse.

(6) Catholicism Is More Damaging Than Childhood Sexual Abuse

Richard Dawkins is perhaps one of the last men on Earth who should be discussing what is the right and proper way to raise children, given that the number of his wives outnumbers his offspring. But while he can accept both child abandonment and childhood sexual abuse with dispassionate fortitude, it is the horrible crime of raising children in the faith of their fathers that upsets him due to his belief that the fear of Hell is more psychologically damaging than childhood sexual abuse in the long term.[25]

In his letter to his daughter Juliet, addressed to her at the age of ten and published in A Devil's Chaplain, there is little mention of love, no admission of regret, and no paternal promises. As one British journalist noted, the letter is "coldly impersonal" and "authoritarian."[26]

---

[25] "Once, in the question time after a lecture in Dublin, I was asked what I thought about the widely publicized cases of sexual abuse by Catholic priests in Ireland. I replied that, as horrible as sexual abuse no doubt was, the damage was arguably less than the long-term psychological damage inflicted by bringing up the child Catholic in the first place." Dawkins, The God Delusion, 317.

[26] "The letter highlights his own complex, often contrary, nature—it is intimate and coldly imperson-

There is no expression of interest in what might be important to her. But Dawkins loses no time in informing her what is important to him, and that is "evidence." One has to pity the poor girl, who at ten would have surely rather been assured that she was beautiful in his eyes and of supreme importance to him despite his absence instead of receiving a tedious seven-page lecture on the need to believe in evidence that is not based on tradition, authority, or revelation.

But that's her problem and her therapist's profit. What's much more interesting is the way Dawkins closes "A Prayer for My Daughter" by writing: "And next time somebody tells you that something is true, why not say to them: 'What kind of evidence is there for that?' And if they can't give you a good answer, I hope you'll think very carefully before you believe a word they say." The scientist may not be much of a father, but as it turns out, this particular advice is excellent.

For what kind of evidence is there for Dawkins's controversial assertion of the greater long-term psychological damage inflicted upon children who are raised Catholic than upon those who are sexually abused? He first provides anecdotal information from one woman who was raised Catholic, was sexually abused by a priest, and later had nightmares about Hell. And in the unlikely event that one woman's bad dreams are not enough to completely convince the reader, Dawkins goes on to mention an apocryphal story about Alfred Hitchcock driving through Switzerland, a Protestant haunted house, a letter from a woman seeking a therapist, an American comedienne's routine, and a letter from an upset American medical student whose girlfriend is breaking up with him. Despite posing the proposition as a comparison, Dawkins does not bother to consider what, if any, the negative effects of childhood sexual trauma might happen to be in order to compare them with this comprehensive list of Catholic horrors.[27]

Dr. Jonathan R.T. Davidson of the Duke University Medical Center is not quite so blasé about the psychological damage of sexual abuse, as his 1996 study found that the chances of sexually abused women attempting suicide were three times higher if they had been

al, humble and pompous, innocent and calculated, chummy and authoritarian." Hattenstone, Simon. "Darwin's Child." The Guardian. 10 Feb. 2003.

[27] Half of which aren't even related to Catholicism.

sexually abused before the age of sixteen.[28] In the same study, Davidson determined that women who had been sexually assaulted were six times more likely to attempt suicide than those who had not. As for long-term effects, the *American Journal of Geriatric Psychiatry* reported that 67 percent of women over fifty diagnosed with major depression who had been sexually abused as children had made multiple suicide attempts, compared with 27 percent of depressed women over fifty who had not been abused.[29] The study also found that middle-aged women who were sexually abused were more likely to suffer at least one other major mental disorder and possess a lifetime history of substance abuse.

As for the proposed psychological damage of being raised Catholic, all of the scientific evidence directly contradicts the notion, despite those compelling anecdotes about filmmakers and failed Romeos. A report in the *American Journal of Psychiatry* concluded that the religious faithful, most of whom were presumably raised religious, were much psychologically healthier than the irreligious.

> *Religiously unaffiliated subjects had significantly more lifetime suicide attempts and more first-degree relatives who committed suicide than subjects who endorsed a religious affiliation.... In terms of clinical characteristics, religiously unaffiliated subjects had more lifetime impulsivity, aggression, and past substance use disorder.*[30]

In fact, if suicide is a reasonable metric for long-term psychological damage, and it is hard to imagine a better one, then there is evidence to suggest that children raised Catholic suffer from less long-term psychological damage than the average *religious* individual and much less than the average child raised as an atheist. A 1986 American study showed that the proportion of Catholics in a region was negatively correlated with suicide rates,[31] while the World

[28] J. R. Davidson, D. C. Hughes, L. K. George, and D. G. Blazer, Department of Psychiatry and Behavior Sciences, Duke University Medical Center. "The Association of Sexual Assault and Attempted Suicide Within the Community," *Archives of General Psychiatry.* 6 (1996).

[29] N. L. Talbot, P. R. Duberstein, C. Cox, D. Denning, and Y. Conwell, "Preliminary Report on Childhood Sexual Abuse, Suicidal Ideation, and Suicide Attempts Among Middle-Aged and Older Depressed Women," *American Journal of Geriatric Psychiatry* 12 (2004): 536–538.

[30] K. Dervic, M. A. Oquendo, M. F. Grunebaum, S. Ellis, A. K. Burke, J. J. Mann, "Religious Affiliation and Suicide Attempt," *American Journal of Psychiatry* 161 (2004): 2303–2308.

[31] David Lester, "Religion, Suicide and Homicide," *Social Psychiatry and Psychiatric Epidemiology* 2 (1987).

Health Organization's most recent national suicide statistics show that heavily Catholic countries such as Mexico, Brazil, Italy, and the Philippines have an average suicide rate of 4.2 per 100,000, while historically Protestant countries such as Germany, Sweden, Switzerland, and the Netherlands were more than three times higher at 13.8. And it is the countries of the former Soviet Union that have some of the highest rates of suicide, as Russia, Ukraine, Latvia, and Estonia average 31.1 suicides per 100,000 population.[32]

While there is no evidence that being raised Catholic is more psychologically damaging than being sexually abused as a child, there is a great deal of evidence proving the opposite. I suggest, therefore, that the reader would do very well to follow Richard Dawkins's paternal advice and think very carefully before believing a single word that Dawkins says.

(7) The Infallibility of Sam Harris

As was demonstrated by the unfortunate citation of Harris's erroneous Red State-Blue State argument vivisected in the previous chapter, Dawkins's faith in Sam Harris is both ill-founded and poorly rewarded. Even more damaging to Dawkins's credibility, though, is the foreword to the British edition of *Letter to a Christian Nation* in which he writes:

> *If you are part of the target, I dare you to read this book. It will be a salutary test of your faith. Survive Sam Harris's barrage, and you can take on the world with equanimity. But forgive my skepticism: Harris never misses, not with a single sentence, which is why his short book is so disproportionately devastating.*

While my faith has been tested on more than one occasion, I cannot say that the short slog through *Letter to a Christian Nation* was one of them. I survived the barrage, but it was admittedly difficult to maintain my equanimity and refrain from laughing when informed that the only known cure for poverty is the empowerment of women and

---

[32] "Suicide Rates per 100,000 by Country, Year and Sex." World Health Organization, December 2005. Suicide rates for the atheist-run states of Laos, North Korea, and Vietnam were not provided, the rate for China only represented Hong Kong and unidentified other parts of the country.

their emancipation from reproduction.[33] Take that, Joseph Schumpeter, and your crazy theory of creative destruction! You, too, Hernando de Soto, and your whacky ideas about property rights! And someone do tell that silly old Scot that it's girl power, not self-interest and the division of labor, that produces the wealth of nations!

As the reader has probably come to expect by now, Harris has it backward again. Not only has a causal link between women's suffrage and an immediate increase in the size and spending of government (which decrease societal wealth through their disruption of the free market forces and strictures on private property rights) been proven,[34] but the influx of women into the American labor market has been the primary factor in the 16.8 percent decline in weekly real wages since 1972.[35] This is not a complex issue; because women were already active in the market as consumers, the only significant quantitative effect of the doubling of their participation in the work force since 1950 was to reduce the price of labor without an ameliorating increase in demand. If America had been an immature export-driven economy, this could have been a very positive development, not so much in a mature import economy.

So Harris not only misses on a regular basis, he usually misses by a wide margin when he's not actually shooting himself in the foot. Similar factual errors can be found on pages 7, 20, 39, and 43,[36] to give just a few of many examples.

---

[33] Harris, *The End of Faith*, 35. Harris is actually quoting Hitchens, in another example of the atheist circle jerk.

[34] John R. Lott and Lawrence W. Kenny, "Did Women's Suffrage Change the Size and Scope of Government?" Part 1 of *The Journal of Political Economy* 6 (1999), 1163–1198.

[35] In 1972, the average weekly wage was $331.59 (in 1982 constant dollars), which equaled an annual salary of $34,979 in 2005 dollars. But the weekly wage in 2005 was only $275.90 (in 1982 constant dollars), which works out to $29,105 per year. The negative effect on wages caused by women entering the work force was largely hidden until 1972, when men finally stopped leaving the work force in numbers sufficient to conceal the trend. One could accurately characterize the period from 1950 to 1972 as women from eighteen to thirty-five going to work so that men over sixty could play golf. Source: U.S. Bureau of Labor Statistics.

[36] (7) The way Harris views all religions is not how Christians view Islam. (20) The first four Commandments do not have "nothing whatsoever to do with morality"—Harris is improperly defining morality as "a search for happiness," not "a standard of correct conduct." (39) American teenagers have nearly twice as many sexual partners as European teens, 80 percent more than the famously libertine Dutch. (43) The least religious societies are not the healthiest; the atheist nations of China, Vietnam, North Korea, and Laos are much less religious than the historically Christian nations listed by Harris and rank 54, 83, 110, and 151 in terms of life expectancy.

FRACTAL INTELLIGENCE AND THE COMPLEX DESIGNER

The anthropic principle has been an embarrassing problem for secular scientists in recent decades due to the way in which the probability of the universe and Earth just happening to be perfectly suitable for human life is very, very low. The extreme unlikelihood of everything being not too hot, not too cold, not too big, and not too small, to put it very crudely, has often been cited as evidence that the universe has been designed for us, presumably by God. Now, Richard Dawkins is arguably not an individual particularly well-suited to play around with probability. He may not be quite as mathematically handicapped as Sam Harris, but he is known to have some issues in this regard, being openly mocked for his "comic authority" and "fatal attraction" to mathematical concepts by the French mathematician Marcel-Paul Schützenberger.[37]

Schützenberger's contempt for Dawkins's mathematical abilities is well-founded, as it's generally not considered to be a good idea to adopt a casual approach to mathematical probability, as Dawkins does with the "one in a billion" chance of something like DNA spontaneously arising which he invents *ex nihilo*, before reaching the shocking statistical conclusion that if there are a billion billion planets and a one in a billion chance of life spontaneously arising on a planet, then life must exist on a billion planets throughout the universe! Dawkins is genuinely surprised by his astonishing discovery of mathematical division, so much so that he repeats it twice.

Did you know that if there are four fours[38] of books and a one in four chance of a book being written by a New Atheist, then there must be four New Atheist books? Sweet St. Darwin of the Galapagos, is this really what passes for a public intellectual today?

Encouraged by this successful foray into the realm of higher

---

[37] "But look, the construction of the relevant space cannot proceed until a preliminary analysis has been carried out, one in which the set of all possible trajectories is assessed, this together with an estimation of their average distance from the specified goal. The preliminary analysis is beyond the reach of empirical study. It presupposes—the same word that seems to recur in theoretical biology—that the biologist (or computer scientist) know the totality of the situation, the properties of the ensemble of trajectories. In terms of mathematical logic, the nature of this space is entirely enigmatic." Schützenberger, Marcel-Paul. "The Miracles of Darwinism." <http://www.arn.org/docs/odesign/od172/schutz172.htm>.

[38] Or sixteen, as we non-dysnumeric individuals usually describe it.

mathematics, Dawkins is convinced that his response to the anthropic principle, somewhat confusingly named the Argument from Improbability for the nonexistence of God, is a serious, even unrebuttable,[39] refutation of the Argument from Improbability for the existence of God. Since he informs us that this is the central argument of his book, it behooves us to examine his summary of the argument in detail.

1. *One of the greatest challenges to the human intellect, over the centuries, has been to explain how the complex, improbable appearance of design in the universe arises.*
2. *The natural temptation is to attribute the appearance of design to actual design itself.*
3. *The temptation is a false one, because the designer hypothesis immediately raises the larger problem of who designed the designer. The whole problem we started out with was the problem of explaining statistical improbability. It is obviously no solution to postulate something even more improbable. We need a "crane," not a "skyhook," for only a crane can do the business of working up gradually and plausibly from simplicity to otherwise improbable complexity.*

It would be hard to take any serious issue with step one or two, but in step three, Dawkins's train of thought tumbles off the logic rails, not once, not twice, but thrice. His first mistake is the assumption that the designer is inherently more improbable than the design, based on the assumption that the designer of the universe must be more complex than the universe itself. But because Dawkins does not define complexity, he provides no means of calculating the statistical improbability of the designer, whereas the statistical improbabilities of the design are clearly defined in no little detail in the cosmological applications of the anthropic principle, as Dawkins concedes in his citation of the six fundamental constants examined by the physicist Martin Rees.

While Dawkins's complaint that the theistic answer to the design's

---

[39] Or so Dawkins quotes Daniel Dennett "rightly" describing it, in yet one more example of the endless circle jerking.

improbability is unsatisfying because it leaves the existence of the designer unexplained is fair, his subsequent assertion that "A God capable of calculating the Goldilocks values for the six numbers would have to be at least as improbable as the finely tuned combination of numbers itself"[40] is not. This is his second error, as the statement is certainly true of Rees, who is both capable of calculating the numbers and is a part of the design, but it cannot be true of the designer because the latter fact does not apply. Third, does Dawkins seriously wish to argue that Martin Rees is more complex than the universe? We know Rees calculated the Goldilocks values, so if he can do so despite being less complex than the sum of everyone and everything else in the universe, then God surely can, too.

There is no reason why a designer must necessarily be more complex than his design. The verity of the statement depends entirely on the definition of complexity. While Dawkins doesn't specifically provide one, in explaining his "Ultimate Boeing 747 gambit," he refers to the Argument from Improbability as being rooted in "the source of all the information in living matter." Complexity, to Dawkins, is therefore equated with information.

But as any programmer knows, mass quantities of information can easily be produced from much smaller quantities of information. A fractal is perhaps the most obvious example of huge quantities of new information being produced from a very small amount of initial information. For example, thirty-two lines of C++ code suffice to produce a well-known fractal known as the Sierpinski Triangle.

---

[40] Dawkins, *The God Delusion*, 143.

In the Triangle, each triangle divides into four smaller triangles. As the size of the new triangles progresses toward zero, the total area of the set tends to infinity. What contains more information and is therefore more complex, an infinite total area or thirty-two lines of C++? A BASIC program generating the gorgeous recursive images of the famous Mandelbrot Set is even simpler:

```
CLS
FOR i = 1 TO 300
   FOR j = 1 TO 150
      c1=-2+4*i/300
      c2=2-4*j/300
      x=c1
      y=c2
         FOR n = 1 TO 30
          x1=x*x-y*y+c1
          y1=2*x*y+c2
          r=x1*x1+y1*y1
          IF r > 4 THEN GOTO 1000
          x = x1
          y = y1
          NEXT n
      PSET(i, j)
      PSET(i,300-j)
   1000 NEXT j
NEXT i
END[41]
```

[41] http://library.thinkquest.org/3493/src/fractal/mandelbrot.bas.

Despite their informational simplicity, fractals are not only considered to be complex, but infinitely complex. Nor do they require human intelligence or computers to produce them, as approximate fractals can be found in clouds, snowflakes, lightning, mountains, and other natural examples. This demonstration of complexity from simplicity could be termed the Fractal Intelligence response to the theoretical problem of the Complex Designer posed by Dawkins.

But there are other means of proving the relative probability of the designer versus the design. The human genome possesses 30,000 genes while the *indica* rice genome possesses between 46,022 and 55,615 genes. However, the average length of those rice genes is only 4,500 gene pairs, one-sixteenth the length of the average human gene at 72,000 gene pairs. While the Chinese scientists developing a rice known as Xa21, a new strain of genetically modified rice resistant to bacterial blight, have not yet published the exact number or length of Xa21's genes, it almost surely possesses more and shorter genes than the scientists who developed it. So, in terms of genetic information, the design may or may not be more complex than the designer, depending on whether we choose to define information in terms of genes or gene pairs. In any case, it proves that the designer does not have to be more complex than his design if information is the measure.

Dawkins makes three even more serious mistakes in attempting to demonstrate the improbability of divine complexity when he argues that a designer capable of not only designing, but continually monitoring and controlling the individual status of every particle in the universe must be complex, especially if the designer's consciousness is also occupied with the activities of every single sentient being across the billions of galaxies, answering his prayers, inflicting suffering on him and so forth. But here he is confusing the design of the universe, which is the topic under discussion, with the active management of the universe, which is not.

The designer of the universe need not monitor it, in fact, the concept of a hands-off Creator God has been around for centuries, it is the deity of the nineteenth-century Deists whom today's atheists regard as spiritual ancestors. A distinction between the divine designer and an active divine monitor is not only inherent to the Gnostic heretics, but to Bible-believing Christians as well. The common, but misguided, concept of divine puppet mastery, or omniderigence, is addressed in detail in Chapter XV, but for now it is sufficient to state that because Christian and other theologies do not require any belief in ongoing divine monitoring or active control (even if they permit it), that particular aspect of God's supposed complexity does not belong in any Argument from Improbability.

Third, the network analyzers known as packet sniffers, which capture each packet from the data stream passing through the network and can log, analyze, or decode the information contained therein, are orders of magnitude smaller in terms of digital bytes than the information they are monitoring. They are much less complex by Dawkins's definition, therefore, one would also expect a universal divine monitor to be significantly less complex than the universe monitored.

His supposedly "unrebuttable argument" is already refuted at this point, but it's only fair to follow its last three steps.

4. *The most ingenious and powerful crane so far discovered is Darwinian evolution by natural selection. Darwin and his successors have shown how living creatures, with their spectacular statistical improbability and appearance of design, have evolved by slow, gradual degrees from simple beginnings. We can now safely say that the illusion of design in living creatures is just that—an illusion.*

5. *We don't yet have an equivalent crane for physics. Some kind of multiverse theory could in principle do for physics the same explanatory work as Darwinism does for biology.*

Dawkins visits the wreckage of his train of thought, pours lighter fluid over it, and sets it on fire by bringing up the multiverse concept, an utterly non-scientific theory invented solely to get around the problem of the anthropic principle. The anthropic principle is an explanation for the great mystery of physics: the improbable coincidence of various fundamental constants being set at just the right levels in order to support life in the universe. First announced by astrophysicist Brandon Carter in 1973 at a symposium celebrating the

500th birthday of Nicolaus Copernicus, the principle suggests that the tremendous improbability of life in the universe suggests that its existence is not an accident. In explaining this principle, which is an extremely embarrassing thorn in the side of secular science, a former atheist named Patrick Glynn comments wryly that "the more physicists have learned about the universe, the more it looks like a put-up job."[42] Carter conceived the anthropic principle based on the odds against a relatively small number of fundamental constants being set precisely enough to permit life, but the current count is reportedly up to 128 of these fortuitous coincidences.[43]

Those indisposed to accept the anthropic principle attempt to get around the massive improbability problem it presents by imagining that there are billions and billions of universes, for all things are possible through the scientist who postulates very large numbers. Only by postulating a potentially infinite number of universes can our wildly improbable universe become mathematically probable. Of course, there are no signs of any of these other universes, nor did science ever take the idea of parallel universes seriously until the alternative was accepting the apparent evidence for a universal designer. But not only is multiverse theory every bit as unfalsifiable and untestable as the God Hypothesis, it is demonstrably more improbable. If we accept Dawkins's naked assertion that a universal designer is more complex than the one known universe, a designer is probably less complex than any two universes and infinitely less complex than an infinity of them.

Dawkins does not inform us of the degree to which God's complexity exceeds the complexity of the universe, but if we concede, for the sake of argument, that a universal designer must be 1,000 times more complex than the universe in order to create it, and therefore 1,000 times more improbable, a universal designer is still more mathematically likely than the squared improbability of there being two universes of similar complexity. For example, if the probability of one universe is one in one million, then the probability of the universal designer would be one in one billion, but the probability of

---

[42] Patrick Glynn, *GOD The Evidence: The Reconciliation of Faith and Reason in a Postsecular World* (Rocklin, 1999), 22.

[43] Ian Wishart, *Eve's Byte* (North Shore, 2007) 77.

there being two universes of similarly complex natures would be a much more improbable one in one quintillion.

> 6. *We should not give up hope of a better crane arising in physics, something as powerful as Darwinism is for biology. But even in the absence of a strongly satisfying crane to match the biological one, the relatively weak cranes we have at present are, when abetted by the anthropic principle, self-evidently better than the self-defeating skyhook hypothesis of an intelligent designer.*

Dawkins's "unrebuttable argument" ends laughably with a desperate appeal to the reader not to give up the faith, even though evidence, logic, and mathematics all refute this crown jewel of *The God Delusion*. Lacking any means of proving his conclusion, Dawkins simply throws up his hands and declares it to be self-evident![44] I ask you this, dear atheist reader, would you accept an argument this poorly constructed as conclusive and irrefutable evidence of the existence of God?[45] And yet, on the basis of this burned-out train wreck of an argument, Dawkins declares the God Hypothesis to be untenable. I believe, on the other hand, that on the basis of this argument and the many errors mentioned previously in this chapter, any reasonable individual, regardless of his religious faith or lack of religious faith, can only conclude that it is Dawkins's entire foray outside of his realm of scientific expertise that is hopelessly untenable.

Sir Isaac Newton was fortunate that his obsessions with alchemy and occultic rediscovery did not tarnish his splendid record of intellectual achievement. Unfortunately for Richard Dawkins, his penchant for publishing his cognitive indiscretions make it unlikely that his reputation will survive similarly unscathed. But if science cannot inspire great art, never let it be said that a scientist cannot inspire great comedy, for who can possibly forget the classic episode of *South*

---

[44] Sam Harris likes this "argument," too. So do I. I am a super sex machine to all the chicks. It is self-evident. Q.E.D.

[45] How is the hypothesis of an intelligent designer "self-defeating" anyhow? Some arguments for an intelligent designer make use of the anthropic principle, but the two are not the same. Dawkins's logic isn't so much incompetent here as it is simply weird.

Park featuring the famed evolutionary biologist getting his gene-replicating groove on. For inspiring that, if nothing else, we owe him an eternal debt of gratitude.

> *A fish-squirrel boned a monkey in the Cambrian stream;*
> *Satan shrieked "Let Dawkins be" and brought forth a meme.*[46]

---

[46] This isn't precisely the original form, but I am informed that certain words are frowned upon at Westminster Abbey and I shouldn't wish to deprive the Dawkins family of the chance to use this tribute to the great man on the occasion of his demise. Should the families of Sam Harris, Christopher Hitchens, or Daniel Dennett find themselves requiring a similar epitaph, they may rest secure in the knowledge that my poetic services are available.

IX

A MARXIAN APOSTATE

One of Lenin's great achievements, in my opinion,
is to create a secular Russia.

—CHRISTOPHER HITCHENS,
Heaven on Earth: The Rise and Fall of Socialism

C HRISTOPHER HITCHENS IS THE LAST AND LEAST of the Unholy Trinity. A respected political journalist, iconoclast, and, according to the *Economist*, one of the greatest living English conversationalists, he has neither the professional authority of Richard Dawkins nor is he accorded the intellectual cachet preposterously granted to Sam Harris. However, his book, *god is not Great*, has the virtue of being presented to the reader in a commendably honest and straightforward manner. Hitchens is not marketing humanism with a scientific brand, he is not pushing for global government under the guise of godlessness, he is merely venting about his personal hatred for religion in general and Christianity in particular.

And he vents well. Hitchens is a literary creature and the effortless

prolixity of his acidulous anti-religious ranting betrays his familiarity with some of the great writers of the past. The self-righteousness
of his outrage does credit to his Marxist background;[1] throughout
the thunder of his prose one can feel the same burning sense of in-
dignation that previously fueled Eugene Debs, Upton Sinclair, and
the great prophet of scientific socialism himself. But Hitchens is seldom overly bombastic and he remains entertaining even at his most
vicious, as there is more Wodehouse than Brecht in his most pointed wit.

A globe-traveling journalist, Hitchens has seemingly been almost
everywhere. He has had personal experience of the religious faithful
from Protestant Unionists in Ulster to Buddhist monks in Tibet. But
as with most journalists, his knowledge is far wider than it is deep
and his unsophisticated reasoning reflects this superficiality.

To the journalistic mind, to have heard of something is to know
it and to write about something is to understand it. This is absurd, as anyone who has ever read a newspaper account of their
own doings or even a story related to an area of their expertise
well knows; I am hardly a public figure, but I have noticed that
every single time a media publication has done a story or broad-
cast related to me, it has contained at least one major error and
more often than not betrays a failure to understand something
significant about the subject.[2]

Because Hitchens is more intelligent than the average journalist,
his personal experiences do tend to shed a degree of relevant light
on the topics he is discussing; even so, he is obviously subject to the
common journalistic misconception that the plural of anecdote is
data. While Harris constructs incompetent arguments and Dawkins
constructs illogical ones, Hitchens doesn't even attempt to construct
an intelligible case at any point along the way; instead he relies on
argumentation by anecdote, avoidance, and aspersion.

Like any good storyteller, Hitchens sees no problem in casually
adjusting the facts in order to make for a more entertaining story.

---

[1] To this day, the former Trotskyite still "*won't have a word said against Marxist dialectical materialism.*" Nor will he accept it being described as a religion, although he admits that one can call it "*a
terrible idea.*"

[2] This includes *The New York Times*, *Minneapolis Star-Tribune*, Knight Ridder, and the Twin Cities
NBC-affiliate.

When he relates how radio host Dennis Prager once asked him about whether the knowledge that a large group of men approaching him at night were coming from a Bible class would make him feel safer or less safe, Hitchens changes the words "Bible class" to "prayer meeting" and then "religious observance" in order to give himself an excuse to spend eleven pages rambling on about his negative experiences with militant religious extremists in Belfast, Beirut, Bombay, Belgrade, Bethlehem, and Baghdad.[3] Given his alliterative theme, you'd think he would have been happy to stick with the Bible scenario, but then, that would have eviscerated the story and shortened the book by nearly 4 percent.[4]

Hitchens writes as he debates, as if there is a team of judges keeping track of the total number of punches thrown and awarding points for each one landed. While this is entertaining and an effective means of rousing the already convicted rabble, it is entirely useless in attempting to present a coherent and convincing case to either the neutral or the dubious reader. Because of this pugnacious approach, he always seeks to come up with a rationale to avoid answering even the most direct questions instead of taking them on in a headfirst manner that will allow him to defend his assertions.

For example, when asked on another occasion about his theoretical reaction to a dozen black men appearing on a deserted subway platform late at night, Hitchens is delighted to relate that he once found himself in just such a situation when he happened to encounter a repair crew and "felt instantly safer." But his response is just an evasion, and the question is not, as Hitchens describes it, a "trick" one; it is merely a simple and somewhat silly question designed to determine whether the supposedly color-blind individual is, in practice, free of racial prejudice.[5]

This preference for intellectual evasion is harmless enough when it comes to unimportant matters such as one Englishman's embrace of

---

[3] Prager, Dennis. "10 Men Approaching in a Dark Alley." WorldNetDaily. 2 July 2007.

[4] When called on this substantive substitution, Hitchens simply asserted that he still would not feel safer in the knowledge that he was encountering a Bible study group and not, say, a set of the Gangster Disciples or Venice 13. Of course, this is merely his characteristic iconoclasm for iconoclasm's sake and should not be taken as evidence that he is a complete moron.

[5] Hitchens does seem to get asked a lot of stupid questions. I'm not sure if that reflects more poorly on his choice of interlocutors or his decisions regarding which of his past triumphs he wishes to share with the reader.

multiculturalism. It is much more significant, however, when Hitchens exhibits the same behavior when dealing with one of the central issues involved in the ongoing debate between Christians and the New Atheists, especially one that Hitchens discusses in some detail in *god is not Great*, namely, the inability of atheists to hold others accountable to a universally applicable moral standard.

The two senior members of the Unholy Trinity deal with this inherent problem in a perfectly reasonable manner, as they have embraced, however surreptitiously, secular humanism as a replacement religion in the place of Christianity.[6] While the humanist standard can be legitimately criticized as nothing more than warmed-over utilitarianism with a flower child's face, it must nevertheless be recognized as an alternative moral system by which one individual can judge another's behavior and hold him accountable.[7] But Hitchens, being more concerned with avoiding concessions than making any sense, repeatedly failed to grasp this point in his 2007 debate with theologian Douglas Wilson hosted by *Christianity Today*.[8]

From the very first of his six responses to Hitchens, Wilson is forced to repeatedly ask Hitchens for his atheist basis of respect for the individual, for the reason why an individual should care one way or another about what Hitchens, or anyone else, happens to believe is good or evil, and exactly what the fixed standard by which Hitchens declares Christianity to be not good happens to be. After initially ignoring the question, followed by evasive digressions into everything from etiquette to Epicurus, from Spinoza to innate human solidarity, from slavery to stem cell research, Hitchens finally breaks down under the unrelenting pressure and answers:

> Quo warranto *is a very ancient question, meaning "by what right?" You ask me for my "warrant" for a code of right conduct and persist in mistaking*

---

[6] I admit that only Dawkins has done so in an explicit manner, but the theoretical morality described by Harris is implicitly humanist given that it is based on precisely the same happiness-suffering metric as Russell's and Dawkins's secular humanism. And, as previously shown, he has the same ultimate goals in mind.

[7] Indeed, this is where the danger of humanism becomes evident, as humanism provides for both moral accountability and moral authority without ever providing an objective device to which the moral authority can be held answerable. Theoretically immutable holy texts, however nonsensical they might appear, actually tend to provide a means of limiting authoritarianism, not increasing it.

[8] "Is Christianity Good for the World?" *Christianity Today*. 8 May 2007.

my answer for an evasion. I in turn ask you by what right you assume that a celestial autocracy is a guarantee of morals, let alone by what right you choose your own (Christian) version of it as the only correct one. All deities have been hailed by their subjects as the fount of good behavior, just as they have been used as the excuse for inexcusable behavior. My answer is the same as it was all along: Our morality evolved.[9]

The reason Hitchens was so reluctant to provide this answer, which the reader can confirm that he most certainly did not provide at any previous point during the debate,[10] is explained by the logical hammer that Wilson drops on Hitchens as the debate comes to a close. Wilson's correct response is that a constantly evolving standard is, by definition, not a fixed one, and moreover, the less-evolved cannot be reasonably held to the same standard as the more highly evolved. We do not put cats on trial for murdering mice. These are not the only flaws in Hitchens's belated answer, for he has no explanation for the unknown mechanism for moral evolution in the apparent absence of a morality gene, nor does he explain the evidence that the pace at which morals "evolve" must be variable and speeding up dramatically of late if one is to accept some of the newly evolved "morals," such as the sin of being insufficiently enthusiastic about homosexual activity, as genuine.

Strangely, not long after being roundly thumped by a pastor from a small church in Idaho, this international public intellectual boasted that he has never been asked a question about religion and morality that surprised him. Like Sam Harris, Christopher Hitchens does not seem to understand that it is not the ability to foresee a question that counts, but the ability to respond to it with a convincing answer.

---

[9] I note that Hitchens doesn't seem to understand what a warrant, or universally applicable moral standard, is. The fact that the claimed issuing authority cannot be confirmed to either exist or be the proper authority does not call into question the undeniable *existence* of the Christian warrant. To summarize: Hitchens is questioning the legitimacy of Wilson's warrant, Wilson is looking at Hitchens's empty hands and asking where his warrant is.

[10] In the fifth exchange, Hitchens does quote Charles Darwin and spends two paragraphs discussing evolution in connection with morality, but he never does so in the context of a direct answer to Wilson's question.

AN EXERCISE IN SELF-EVISCERATION

It is a bit disappointing that for all his famously intransigent iconoclasm, Hitchens's attacks on religion are nearly identical to those made
by Dawkins and Harris, aside from a bizarre little chapter in inexplicable defense of *S. domestica* entitled "Why Heaven Hates Ham."[11]
There are the expected complaints about the Christian church's failure to embrace homosexuality or stem cell research, the supposed
threat to science, the defense of abortion,[12] the half-hearted attempt
to connect religion with war, the usual hand-wringing over sexual
moderation, and, of course, the desperate attempt to blame Joseph
Stalin's evil deeds on his youthful religious training.[13]

To his credit, however, Hitchens doesn't worry overmuch about
what he terms the "inculcation of compulsory 'creationist' stupid-
ity in the classroom" despite his general enthusiasm for evolutionary theory. Perhaps this is because, unlike Dawkins, Hitchens does
not sell DVDs marketed to schools and libraries from his Web site,[14]
or more likely because the highly literate Hitchens recognizes that it
does not matter if school children who cannot read or do arithmetic
are taught that they were created by natural selection, God, or space
aliens.[15]

There are some noteworthy aspects to *god is not Great*, however,
particularly on page 150, where Hitchens performs an epic feat of intellectual self-evisceration that is impressive even by the lofty standards of one who has survived the tedious slog through the morass
of Sam Harris's two exercises in self-parody. Incredibly, Hitchens declares that "what can be asserted without evidence can also be dismissed without evidence," thus granting the critic *carte blanche* to

---

[11] This porcine digression is apparently supposed to demonstrate how religion interferes with even
the most trivial aspects of life, but the point is more than a little muddled when Hitchens admits
that humanists aren't particularly enthusiastic about seeing pigs farmed for food, either.

[12] Surprisingly moderate, though.

[13] Of course, there's no mention of Mao, Mengistu, Sar, Hoxha, or any other atheist fellow traveler,
who, unlike Dawkins and Hitchens himself, never belonged to any Christian church.

[14] "*Richard Dawkins, author of the* New York Times *bestseller* The God Delusion, *and now the Galaxy
British Book Awards AUTHOR OF THE YEAR—brings you the first DVD from The Richard Dawkins
Foundation for Reason and Science:* Growing Up in the Universe. *Order the* Growing Up in the Universe *2-Disc DVD Set Now! All proceeds go to the Richard Dawkins Foundation for Reason and Science.*" From http://www.richarddawkins.net on 2 April 2007.

[15] I am an evolutionary skeptic myself, but I could not care less what is taught in the public schools.
It's like worrying about what cattle are being taught in the meat-packing factory.

legitimately dismiss the greater portion of Hitchens's own book.

One would assume that having staked out such a position, Hitchens would have been careful to supply substantial evidence in support of all his arguments. This is not the case. Here is a table of fifty-one assertions made by Hitchens, each made completely sans evidence, taken from every single one of the nineteen chapters of *god is not Great*. The astute reader will note that many of these auto-refutable statements are not only made without any support whatsoever, they can often be confirmed to be downright incorrect should the reader trouble himself to examine the relevant evidence.

Page #	Quote from god is not Great
5	(1) Our belief is not a belief. Our principles are not a faith....(2) What we respect is free inquiry, openmindedness, and the pursuit of ideas for their own sake....(3) We do not believe in heaven or hell, yet no statistic will ever find that without these blandishments and threats we commit more crimes of greed or violence than the faithful.[16]
8	(4) Past and present religious atrocities have occurred not because we are evil, but because it is a fact of nature that the human species is, biologically, only partly rational.
17	(5) [Religion] must seek to interfere with the lives of nonbelievers...it wants power in this [world]....(6) [I]t does not have the confidence in its own various preachings even to allow coexistence between different faiths.[17]
40	(7) Nothing optional is ever made punishable unless those who do the prohibiting have a repressed desire to participate.
41	(8) In the hands of eager Christian fanatics, even the toothsome jamón Ibérico could be pressed into service as a form of torture.[18]

---

[16] It seems Mr. Hitchens didn't look very hard. Or, in light of how easy it was to find several such statistics, at all.

[17] I note that religion is strikingly busy for an inanimate, abstract concept. Forget the absence of evidence, this is simply anthropomorphizing run amok.

[18] One wonders which of the three approved means of inquisitorial torture Hitchens has in mind: the *garrucha,* the *toca,* or the *potro.* Was the cured ham suspended as a counterweight on the *strappado*? No, it's merely rhetorical silliness.

46	(9) It is a certainty that millions of other harmless and decent people will die, very miserably, and quite needlessly, all over the world as a result of this obscurantism [AIDS denial]. (10) The attitude of religion to medicine, like the attitude of religion to science, is always necessarily problematic and very often necessarily hostile.[19]
48	(11) To accept the spread of cervical cancer in the name of god is no different, morally or intellectually, from sacrificing these women on a stone altar.[20]
63	(12) Faith of that sort—the sort that can stand up at least for a while in a confrontation with reason—is now plainly impossible.
64	(13) All attempts to reconcile faith with science and reason are consigned to failure and ridicule....
71	(14) If one must have faith in order to believe something, or believe in something, then the likelihood of that something having any truth or value is considerably diminished. The harder work of inquiry, proof and demonstration is infinitely more rewarding....[21] (15) [Religion] often doesn't rely on "faith" at all.
74	(16) Since human beings are naturally solipsistic, all forms of superstition enjoy what might be called a natural advantage.
86	(17) However, all these disputes [between evolutionists], when or if they are resolved, will be resolved by using the scientific and experimental methods that have proven themselves so far.
98	(18) The syncretic tendencies of monotheism, and the common ancestry of the tales, mean in effect that a rebuttal to one is a rebuttal to all.[22]
102	(19) The Bible may, indeed does, contain a warrant[23] for trafficking in humans, for ethnic cleansing, for slavery, for bride-price, and for indiscriminate massacre, but we are not bound by any of it because it was put together by crude, uncultured human mammals.

---

[19] This historical antipathy for medicine is no doubt the reason so many religious individuals and organizations founded hospitals.

[20] Despite discussing condoms in this very paragraph, Hitchens conspicuously fails to mention that condoms are useless at even slowing down the transmission of the HPV virus, that this miraculous vaccine only targets two of the nineteen strains of the virus that cause cancer, and that most sexual education programs fallaciously teach that condom use will stop HPV transmission. It is Hitchens and his advocacy of sexual license combined with a vaccine that the *New England Journal of Medicine* determined to be applicable to only 18 percent of infected women that is much more likely to cause women to die of cervical cancer than the religious advocates of abstinence.

[21] Hard work to which Hitchens is demonstrably not amenable.

[22] This is just stupid. Certain proof that Jesus Christ did not rise from the dead would encourage, not dishearten, a Jew. And there is no shortage of Christians who do not believe that Allah is the same god as Jehovah.

[23] Hitchens simply does not grasp what a warrant is. A specific order to kill Amalekites, for example, should not be confused with the right to commit ethnic cleansing at will. Christians are not bound by the Old Testament "warrants" he cites because we're not Mosaic-era Jews living in Canaan.

111	(20) The Passion of the Christ…is also an exercise in sadomasochistic homoeroticism starring a talentless lead actor who was apparently born in Iceland or Minnesota.[24]
115	(21) The contradictions and illiteracies of the New Testament have filled up many books by eminent scholars and have never been explained by any Christian authority except in the feeblest terms of "metaphor" and "a Christ of faith."
125	(22) All religions take care to silence or execute those who question them.
129	(23) There is some question as to whether Islam is a separate religion at all.
133	(24) The Christian world was so awful in this respect, and for so long, that many Jews preferred to live under Ottoman rule and submit to special taxes and other such distinctions.[25]
150	(25) Miracles are supposed to happen at the behest of a being who is omnipotent as well as omniscient and omnipresent. (26) The "Argument from Authority" is the weakest of all arguments.
151	(27) When I was a Marxist, I did not hold my opinions as a matter of faith.
158	(28) Is it not further true that all religions down the ages have shown a keen interest in the amassment of material goods in the real world?
160	(29) the whole racket of American evangelism was just that: a heartless con run by second-string characters from Chaucer's "Pardoner's Tale."
169	(30) And we shall not hear again, in any but the most vestigial and nostalgic way, of Pan or Osiris or any of the thousands of gods who once held people in utter thrall.
176	(31) In no real as opposed to nominal sense, then, was he [Dr. Martin Luther King, Jr.] a Christian.
180	(32) Even a glance at the whole record will show, first, that person for person, American freethinkers and agnostics and atheists come out the best.
181	(33) As far as I am aware, there is no country in the world today where slavery is still practiced where the justification of it is not derived from the Koran.[26]
195	(34) the numberless ways in which religious morality has actually managed to fall well below the human average.

[24] James Caviezel may be a handsome fellow, but he doesn't look the least bit Minnesotan or Icelandic. Josh Hartnett and Scarlett Johanssen, on the other hand, look like they should be walking hand-in-hand through Southdale. I grew up surrounded by Johnsons, Johnsens, Olsons, Olsens, Swensons, and Swensens, and believe me, I know what a Minnesotan looks like.

[25] No doubt this is why 40,000 of Spain's 80,000 Jews elected to convert to Christianity rather than accept exile across the Straits of Gibraltar. Jews were seldom permitted residence in medieval Christendom; as soon as they were permitted to re-enter a kingdom from which they had previously been expelled, they usually did.

[26] I'm sure those Eastern European atheists who buy and sell thousands of women every year would be very surprised to know that their acts are justified by the Koran, not *The Wealth of Nations* and *The Origin of Species*.

198	(35) the mind and the reasoning faculty—the only thing that divides us from our animal relatives.
205	(36) There are, indeed, several ways in which religion is not just amoral, but positively immoral.
208	(37) [Suttee] was put down by the British in India for imperial as much as for Christian reasons.
213	(38) Humans are not so constituted as to care for others as much as themselves: the thing simply cannot be done.
214	(39) Perhaps we would be better mammals if we were not "made" this way, but surely nothing could be sillier than having a "maker" who then forbade the very same instinct he instilled.[27]
217	(40) We can be sure that religion has always hoped to practice upon the unformed and undefended minds of the young, and has gone to great lengths to make sure of this privilege by making alliances with secular powers in the material world.
218	(41) The museums of medieval Europe, from Holland to Tuscany, are crammed with instruments and devices upon which holy men labored devoutly, in order to see how long they could keep someone alive while being roasted.[28]
220	(42) If religious instruction were not allowed until the child had attained the age of reason,[29] we would be living in a quite different world.
223	(43) As to immoral practice, it is hard to imagine anything more grotesque than the mutilation of infant genitalia.[30]
232	(44) the object of perfecting the species—which is the very root and source of the totalitarian impulse—is in essence a religious one.[31] (45) In the early history of mankind, the totalitarian principle was the regnant one.[32]
247	(46) There is nothing in modern secular argument that even hints at any ban on religious observance....
250	(47) Totalitarian systems, whatever outward form they may take, are fundamentalist and, as we would now say, "faith-based."
254	(48) [Atheists] have in all times and all places been subject to ruthless suppression.[33]

[27] And yet even Christopher Hitchens seems to be able to manage the supposedly impossible task of keeping his hand out of his pants when he's on national television.

[28] See Chapter XII on the Spanish Inquisition.

[29] Which is what?

[30] Hitchens objects to both male and female circumcision. Based on the increasing popularity of Brazilian waxes and labiaplasties, porn will likely have a greater influence on the future of male circumcision than religion anyhow.

[31] How strange, then, that it's atheists like Lenin, Russell, and Harris who always go in for that sort of thing. It's not the Pope and the Southern Baptists who are pushing for eugenics these days.

[32] Hardly, as the word wasn't even needed until the twentieth century.

[33] Drama queen much? Precisely what "ruthless suppression" has Hitchens ever suffered?

259	(49) Atomism was viciously persecuted throughout Christian Europe for many centuries, on the not unreasonable ground that it offered a far better explanation of the natural world than did religion.
278	(50) It is better and healthier for the mind to choose the path of skepticism and inquiry in any case
280	(51) Until relatively recently, those who adopted the clerical path had to pay a heavy price for it. Their societies would decay, their economies would contract, their best minds would go to waste or take themselves elsewhere, and they would consistently be outdone by societies that had learned to tame and sequester the religious impulse.[34]

Since we are reliably informed that assertions made without evidence can be refuted without the need to supply any refuting evidence, all fifty-one statements listed above are hereby dismissed with prejudice. *Qui nimium adseverat sine indicio nihil adseverat.*

HOLISTIC TOXICITY

Even the most skilled polemicist occasionally gets carried away on the winds of his own rhetoric. It happens—one minute Ann Coulter is the shining blonde star of National Review Online, and the next she is gone, blown off the pixel pages due to the fallout from her notorious post-9/11 column.[35] It is rare, though, that a writer manages to get so completely carried away on the cover of his own book.

The first reaction to the subtitle of *god is not Great: How Religion Poisons Everything* is one of mild surprise. Everything? Seriously? While one is rather unlikely to begin reading the book under a misapprehension that an atheist attack on God is going to be especially enthusiastic about religion in general, blaming it for poisoning literally everything should strike even the most avowedly militant atheist as perhaps being a bit of an exaggeration. And although one hardly

---

[34] That's why Christendom was so notoriously backward compared to non-clerical Africa.

[35] *"We know who the homicidal maniacs are. They are the ones cheering and dancing right now. We should invade their countries, kill their leaders and convert them to Christianity."* Although in fairness to Miss Coulter, whom I admire greatly, I note that invading their countries, killing their leaders, and handing government authority over to Shiite mullahs hasn't turned out quite as well as George W. Bush and Christopher Hitchens had hoped. And in fairness to NRO, Jonah Goldberg and Rich Lowry didn't kick Miss Coulter out, she reached the reasonable conclusion that they didn't have her back and elected to end the relationship.

expects Hitchens to provide an encyclopedic demonstration of religion's destructive venom, the truth is that once one finishes reading his book, one is forced to conclude The Sports Guy makes a much more convincing case in support of his mantra that it is, in fact, women who ruin everything.[36]

The problem is not that Hitchens doesn't make an effective argument that religion ruins everything, it's that he doesn't even try make the case that it ruins much of anything except possibly one's sex life.[37] Nearly everything about which he complains continues apace despite religion's baleful influence: stem cell researchers are still researching, circumcised penises are still functioning,[38] homosexuals are still homosexualizing, people are still masturbating; really, the only point he substantiates is the way he personally witnessed how religion interfered with the polio eradication programs in India in 2001. And even this turns out to have been a minor setback, as the World Health Organization declared in June 2007 that "in all four endemic countries, type 1 polio has been successfully cornered."[39] This is no credit to the religious lunatics who interfered and delayed this success, but it also shows that religion is not the lethal obstacle to manifestly decent and worthwhile human endeavors that Hitchens portrays it to be.

Hitchens does not mention any aspect of economics, any science except evolutionary biology and cosmology, he makes no references to sport, to technology, or to fashion. While he mentions literature, he does not claim that religion threatens it in any way even though he proposes it as a substitute for the holy texts from which it borrows

---

[36] "The lesson here, as always: Women ruin everything." Bill Simmons, ESPN.

[37] And even there his assertion flies in the face of the evidence that reports that married religious couples are the most sexually satisfied. Remember that for every well-satisfied single swinger, there are probably twenty losers making do with romance novels, chocolate, and pixels.

[38] And, incidentally, proving more resistant to AIDS and other venereal diseases than the untrimmed variety.

[39] "In all four endemic countries, type 1 polio has been successfully cornered, a major step toward a polio-free world, given type 1's historically higher disease burden and potential to spread internationally. This year: in western Uttar Pradesh, India, only one type 1 case has been reported (compared to 18 type 1 cases for the same period in 2006); in northern Nigeria, from the three highest-risk states of Jigawa, Kano and Katsina, only one type 1 case has been reported (compared to 256 type 1 cases for the same period in 2006); Pakistan marked its longest period of time ever without type 1 cases—14 weeks between 30 January and 14 May; and in Afghanistan, only three type 1 cases have been reported this year (compared to 10 type 1 cases for the same period in 2006)." Global Polio Eradication Initiative, Monthly Situation Report, June 2007, World Health Organization. 19 June 2007.

so liberally. The truth is that not even Christopher Hitchens believes religion poisons everything, or else he would not volunteer his opinion that he would not prohibit religion even if he thought he could. It is a pity that not all his fellow New Atheists are willing to follow his unexpectedly gracious example.

While the titular case for the holistic toxicity of religion is nowhere to be found in *god is not Great*, Hitchens does mention four irreducible objections to religious faith. If these four objections are truly the basis for Hitchens's hostility toward God and religion, then the irrepressible atheist may be much closer to returning to the faith of his fathers than anyone suspects, because one of these objections is trivial, one is irrelevant, and the other two are simply wrong.

1. *It wholly misrepresents the origins of man and the cosmos.*

Hitchens might as well reasonably reject science on the same petty basis, considering the wide range of abiogenetic hypotheses, cosmological creation myths, and astrophysical fiction currently on offer. Is he similarly opposed to DNA because Francis Crick subscribed to the Directed Panspermia hypothesis and an *X-Files* variant of Intelligent Design dependent upon space-traveling aliens?

2. *It combines the maximum of servility with the maximum of solipsism.*

This is alliteration, not a genuine objection. And it is incorrect. Orwell's "boot in the face forever" is arguably the best conceptual expression of the maximum of servility and it is a secular one, given religion's preference for eschatological scenarios over steady-state theories.

3. *It is the cause of dangerous sexual repression.*

There are loads of evidence that it is not sexual repression, but the absence of sexual repression that is dangerous. Abstinence never killed anyone, but AIDS certainly has. Male homosexuals are the least sexually repressed humans on the planet; they also happen to enjoy the shortest life expectancy.[40] While sexual repression might explain the horrific history of sexual abuse committed by Catholic clergymen, it does not explain the much greater incidence of sexual abuse by secular educators in the public school system.[41]

4. *It is ultimately grounded on wish-thinking.*

This is an irrelevant and tautological statement. "I object to something in which I don't believe because it is not true." All human action is ultimately grounded on wish-thinking, indeed, all technological advancement is. It is not a reasonable basis for an objection to religion; the statement might as easily be applied to the airline industry.

god is not Great reveals another fundamental limitation of the journalistic mindset in Hitchens's over-reliance on personal observation and perfunctory sourcing.[42] This professional habit leads him into error after error, as he is usually content to rely on a single source without ever considering readily available information to the contrary; in many cases, that single source is himself. Consider the similarities in the way he approaches three very different issues: historical biblical accuracy, child abuse, and charity.

In discussing the Bible, Hitchens claims that the four Gospels were not in any sense a historical record and states their multiple authors "cannot agree on anything of importance." His only source is Bart Ehrman, an apostate former evangelical whose *Misquoting Jesus* is an interesting and respected textual criticism of the inerrant inspiration of the New Testament. But Hitchens is apparently unaware that Ehrman has been forced to admit that the Gospels are in accor-

---

[40] While the studies by Hogg and Cameron that conclude male homosexuals live between eight to twenty years less than their heterosexual counterparts are angrily disputed by a homosexual population that is by all accounts inordinately disposed to snorting meth, committing suicide, and trading venereal diseases, I was unable to find any scientific studies contradicting their findings.

[41] *"The physical sexual abuse of students in schools is likely more than 100 times the abuse by priests."* Shakeshaft, C. Ph.D., U.S. Department of Education report. 2002.

[42] Hitchens's statement about the weakness of the Argument from Authority is particularly amusing considering his background as a journalist, since it is the sole basis for most news reporting. Journalist: "Is it true the DEA is breaking the law, Mr. DEA Press Agent?" DEA Press Agent: "No, that is not true." Newspaper the next morning: "Accusations of DEA wrongdoing are unfounded."

dance that 1) Jesus was crucified and buried, 2) his tomb was discovered to be empty, 3) his disciples believed they encountered him after his death, and 4) his disciples sincerely believed that Jesus had risen from the dead.[43] The reason Ehrman claims these are not reliable historical accounts is because there is divergence between details relating to what time of day Jesus died, whether he carried his cross alone or not, who went to the tomb, and whether the disciples went to Galilee and then returned to Jerusalem. But as the journalist Hitchens should be aware, even eyewitness accounts tend to vary greatly when it comes to the particulars. In any case, it is a substantial exaggeration to state that the Gospels do not agree on anything of importance.

This is especially true because by the standards normally used by historians to evaluate ancient texts, the fact that there are several texts written by multiple primary sources within decades of the historical event strengthens the historical case for the Bible. The textual case for the historical Jesus is orders of magnitude stronger than the one for the historical Alexander the Great,[44] and as archeologists have learned the hard way, it is unwise to assume the historical inaccuracy of the Bible based on missing evidence. While it's true, as Hitchens happily points out, that Israeli archeologists haven't located archeological evidence of the exodus from Egypt, this was also once true of the "mythical" Nineveh, discovered in 1850,[45] and the "nonexistent" Hittite Empire discovered in 1906.

Even worse, Hitchens revealed in a debate with Dr. Mark D. Roberts on "The Hugh Hewitt Show" that his reliance on Ehrman for New Testmant criticism was misplaced because he did not know that Ehrman has been an agnostic for more than twenty years. Roberts, a seminary professor, also explains that Hitchens made fifteen factual errors and sixteen substantial distortions or misunderstandings of the evidence in *god is not Great*.[46] He lists the fifteen factual errors as follows:

---

[43] Craig, William Lane and Bart D. Ehrman, "Is There Historical Evidence for the Resurrection of Jesus?" College of the Holy Cross, 28 March 2006.

[44] There are no primary sources for Alexander and the most trustworthy of the five secondary sources was written by Arrian approximately 470 years after Alexander's death.

[45] Prior to the discovery of King Sennacherib's palace in 1847, the "missing" city of Nineveh was cited as reason for doubting the Old Testament books of Jonah and Nahum.

[46] <http://www.markdroberts.com/htmfiles/resources/godisnotgreat.htm>.

1. Scholars estimate the date of Jesus's birth to be 6 B.C., not 4 A.D.
2. Bart D. Ehrman's name is not Barton.
3. The four Gospels are in accord regarding thirty-three key facts about Jesus, not zero.
4. Not all four Gospels are supposed to be based on Q, only Matthew and Luke.
5. Jesus was not the only one to mention Hell. Paul, Peter, Jude, and John did as well.
6. Jesus did not invent the concept of Hell. It is mentioned in earlier Jewish writings.
7. The Nag Hammâdi "Gospels" were codices, not scrolls, and they were not written in the same period as the canonical Gospels, but later.
8. No one was killed over the debate regarding which of the Gospels should be considered divinely inspired. Hitchens writes that "many a life was horribly lost."
9. H. L. Mencken was a journalist who had no capacity for judging whether the New Testament documents were tampered with or not. His assertion is by no means "irrefutable."
10. Tacitus does mention an Augustan Census in the *Annals*. Augustus himself mentions three, 28 B.C., 8 B.C., and 14 A.D., in his *Acts of Augustus*.[47]
11. Scholars do not consider the eyewitness claims to have witnessed the Crucifixion to be fraudulent, let alone patently so.
12. The Apostle Paul never expresses either fear of women or contempt for them.
13. It is not true that no Christian authority has ever addressed the perceived "contradictions and illiteracies of the New Testament" except in terms of "metaphor" and "a Christ of Faith."[48]
14. All scholars agree that the nature of the Gospels is at least partially literal.
15. Hitchens invents and exaggerates disagreements about the Gospels. The "disagreement" about Peter's denial is whether

---

[47] If Jesus was born in 6 B.C., the census announced in 8 B.C. would appear to be the likely culprit.
[48] Many have, including two published theologians with whom I am personally acquainted. Hitchens simply hasn't read them. I'd be happy to send him their books if he likes.

the cock crowed once or twice; it is not a matter for scholarly theological debate.

In addition to these demonstrable errors, Hitchens doesn't provide a single source or even anecdote for his absurd declaration that charity and relief work are "the inheritors of modernism and the Enlightenment," he merely draws upon his recollection of the relief workers he has personally encountered. Not only have Christians operated under the mandate of Jesus Christ to heal the sick and feed the hungry since the Crucifixion, but to this day, relief work around the world is dominated by Christians. The fact that the name "Red Cross" is synonymous with disaster relief is not exactly a coincidence.

And Hitchens abandons even personal experience when he declares that revulsion for various forms of child abuse is innate and does not need to be taught. Instead, he dramatically informs the reader that if he were to harm a child, he would commit suicide, indeed, he might even consider it if he were wrongly suspected of it. But this moral posturing notwithstanding, the literally millions of such crimes that have taken place during the twentieth century, to say nothing of the large market for child prostitutes that exists today in countries such as Cambodia, Vietnam, and Thailand, a significant percentage of whom were sexually abused prior to being forced into prostitution,[49] prove that not everyone is so morally evolved as to be gifted with the same innate revulsion. Hitchens then proceeds to announce that religion's failure to protect children from abuse is "uniquely delinquent," *and on that sole basis* claims justification to conclude that religion is manufactured, that ethics and morality are independent of faith, and that religion is not just amoral, but immoral.

His argument, if one can even call it that, isn't even wrong, it's not coherent enough to be described as incorrect. It is nothing less than a revelation of a deep-rooted irrationality that harks back to the teary-eyed emotionalism of Jean-Jacques Rousseau, not cold, dispassionate reason.

---

[49] "*In Vietnam 49% of girls in prostitution were victims of prior sexual abuse.*" "Asia's Child Sex Victims Ignored." BBC News, 15 Sept. 2000. Of course, prostituting children is itself a form of sexual abuse.

It is this emotional aspect that redeems Hitchens as a human being even as it precludes any possibility of taking *god is not Great* seriously as an attack on religion. The theist critic is left to conclude—and oh, the irony!—that one cannot dismantle an argument that does not exist. For where there is no logic, there can be no logical analysis. And if Hitchens reveals himself to be a snide, petty, self-righteous, and superficial character throughout the course of the book, he also comes off as an eminently likeable individual, even charming at times. Whereas one finishes *The God Delusion* and *The End of Faith* resenting the authors for forcing one to immerse one's mind in such a sneering slough of asininity, the third member of the Unholy Trinity rather makes one feel like buying him a drink and asking if the subject of total consciousness ever came up when he was playing golf with the Dalai Lama.[50]

In the first chapter of his book, Christopher Hitchens asks an important question.

> *Religious faith is, precisely because we are still-evolving creatures, ineradicable....For this reason I would not prohibit it even if I thought I could. Very generous of me, you may say. But will the religious grant me the same indulgence?*

I cannot speak for those who follow other religions, but for the Christian there is only one answer: by all means!

If God, whose power is infinitely greater than my own, does not see fit to force Christopher Hitchens to worship him, then how can I, or any other Christian, fail to do other than follow that divine example? Free will is at the heart of the Christian faith. To follow or not to follow is a choice, and I would not, indeed, I could not, rob Christopher Hitchens of his right to make that decision on his own.

---

[50] Big hitter, the Lama.

X

THE PRAGMATIC
PHILOSOPHER

When the gods are toppled, new ones will soon be invented.
—CAMILLE PAGLIA

THIS BOOK DID NOT PROCEED exactly according to plan. Originally inspired by a trilogy of columns entitled "The Clowns of Reason," it was supposed to be devoted to dissecting the anti-theistic arguments of Richard Dawkins, Daniel C. Dennett, and Sam Harris. However, when Christopher Hitchens appeared on the scene and began wreaking such a wide path of intellectual devastation by trouncing noted theologians such as the Rev. Al Sharpton and Chris Hedges, the author of *The Christian Right and the Rise of American Fascism*, it became clear that Hitchens was an atheist *tour de force* who must be addressed at all costs!

Also, when I finished reading *Breaking the Spell, Darwin's Dangerous Idea,* and *Freedom Evolves,* I was embarrassed to discover that

I had done Dr. Dennett somewhat of a disservice by lumping him in with those who can more legitimately be described as Reason's clowns. It may be a forgivable error, given Dennett's public anointing as a New Atheist of note by *Wired* magazine and the way in which he shares top billing with the Unholy Trinity at events such as the 2007 Atheist Alliance International Convention, but it was a mistake nevertheless. My apologies to the good professor, and I hope the excellent rating I gave *Darwin's Dangerous Idea* in a subsequent column[1] may have in some small way alleviated the deep anguish he surely suffered.

Breaking the Spell is substantially different than any of the four books on religion written by the Unholy Trinity. Despite being every bit as ignorant of the theological, historical, and demographical basics as Dawkins, Harris, and Hitchens, Dennett's book is far from a polemic, even if he can't quite resist giving in to the customary atheist chest-thumping.[2] I suppose one shouldn't condemn a man who believes he descended from apes[3] for behaving like one; at least the feces-flinging is kept to a minimum. For in *Breaking the Spell*, instead of assuming that God is a delusion, asserting that religion is bad, and announcing that science is finally on the verge of bringing an end to faith, Dennett merely argues for putting both our positive and our negative assumptions about religion aside in order to take a rational scientific look at precisely what religion offers Mankind.

This is an eminently reasonable perspective, especially in contrast with the wild-eyed scaremongering of the Unholy Trinity, although it is a little strange that it should take an academic philosopher to remind the ex-scientist and the would-be scientist that if one hopes to make a convincing scientific case, it helps to actually gather the evidence and examine it. Dennett's intellectual honesty, at least in comparison with his peers, is also refreshing. After being forced to endure Harris's sophomoric deceptions and Dawkins's incessant shell games, it is a sheer pleasure to consider the fair and sometimes

---

[1] It wasn't really a book review, but I did give *Darwin's Dangerous Idea* a rating of nine out of ten. The book is well worth reading regardless of your position on evolution.

[2] Yes, professor, in spite of my eschatonic beliefs, I was somehow able to reach deep inside and summon the "intellectual honesty and courage" required to read your book all the way through. Including the appendices and notes!

[3] I know, I know. Shared a common ancestor and all that. I claim the right of rhetorical license.

even insightful questions that Dennett poses relating to the potential costs and benefits of the God Hypothesis. Whereas the Unholy Trinity attempt to browbeat the unthinking reader into unquestioningly accepting their assertion that Man is on the verge of vanishing in nuclear fire unless billions of idiots can be forcibly stripped of their belief in nonexistent sky fairies, Dennett calmly asks the thoughtful reader to consider why religious faith exists in the first place, why it persists so stubbornly, and why so many individuals place such a high value upon it.

Dennett is also forthright about the arbitrary nature of his own beliefs. He admits to holding sacred values and declares that he would never consider abandoning them, although one wonders if he may not want to give some thought to demoting democracy from his list of the unquestionable in light of the results of various elections across the Middle East. His other values are justice, life, love, and truth, and although he puts them in no order of priority, it would have been most enlightening to know which of these values trumped the others, and why. It's also interesting to see that he left out liberty and equality as well as the humanist happiness/suffering quotient; one suspects that being a competent philosopher, Dennett is aware of the ultimate moral bankruptcy of utilitarianism. Unlike many intellectuals, Dennett is quite willing to admit when he doesn't know something or has no opinion on it—in one long interview with an obnoxious interviewer far more interested in talking about his own ideas than asking questions about Dennett's,[4] the philosopher responds with no less than ten variants on a neo-Socratic theme, repeatedly stating "I have no idea," "I haven't a clue," and "I have nothing to say about this."

And while Dennett's declaration of unabashed atheism leaves no doubt about his personal opinion regarding the existence of the supernatural, which he equates with the Easter Bunny and the Tooth Fairy, he is at least open to the possibility that there are numerous aspects of religion that neither he nor anyone else truly understands.

---

[4] "The M&C Interview 2: Daniel Dennett," Monsters and Critics. 1 July 2007. And to Dennett's additional credit, he declines to take the opportunity to agree with the interviewer's ridiculous assertion that it is "wholly inaccurate" to equate Communism with atheism because Communism "was really a secular religion." Apparently it was just an amazing coincidence that every Communist of historical note publicly declared his atheism. See chapter XIII.

It is this recognition of the near-complete scientific ignorance on the matter that inspires Dennett to propose that scientists make a serious effort at investigating religion instead of merely insulting it. His confidence that the evidence collected will eventually support his hypothesis appears to ebb and flow throughout the book, but it is to his credit that he never asks his reader to accept it at face value or on the strength of his rhetoric.

In looking at the matter from an evolutionary perspective, Dennett suggests several possibilities to explain how religion might be of benefit to someone, somewhere. *Cui bono?* he asks. His first suggestion is to consider the way it can bring out the best in individuals. Religion may not be the only phenomenon to do so, but Dennett does not question that it does. While he suggests that it could be possible to design a synthetic replacement that would do so even more efficiently, the suggestion is weakened by his incorrect insistence that atheists are more law-abiding, more sensitive to the needs of others, and more ethical than others. While this may be true if one cherry-picks the data and looks only at the High Church atheist, there is a plethora of evidence that a comparison of all atheists to all Christians will not favor the former, whether one looks at crime rates, divorce rates, birth rates, democratic participation, or charitable giving.[5]

His second suggestion is that religion could be a memetic symbiont or parasite, which benefits itself at the expense of humanity. This is an intriguing concept, but largely a pointless one since there is absolutely no evidence that memes even exist and the idea smacks of confusing metaphor with reality. Consider the protests from his fellow atheists if Dennett had instead tried to argue that religion exists in order to benefit God. It's certainly an unusual argument for a materialist to make, given the obvious difficulties presented in trying to weigh religion or measure the wavelength of a meme.

His third suggestion is that if religion benefits any human group, the important question would be to determine whom. He suggests three possibilities: all the individuals in society, the members of the controlling elite, or societies as a whole, and while he doesn't answer the question himself, he expresses a certain skepticism of the last one due to his doubts about evolutionary group selection. The

---

[5] See chapters IV and XIII for evidence in support of this statement.

evidence, however, suggests that his first and third options are the strongest here. The idea that religion exists to benefit the elite is weakened by the fact that the ranking members of one of the eldest and most powerful religious elites, the Catholic Church, are neither allowed to have genetic heirs or enjoy many material benefits from their elite status, whereas the competing concept of societal benefit is supported by the evidence that irreligious individuals and societies do not show much enthusiasm for propagation.[6]

Finally, he raises a fourth possibility that religion is merely a by-product of evolution, otherwise known as a spandrel. It's here that the philosopher finds himself in logical trouble. Both of Dennett's memetic proposals and his subsequent argument against Starke and Finke's economic case for the rational value of religion directly contradict his assertion of the way that evolution's remarkable efficiency means that a persistent pattern amounts to proof—"we can be quite sure"—that the pattern is of benefit to something in the evolutionary currency of differential reproduction.[7] How, one wonders, does Dennett fail to grasp that a creed that explicitly states "go forth and multiply" is likely to be inordinately successful in evolutionary terms, be they genetic or memetic?

And yet, the philosopher shows himself to be repeatedly susceptible to missing similarly obvious things, usually due to a failure to draw a correct logical conclusion from the evidence on hand. Consider, for example, the way Dennett attempted to explain the ant analogy with which he begins *Breaking the Spell* to an interviewer for Salon:[8]

Tell us the story from your new book about the ant and the blade of grass.

Suppose you go out in the meadow and you see this ant climbing up a blade of grass and if it falls it climbs again. It's devoting a tremendous amount of

---

[6] Dennett presumably considers this, since he mentions cultural as well as genetic heirs, but seriously, no one goes into the priesthood to have a good time. There's a reason it's considered a renunciation. And even the life of a Protestant minister leaves much to be desired, as anyone who has ever survived a Sunday basement buffet in the Midwest well knows. Life is too short to eat microwaved casseroles topped with Corn Flakes.

[7] Dennett, *Breaking the Spell*, 62.

[8] Slack, Gordy. "Dissecting God." Salon. 8 Feb. 2006.

energy and persistence to climbing up this blade of grass. What's in it for
the ant? Nothing. It's not looking for a mate or showing off or looking for
food. Its brain has been invaded by a tiny parasitic worm, a lancet fluke,
which has to get into the belly of a sheep or a cow in order to continue its
life cycle. It has commandeered the brain of this ant and it's driving it up
the blade of grass like an all-terrain vehicle. That's how this tiny lancet
fluke does its evolutionary work.

Is religion, then, like a lancet fluke?

The question is, does anything like that happen to us? The answer is,
well, yes. Not with actual brain worms but with ideas. An idea takes over
our brain and gets that person to devote his life to the furtherance of that
idea, even at the cost of their own genetics. People forgo having kids, risk
their lives, devote their whole lives to the furtherance of an idea, rather
than doing what every other species on the planet does—make more chil-
dren and grandchildren.

It somehow escapes the professor's attention that it is not the religious portion of the population that is having trouble doing what every other species on the planet does, but rather, the irreligious one.[9] If
there is a metaphorical lancet fluke to be blamed for anti-evolutionary
human behavior, then it is atheist secularism that most accurately fits
the analogy now that the Shakers and Skoptsi are no more. Indeed, the
demographic performance of secular post-Christian societies over the
last fifty years suggests that from a grand historical perspective, modern atheist secularism will be seen as a fluke indeed.

Dennett also digs another logical hole for himself when he admits that only a tiny fraction of humanity understands what he describes as "the ultimate talismanic formula of science," Einstein's
$E=mc^2$ equation. He has no problem with the fact that most people
are content to accept this scientific dogma on faith and leave the
burden of understanding the details to the priesthood of scientific
experts, then, seventy-seven pages later, turns around and declares
that it is personally immoral for the religious faithful to practice this
very same division of doxastic labor by placing trust in their pastors,

---

[9] *"Conservative, religiously minded Americans are putting far more of their genes into the future than*
their liberal, secular counterparts." Longman, Phillip. "Political Victory: From Here to Maternity."
The Washington Post, 2 Sept. 2004.

priests, rabbis, and imams to make their moral decisions for them. Dennett attempts to justify these contrary stances by stating that the difference is that the scientific priesthood really know what they're doing, that they understand their formulas and use them to achieve amazingly accurate results, while the religious priesthood do not.

But Dennett is demonstrably incorrect on both scores. Dennett's two favorite sciences, cognitive science and evolutionary biology, are primarily distinguished by the way in which no one understands exactly how anything works nor has managed to construct any significant formulas, let alone achieve any results demonstrating the precision of the quantum electrodynamic calculations cited in Dennett's example. Dennett himself confesses that human consciousness is a mystery, a phenomenon that people don't even know how to think about yet,[10] and while he is rather more sanguine about the achievements of evolutionary biology, he admits that the science which began with the *Origin of Species* still regards the way in which species begin to be a mystery, too, albeit one with more of the details filled in.[11]

So while some sciences have proven themselves worthy enough of our complete confidence that we need not trouble our pretty little heads about them, to claim that we are justified in placing blind trust in cognitive scientists, evolutionary biologists, and sociologists because physicists really know what they're doing is absurd. It's a bait-and-switch worthy of Dawkins. And Dennett offers absolutely no evidence that any religious faithful are any more prone to unquestioning obedience of their priesthood than science fetishists are of the various secular bulls issued regularly from the archbishoprics of Oxford, Cambridge, M.I.T., and Stanford.

Conversely, the very existence of the Protestant church and the ubiquitous suburban Bible studies held across America on weekday evenings prove that the majority of Christians do not subscribe to any doxastic division of labor regarding either their fundamental beliefs or their individual moral decisions. And how could they, considering their belief that their every act will one day be judged before the throne of the Almighty? One could even argue that the belief of the average

---

[10] Dennett, Daniel C. *Consciousness Explained.* London: Penguin Books Ltd., 1993. 21.
[11] Dennett, Daniel C. *Darwin's Dangerous Idea.* London: Simon & Schuster, 1996. 44.

secular non-scientist in science's latest mystical pronouncements is far more blind than that of the average churchgoer, who usually knows his pastor well enough to know when even the most firmly held pastoral opinion is best disregarded. I very much like and admire Greg Boyd, who was my pastor when I attended Woodland Hills Church in St. Paul a decade ago, and I tend to agree with him on a number of theologically controversial matters such as Open Theism and warfare theodicy. This did not stop me from rolling my eyes when Greg decided that it was necessary to publicly apologize to the blacks of the congregation for eighteenth-century slavery and beg them for forgiveness; my amusement devolved into inappropriate laughter when my wife chose that deeply emotional moment to whisper an apology for the sins her Viking ancestors committed against my English forebears.

The reality is that no one ever stops and reasons for himself from first principles on every issue, be it scientific, religious, or moral. Dennett points this out himself in *Darwin's Dangerous Idea* as the reason behind humanity's need for a moral first-aid manual, because it will not do for people to waste time philosophizing instead of acting in response to every new moral dilemma that presents itself.[12]

The occasional logical errors and assertions in the face of evidence such as these show that while *Breaking the Spell* is unquestionably superior in almost every way to the Unholy Trinity's four books on religion, the scientific-sounding speculation that fills it is nothing more than that, speculation. The literary editor of *The New Republic* underlined this point in an utterly brutal review of the book that appeared in the *New York Times*, reminding the reader that at the end of the day, *Breaking the Spell* is not science, but a book of speculative philosophy written by a science fetishist.

There is no scientific foundation for its scientistic narrative. Even Dennett admits as much: "*I am not at all claiming that this is what science has established about religion.... We don't yet know.*" So all of Dennett's splashy allegiance to evidence and experiment and "*generating further testable hypotheses*" notwithstanding, what he has written is just an extravagant speculation based upon his hope for what is the case, a pious account of his own atheistic longing.[13]

---

12 Ibid., 504.
13 Wieseltier, Leon. "The God Genome." *The New York Times*. 19 Feb. 2006.

LIFTING THE CURTAIN

"I'll have you hung, drawn and quartered! And whipped! And boiled... until... until... until you've had enough.... And then I'll do it again!" yelled Arthur. "And when I've finished I will take all the little bits, and I will jump on them!"

—Douglas Adams, *The Hitchhiker's Guide to the Galaxy*

Leon Wieseltier's review is too hard on Dennett in my opinion; one shudders to think what he might have done to *The God Delusion*, let alone *The End of Faith*, but it's hard to argue with his conclusions when Dennett himself can't offer a better defense than to suggest that his matter-of-fact, non-disrespectful approach to religion has somehow frightened Wieseltier.[14] But this is a response better suited to a rejected forty-something blaming her single status on being too strong and independent for prospective suitors than to a philosopher and serious intellectual disputant. Wieseltier sums up his review by stating that the most conclusive thing proved by Dennett is that there are many spells that need to be broken, and *Breaking the Spell* indeed inspires one to conclude that everything from material reductionism to moral relativism to science itself would probably benefit from a good dose of the scientific analysis that Dennett recommends for religion.

If Dennett's weak logic merely provided some ironic amusement with regards to his parable of the parasitic ant, it threatens to become problematic when he attempts to solve the dilemma of moral origins by positing an evolved free will that gives humanity the opportunity to usurp the Blind Watchmaker of natural selection and begin to guide its own evolution. For when asked where society will find its moral foundation, if not from religion, Dennett responds with a tautology:

---

[14] "*(Somebody asked me if perhaps I'd stolen his wife or raped his daughter, but no, his loathing for me and my book is, I gather, entirely generated by the book itself.) I can only guess why he was rattled. Some people are deathly afraid that if religion falls into disrespect, the world of morality and goodness will collapse—the moral heat death of the universe! To somebody of that conviction, my matter-of-fact attitude toward religion (not DISrespectful, but not displaying the standard hyper-respect religion tries to command in our society) is scary indeed.*" The M&C Interview.

Rules that we lay down ourselves....Now we can continue to expand the circle and get more people involved, and do it in a less disingenuous way by excising the myth about how this is God's law. It is our law.

As evidence that moral democracy is theoretically functional, he asserts without evidence that the prison population is distributed according to religious affiliation in the general population, an incorrect assertion that was belied in chapter I. Dennett further claims that "brights" have better family values than born-again Christians based on "the lowest divorce rate in the United States" which depends on the flawed 1999 Barna study[15] instead of the 2001 ARIS study he makes use of later in the book, a much larger study that reaches precisely the opposite conclusion. It is certainly a quixotic assertion, considering that these family value atheists are half as likely to get married, twice as likely to divorce, and have fewer children than any other group in the United States.

Another obvious flaw is that moral democracy suffers from the same structural weakness as its political counterpart, an inherent mandate to appeal to the lowest common denominator. This should be clear to anyone who has entered a voting booth and looked upon his choices with despair. Is the opportunity to select between the moral equivalents of George W. Bush and Al Gore really to be considered a step forward for Mankind? And yet, not even the electoral horrors of 2000 come close to representing the historical dregs of democracy—it's worth remembering that the National Socialists not only won more seats in the Reichstag than the eight political parties with whom they competed in the three parliamentary elections between July 1932 and March 1933, but also won more than 95 percent of the vote in the four plebiscites held to confirm popular approval of the withdrawal from the Geneva disarmament conference, Hitler's assumption of dictatorial rule, the seizure of the Rhineland, and the annexation of Austria.[16]

---

[15] Barna calculated divorces as a percentage of the entire group, not as a percentage of marriages within that group. Since according to ARIS 2001 more than half of all atheists and agnostics don't get married, this is an apple-orange comparison. If one correctly excludes the never-married from the calculation, then atheists are 58.7 percent more likely to get divorced than Pentecostals and Baptists, the two born-again Christian groups with the highest rate of divorce, and more than twice as likely to get divorced than Christians in general.

[16] What's staggering about Hitler's democratic appeal is not that he managed to win an average of 95.9 percent of the vote in the four plebiscites, but that he did so with 95.5 percent of the registered

When one considers that Hamas won a 56 percent majority of the Palestinian parliament with 75 percent voter turnout in 2006, one is forced to conclude that an atheist would not only have to be irrational, but entirely insane to even consider embracing the concept of moral democracy.

Of course, it's also possible that despite his elevation of democracy to sacred status, Dennett isn't actually envisioning democratic morality per se when he refers to getting more people involved, but was merely thinking of an expanded circle of elders who would take responsibility in laying out this new self-determined morality for the rest of Mankind. It's not exactly unheard of for philosophers to reach the conclusion that rule by philosopher-kings is the ideal form of human governance, after all.

Dennett doesn't ignore the possibility that looking too closely at religion could blow up in the examiner's face; he even has a section entitled "Wouldn't neglect be more benign?" But he is ultimately convincing when he points out that simply ignoring the issue and hoping it will go away really isn't much of an option, since whatever evidence that is turned up by the curious is bound to eventually find its way in front of anyone who is interested. His case is bolstered by the recent admission of a senior Chinese Communist Party member that not even a ruthless totalitarian government is capable of controlling the news any longer.[17]

The biggest problem is that even if Dennett is correct and there is no magician behind the moral curtain, the positive consequences of revealing this absence may well outweigh the negative ones. Needless to say, philosophers from Socrates to Voltaire and Nietzsche have strongly disagreed with Dennett's optimistic view despite their similar skepticism about the truth of God's existence, and what historical and scientific evidence exists tends to support their pessimism. Given that Dennett is not dogmatically opposed to the idea that some knowledge is simply too dangerous to be freely shared with all humanity, it is surprising that he is so willing to roll the dice with civilization in this regard.

In considering the operation of a functional moral system, Dennett

---

voters showing up to vote. That's a serious democratic mandate!

[17] McCartney, James. "Web Censorship Is Failing, Says Chinese Official." *The Times*, 16 July 2007.

simply ignores the practical need for an objective basis and claim to universal authority, Wilson's "warrant," if you will. Theists have a perfectly logical and objective basis for the application of their god-based moralities that even the most die-hard rational atheist cannot reject, given the theistic postulate that God actually exists and created the universe. In short, God's game, God's rules. If you're in the game, then the rules apply to you regardless of what you think of the game designer, your opinion about certain aspects of the rule book, or the state of your relationship with the zebras.

Atheists, on the other hand, enjoy no similar logical basis, no objective foundation or universal warrant, which leaves every individual playing his own game and making up his own rules as he goes along. So Dennett finds himself caught in the seemingly senseless act of lauding atheists for behaving in a moral manner according to a morality that he considers groundless and in need of democratic modification.

This is somewhat less senseless than it initially appears, because the primary alternative is to pursue the Harris strategy and claim that atheists are behaving according to a morality that someone could invent if he were to sit down and think hard about it, although no one ever seems to actually have done so. This alternative leaves the atheist to decry actions performed by Muslims and Christians inspired by the dictates of imaginary beings on the basis of a hypothetical morality. Of course the imaginary aspect of his morality does not stop the Harrisian atheist from asserting ontological proof of its existence, to say nothing of its obvious superiority to Christian morality because he hasn't personally engaged in any Crusades or Spanish Inquisitions. And yet, not only do we know these reason-based moralities don't exist, we are informed by an unimpeachable source that it is "quite obvious" that they do not exist and have never existed:

> "I do not intend this to be a shocking indictment, just a reminder of something quite obvious: no remotely compelling system of ethics has ever been made computationally tractable, even indirectly, for real world moral problems. So, even though there has been no dearth of utilitarian (and Kantian, and contrarian, etc.) arguments in favor of particular policies,

institutions, practices, and acts, these have all been heavily hedged with ceteris paribus clauses and plausibility claims about their idealizing assumptions."[18]

That's Professor Daniel C. Dennett in *Darwin's Dangerous Idea*. In that passage, Dennett sounds much more like the great anti-socialist von Hayek demonstrating the impossibility of socialist calculation than a committed socialist desperate to prove socialism is capable of rationally determining necessary price information. But reason can no more deliver functional moral systems than socialism can provide functional pricing models.

One must give Dennett his due for his honesty in admitting that the "universal acid" of Darwin's dangerous idea tears a huge and gaping hole in the universal moral fabric, and he deserves credit for manfully attempting to lay the groundwork for a means of addressing that hole in the seventeenth chapter of *Darwin's Dangerous Idea*. And if in the course of *Breaking the Spell* he happens to fall into the very trap he previously had described so eloquently, well, it has happened to many an intellectual before.

SCIENCE, SATAN, AND THE NEO-NEWTONIAN SYNTHESIS

I'm on Aslan's side even if there isn't any Aslan to lead it. I'm going to live as like a Narnian as I can even if there isn't any Narnia.

—C. S. Lewis, *The Silver Chair*

The most interesting thing about *Breaking the Spell* is not the way it differs from the other three atheists' cases against religion, but the way it specifically refutes them. After Harris does his excellent Chicken Little imitation by clucking about how religion is going to end life on the planet at any moment, Hitchens metaphorically calls the poison control center on it, and Dawkins slanderously asserts that it is worse than child molestation, it comes as a bit of a shock to read Dennett's calm declaration that the secular proposition that religion does more harm than good, to an individual or to society, "has

---

[18] Dennett, *Darwin's Dangerous Idea*, 500.

hardly begun to be properly tested," let alone conclusively proved.[19]

In fact, when asked by the Salon interviewer if he would recommend that a believer abandon his faith in favor of presumably more rational truths about the universe, Dennett's reply was that he does not pretend to have the answer yet. It is this lack of pretense and, yes, intellectual courage that makes it necessary for the honest truth-seeker of any faith to respect him, regardless of his occasional short-comings, and his restraint makes the Unholy Trinity's histrionics look all the more contemptible in comparison. Dennett's position, that religion interacts with many of the world's major problems, is a much more reasonable and defensible point than the idea that religion causes all of them. And the distinction is vital, because interaction indicates that while in some cases religion may be a causal factor, in others religion could prove to be part of the solution.

Given Dennett's flexible approach, the title of his latest book is unfortunate, because *Breaking the Spell* tends to lead one to believe that Dennett is attempting to break the spell that religion has cast over Mankind by eliminating religion entirely. But Dennett specifically denies this[20] and shows some genuine sympathy for various religious traditions that he himself values; the appendix of *Darwin's Dangerous Idea* consists solely of a Sunday School song that closes with the words "because God made you, that's why I love you."[21] And he demonstrates genuine compassion for the defensive feelings of the religious faithful when he imagines his own reaction to a hypothetical scientific assault on the social costs of music. On the other hand, the distinction Dennett makes between good spells and bad spells such as Jonestown, jihad, and abortion clinic bombings, and his reference to the desirability of breaking the latter, indicates that the title may actually have multiple layers of significance.

Whatever its true meaning, *Breaking the Spell* is obviously the expansion of the final two chapters of *Darwin's Dangerous Idea,* which are entitled "Redesigning Morality" and "The Future of an Idea." But in some ways, it also represents somewhat of a retreat from the more

---

[19] Dennett, *Breaking the Spell*, 311.

[20] "*I'm proposing we break the spell that creates an invisible moat around religion, the one that says, 'Science stay away. Don't try to study religion.'*" Daniel Dennett. "Dissecting God."

[21] Richard Dawkins must not have read the appendix or else he surely would have called Child Protective Services on his old friend.

militant message with which the previous book was concluded eleven years before. Whereas the younger Dennett pugnaciously threatens the keepers of the wild, untamed religious memes with combat, caging, disabling, and intellectual disarmament, the older and presumably wiser Dennett refrains from such language of conflict. Instead, he advises open inquiry and education.

It would be interesting to know what has inspired this apparent mellowing on the part of the philosopher. Was it his recognition of the difficulty in designing a morality capable of functioning as well as those laid out centuries, even millennia ago? Has the resurgence of Islamic fundamentalism and Christian evangelism caused him to recognize that utopian Enlightenment is not inevitable and looks increasingly less likely with every passing year? Or is it merely a pragmatic realization that it is the height of foolishness for a small and unpopular minority to declare intellectual war on the rest of the human race?

Whatever his reasons, Dennett's call for an open spirit of inquiry into religion is worthwhile and should be welcomed by Christians and other religious individuals. I like the idea of a rapprochement and find the idea of a neo-Newtonian synthesis as the basis for mutual exploration of the unknown to be tremendously appealing. However, Dennett's admirable call for science and religion to lay down their arms and proceed in a spirit of amiable curiosity is subject to one final logical flaw, from at least one religious perspective. Many religious worldviews postulate the existence of intelligent, supernatural beings whose actions affect the physical world, but the Christian view, in particular, puts forth the disturbing notion that our present world is not ruled by God, but by an evil supernatural being, one who long ago usurped humanity's God-given sovereignty. This being, Satan, is not only self-aware, but has been intelligent enough to fool the mind of Man from the very start, beginning with the first temptation in the Garden of Eden.

There can be no doubt that Satan, if he exists, is a powerful being. When Satan showed Jesus all the kingdoms of the world and offered them to him, Jesus did not question that this was a meaningful offer, nor did he dispute that the world was Satan's to give. If it was not, then it wouldn't have been much of a temptation. Jesus also indicated that

Satan was skilled in the arts of deception and specifically referred to Satan as the Deceiver on several occasions. And significantly, the Apostle Paul mentions how the "god of this age" has exerted himself to blind the minds of unbelievers.

So put yourself in the hypothetical position of this evil being ruling over all the Earth. Is it in your interest to reveal yourself to humanity? Or is it better to lie in wait, hidden in the shadows, as the mortal world convinces itself that neither you nor your plane of existence is real? Given the disastrous results of this past century in parts of the world that intentionally turned away from the Christian God and His truth in favor of Man and his scientific proofs, the evidence would seem to suggest that unbelief in the supernatural serves the interests of this evil being.

If, for the sake of argument, we postulate that this is the case, the next question naturally follows: Does this Deceiver possess the power to hide the spiritual world from us? The logical answer, given his apparent power over the physical world, would appear to be yes, which Dennett would no doubt consider to be a sophisticated version of the diabolical lie used to shut down skepticism and prevent the weak believer from encountering the fatal doubts that might kill his faith. In fact, it's nothing of the kind, although I cannot blame the atheist who is inclined to scoff at this objection based on its absurdity from a purely materialistic standpoint. Still, the spirit of open inquiry demands consideration of these ideas, and when viewed from a purely logical point of view, the obstacle presented is a formidable one.

Fortunately, the Bible offers a way out of this apparent dilemma. It teaches that although the Deceiver rules over the Earth as the god of this age, he does not have the authority to prevent God from manifesting power on Earth through the person of Jesus Christ. It is here, then, to Jesus and those who worship him as Lord and Savior, that science will have to turn if it is to truly put Christianity to the scientific test and glimpse behind the veil of the supernatural. Following this logic, it becomes clear that scientists will find nothing if they continue to seek for evidence of the supernatural by examining occult phenomena such as ESP, telepathy, fortune-telling, and witchcraft. Satan is the lord and master of such things, and he does not deign to be unmasked, at least, not yet.

And we can also be sure that no amount of scientific evidence will ever convince those who are determined not to believe. There will always be socialists no matter how many times socialism is proven to be bankrupt, there will always be atheists, and as the Marsh-wiggle says, there will always be Narnians, too. Science, for all of its magnificent accomplishments, is merely the epitome of Man's knowledge, and by itself it is incapable of seeing through the Deceiver or understanding the will of God. Even so, I propose that the religious faithful accept Daniel Dennett's reasonable proposal, for Christians have nothing to fear from the truth. The biblical injunction was not to put the Lord your God to foolish tests, not to shy away from trying to understand the world that He created, and Jesus Christ himself instructed us to ask and seek, with the promise that we would find the answer. Surely the God who created Man and blessed him with intelligence expects him to make use of it!

But let there be just one caveat. Let us reach a mutual agreement to examine the available evidence and use the scientific method to study religion and all three aspects of science as well, so that we might best learn what is truly of lasting benefit to all humanity.

XI

THE ROBESPIERRE OF ATHEISM

Io non rifiuto la spiritualità in generale, rifiuto la spiritualità cristiana e invito a una spiritualità laica. Se si sopprime la teologia, rimane la filosofia.[1]

—MICHEL ONFRAY

ICHEL ONFRAY is almost completely unknown in the English-speaking world, but in France and Italy, he is more famous than Richard Dawkins and the rest of the New Atheists combined. He is a prodigious wordsmith of Rabelaisian proportions, having published thirty-one books that cover everything from the dietary habits of the famous philosophers to a multi-volume explication of his philosophy of hedonism. Describing himself as a Left Nietzschean, he is a professor of philosophy and the founder of the People's University, an institution where he and a few like-minded left-wing intellectuals teach philosophy to ghetto scholars.

---

[1] *"I do not reject spirituality in general, I reject Christian spirituality and propose a profane spirituality. If theology is abolished, philosophy still remains."* Belloni, Daniele. "Onfray: il Robespierre dell'ateismo," *Il Giornale.* 20 Sept. 1995.

Needless to say, he is the epitome of the philosophical sport that exists only in France. As a public intellectual, Onfray bears some small resemblance to Umberto Eco, if the *maestro* smoked crack, forgot everything he knew about history, and used smaller words while writing enthusiastically about the primacy of desire and the connection between knowledge and human genitalia.

Like so many French philosophers of the recent past, Onfray's primary use for Occam's Razor is to repeatedly slash his own throat. He describes himself as a believer in libertarian options[2] and yet publicly endorses the Revolutionary Communist League, a minor French party that subscribes to the ideology of Leon Trotsky. In 2006 he was hailed as an honorary priest by Raël, the leader of the atheist International Raëlian Movement, which occasioned somewhat of a scandal in the French press even though Onfray publicly disavowed the honor.[3]

None of this has prevented his *Traité d'athéologie* from selling more than 300,000 copies. *"Treatise on Atheology"* is the first of his books to be translated into English, although it has been somewhat misleadingly published as *In Defence of Atheism* in England and *Atheist Manifesto* in the United States. But it is neither a defense of atheism nor is it a coherent manifesto of any kind; it is nothing more than a wild-eyed rant that manages to combine the worst of Sam Harris with the worst of Christopher Hitchens, all flavored with a heavy dash of pompous Gallic gall. Despite the occasional flash of insight, his concept has met with a skeptical audience—the Italian writer Beppe Sebaste dismissed atheology as *"un'idea non so se più sciocca o più ignorante."*[4]

From the very first page, Onfray demonstrates a superlative atheist talent for assholery, relating the tale of how he pestered the poor Muslim hired to drive him around the Mauritanian desert for days, picking arguments about the Koran and pointing out how verses from it could be used to justify Hezbollah, the Ayatollah Khomeini,

---

[2] Sarkozy, Nicolas and Michel Onfray. "The Big Questions": *New Statesman*, 4 June 2007. Of course, what "liberty" means in France and what it means in America are two entirely different things, as the world learned between 1776 and 1793.

[3] This elite priesthood includes the French novelist Michel Houellebecq, American atheist Dr. Michael Newdow, Madonna, and Rosie O'Donnell.

[4] *"I don't know if the idea is more silly or ignorant."*

9/11, and al Qaeda's beheadings. He writes: "Abduramane did not like it...we lapsed into silence." One hopes that Onfray did not conclude what must have been an interminable journey for the wretched driver by refusing to pay him in the noble interest of freeing him from the delusion of monetary value.

However, it must be admitted that in his book, Onfray performs the invaluable task of demonstrating that atheism possesses the inherent potential to be every bit as unrepentantly evil by traditional Western moral standards as Christians have always believed it to be. Not for Onfray the temporizing humanism of Dawkins and company; he spits on their spineless embrace of the greater part of Judeo-Christian morality every bit as contemptuously as Sam Harris denigrates religious moderates for providing aid, comfort, and intellectual cover to religious extremists. Like the modern jihadists who strip away the moderate fiction of a religion of peace, Onfray does not hesitate to reveal the grinning skull of atheist post-nihilism that lurks beneath the obsequious smile of secular humanism.

POSTMODERN PHILOSOPHICAL PETAINERY

Monotheism loathes intelligence....Monotheism does not really like the rational work of scientists.[5]

French anti-Semitism is less well-known but is arguably nearly as widespread as the variant that their German cousins made so notorious in the 1940s. It is so widespread, in fact, that the French of unoccupied Vichy did not even bother to wait for the Germans to ask them to begin registering Jews, 75,721 of whom were eventually deported for grim destinations east. More than 73,000 of these unfortunates died, most of them at Auschwitz. According to Paul Webster, the author of *Pétain's Crime, the Full Story of French Complicity in the Holocaust*, even more would have died had Mussolini not ordered the Fascist troops occupying southeastern France to defy French plans for mass Jewish round-ups.[6]

---

[5] Onfray, Michel. *In Defence of Atheism* (London, 2007), 67, 81.

[6] Webster, Paul. "*The Vichy Policy on Jewish Deportation.*" British Broadcasting Corporation. 28 July 2007. <http://www.bbc.co.uk/history/worldwars/genocide/jewish_deportation_01.shtml>.

Onfray's spectacularly absurd assertion that all monotheism, including Judaism, is inherently anti-intelligence and anti-science fits well with this French tendency toward anti-Semitism, which has flared up periodically since the Dreyfus affair in 1894. Philosophy is not science, of course, but one has to wonder just how detached from reality Onfray must be to ignore the undeniable fact that Jews possess the strongest intellectual tradition in human history, have been repeatedly found to possess the highest average intelligence,[7] and account for a much higher percentage of scientific advancements than would be statistically indicated by the small fraction of the global population they represent. I have already shown that it is absurd to claim that Christianity and Islam are intrinsically anti-science in light of the amount of evidence to the contrary, but until reading *In Defence of Atheism*, it never occurred to me that it might be necessary to defend Judaism from the charge as well.

This is not an exaggeration or a peculiar postmodern definition of monotheism either, as Onfray describes the Apostle Paul's rabbinical training as "nonexistent" and explicitly points his finger at Judaism, the Torah, and the Talmud in his chapter entitled "Bonfires of the Intelligence." He argues that because of the leading role played by "the permitted and the forbidden" in all three of the major monotheisms, a logic of licit/illicit is created that imprisons the believer into an anti-intelligent frame of mind. This same prison is the root cause of what Onfray believes to be the monotheistic characteristics of obsession with purity, disdain for the physical world, negation of matter, hatred for science, and hatred for women.

It is astonishing, of course, that a French hedonist should believe that none of the 4.5 billion monotheists on the planet can properly appreciate women the way he can.[8]

By his language, his thought processes, and the title of his book in the original French, Onfray betrays the influence of Michel Foucault's and his *Archeology of Knowledge*, in which the distinction between the Same and the Other creates the boundaries of an epis-

---

[7] Herrnstein, Richard, and Charles. Murray. "*The Bell Curve.*" *Free Press*, Sept. 1994.

[8] And like practically every philosopher from Plato to Dennett, Onfray believes that it is philosophy that is best fitted to dictate how humanity should organize itself. I'm starting to believe that philosophy Ph.D.s should be presented with a mandatory cup of hemlock to go with the diploma.

timeme, Foucault's word for the totality of knowledge that can be discovered at a given level of discourse. However, an epistimeme expressly rejects scientific facts, it is interested in them only insofar as they relate to their position within or without the subject's boundaries of knowledge. Thus, Onfray can blithely set aside the empirical evidence of high-average intelligence and scientific achievement on the part of Jews as well as the Christian roots of scientody—these are mere facts that have no bearing on the higher ontological and epistimemetical truth of his statement that Jews, Christians, and Muslims are all anti-intelligence and anti-intellectual.[9]

INFAMY OF THE OTHER

The immanent ordering of the word distinguishes the Christian atheist from the Christian believer. But not their values, which remain identical. All operate on common ground.[10]

Some of Onfray's harshest words are reserved for those he labels "Christian atheists"—it infuriates him that so many God-deniers are so fascinated by the enemy that they adopt the greater part of its values as their own. In nearly an identical manner to the way in which I described the High Church atheist in the first chapter, Onfray describes the Christian atheist as being one who rejects the existence of God and a part of the values derived from Him, specifically those related to "the Pauline hatred of the body." He declares that this partial atheism is something to get past, in favor of a postmodern atheistic atheism and a hedonistic contract without transcendent obligations or punishment.

Among the values that Onfray wishes to get past are the ideals of charity, temperance, compassion, mercy, humility, love of one's neighbor, forgiveness, and the "ethical asceticism that rejects power honors, and wealth" as false values. Good and evil no longer apply, except as factors in the attempt to supply the greatest possible happiness to the greatest number. Onfray's hedonism is the explicit

---

[9] If this didn't make much sense to you, don't worry about it. It's postmodern French philosophy, it's not supposed to make sense. Or "sense," as Foucault's disciples would have it.

[10] Onfray, 56.

articulation of Harris's fumbling toward a happiness-based ethic and the realization of Dennett's moral democracy, but what the Frenchman makes clear in a distinctly Nietzschean manner is that he will brook no weak-minded influence of the enervating Judeo-Christian disease in tempering the illuminated way toward Enlightenment and the new secular utopia. Nothing is forbidden, no action is unthinkable, and needless to say, if an unpopular minority happen to be in the way of the greatest possible happiness of the greatest number, that minority will simply have to go.

This hedonistic metric looks particularly grim when one compares the New Atheists' need to at least attempt defending past atheist atrocities with Onfray's singular lack of concern for doing the same. Onfray writes not a single word about any of the fifty-two atheist mass murderers of the twentieth century, he does not even mention Stalin or Mao, despite devoting more than six pages of the book to inaccurately claiming that Adolf Hitler was a Christian, based in part upon the *Gott mit uns*[11] belt buckle that the German army inherited from the royal house of Prussia. He is obviously unaware that it was not Hitler who gave the Wehrmacht that motto, but Otto von Bismarck, whose imperial standard contained the slogan in 1870; similar *Gott mit uns* buckles from World War I further prove the falsity of Onfray's argument. Moreover, the Wehrmacht were not Nazis—the 950,000-strong Nazi army personally sworn to Hitler was the Waffen-SS, and their motto was not *Gott mit uns* but *Meine Ehre heißt Treue*.[12]

This silence regarding the historic evils of atheist communists on the part of a sometime communist supporter is particularly damning due to Onfray's claim that the Catholic Church is in some way responsible for the Nazi actions, which is entirely based upon what he considers to be the Church's silence during and after World War II. He complains that the Vatican has demonstrated "a commitment, a militancy, and a vigor" criticizing Marxism and Communism that he believes would have been better spent discrediting the Third Reich. But how can the Catholic Church be held responsible for failing to

---

[11] *"God with us."*

[12] *"My honor is named loyalty."* To put it into perspective, the Waffen-SS was made up of thirty-eight combat divisions. The current U.S. Army has ten.

defend those who reject its authority over them?[13] And what government has ever failed to focus on its openly declared enemies instead of those enemies willing to declare truce?

As Daniel C. Dennett suggests, a truce between Christian believer and "Christian atheist" is possible. But Onfray's hatred for both demonstrates there can be no truce between Christianity and the postmodern atheism of atheology.

NEITHER GOD NOR SCIENCE

Onfray reveals some unexpected talents when he diagnoses the Apostle Paul's sexual dysfunction and psychological ailment from a distance of hundreds of miles and thousands of years. He blames the bombing of Hiroshima on Christianity—though not Nagasaki, for some strange reason—and actually states that "the accumulation of nuclear weapons is not an effective deterrent to war," despite the ongoing absence of large-scale conflict between any of the nuclear powers since 1945. He claims that Christianity did no more than Judaism or Islam to deter slavery, which will no doubt surprise those who have seen the movie *Amazing Grace*, which tells the story of how a devout Christian, William Wilberforce, not only managed to deter slavery but caused it to be abolished in England altogether.

It would be interesting to ask Onfray if he sees any causal connection between the European post-Christianity he celebrates and the rise of sex-slavery throughout Europe. Of course, he might not take exception to the latter, after all, what is the abject misery of one woman who is bringing orgasmic delight to ten or more men every night?[14]

Onfray claims that democracy thrives on reason and the active use of communication. Economists have proven the former to be untrue, due to how the vast majority of voters in all democracies combine

---

[13] I am a Christian, not a Catholic. The Pope has no authority over me, nor does he have any responsibility to defend me. Why Pope Pius XII should be criticized for defending his flock and not defending others who refused to acknowledge him (he actually was a well-known defender of Jews) has never made any sense to me. The fact that the Vatican signed treaties with the Fascists and Nazis in 1929 and 1933 is proof of their astute and early recognition of two dangerous enemies, not a propensity for trans-ideological partnerships (the 1929 treaty established the Vatican as an independent state).

[14] To say nothing of the financial benefit derived by her owner.

ignorance with irrationality. As for the latter, anyone who has paid even the least amount of attention to any electoral campaign since Alcibiades was running for office knows that intentional miscommunication is not the exception, but the democratic rule. A gaffe, as Michael Kinsley defined it, is when a politician accidentally tells the truth; if communication was an integral part of democracy, one would have to conclude on the basis of the history of American political campaigns that none of the 110 Congresses had ever raised taxes.

Onfray complains of the apparent logical contradiction between the Fifth Commandment and the later commands in Deuteronomy to smite, destroy, burn, and dispossess. Setting aside the obvious fact that the Fifth Commandment is generally considered to be "Honor thy father and mother"[15] and that neither burning nor dispossessing can be inherently equated with killing, he is obviously unaware of the consensus that the term "kill" in "Thou shalt not kill" is understood in the sense of a murderous killing. I'm no Hebrew scholar, but like any multilingual individual, I'm aware of the implications of the fact that there are five Hebrew variants on the English theme "to kill": "*ratsach*," "*nakah*," "*muwth*," "*harag*," and "*tabach*." Moses and the Israelites might have been a bit obtuse at times, but even they would have presumably been capable of noticing this superficial dichotomy that so befuddles the philosopher. Even without the obvious linguistic pointers, the distinction really is not difficult, for example, God is reported to have rewarded David for killing a certain large Philistine (*nakah*), while punishing him severely for arranging the death of someone he did not even touch (*harag*). And it would have been very, very strange for Jesus to instruct his disciples to make a priority of buying edged weaponry unless he considered it reasonable for them to make use of it in the appropriate circumstances.

It is not only Onfray's conclusions, but even his direct references that are unreliable. Witness, for example, his statement that the Apostle Paul "called for the burning of dangerous books" in Acts 19:19. This is not true, as the verse actually states that the Jews and Greeks who had been practicing sorcery burned their occultic works

---

[15] Onfray is obviously using the Catholic count. "Thou shalt not kill" is usually considered to be the Sixth Commandment.

of their own accord after converting to Christianity in response to the beating of some false Christians by a demon-possessed man. Paul's only connection to the book burnings was the invocation of his name by the demon. "Jesus I know, and I know about Paul, but who are you?"[16] In a similar vein, Richard Norman, a professor of philosophy at the University of Kent, says of Onfray: "His references look very impressive, but I checked some references to the Koran and he hasn't got it totally right."[17]

Like Hitchens, Onfray is bizarrely fascinated with the uncomfortable subjects of castration and male circumcision, to which he devotes a veritable torrent of text.[18] The book all but shakes with his outrage at what he considers to be mutilation based on nothing more than the monotheistic fear of sexual pleasure. Onfray is the anti-Puritan; he is furious at the thought that someone, somewhere, might not be enjoying himself to the full extent possible. However, his fury is wasted here, as the loss of a thousand nerve endings and 250 feet of nerves that he cites don't actually reduce male sensitivity in any way.[19]

Onfray's atheism is deeply, profoundly, even essentially anti-scientific. For all that he laments the way in which monotheism has historically handicapped what he imagines would have been the rapid progress of science in its absence, both the assertions on which he bases his arguments and the conclusions he reaches are reliably in direct opposition to the current state of scientage. This should come as no surprise, given his statement that "[p]ostmodern atheism divests itself of its theological and scientific trappings in order to construct a moral system. Neither God nor science, neither intelligible heaven nor the operation of mathematical propositions, neither Thomas Aquinas nor Auguste Comte nor Marx."[20]

---

[16] Acts 19:15.

[17] "Atheism à la mode": *New Humanist*, July/August 2007.

[18] It really is astounding how obsessed these atheist writers are with Hitler and circumcision.

[19] Kimberley Payne, Ph.D., Lea Thaler, BA, Tuuli Kukkonen, BA, Serge Carrier, MD, and Yitzchak Binik, Ph.D., "Sensation and Sexual Arousal in Circumcised and Uncircumcised Men," *The Journal of Sexual Medicine* 3 (2007): 667–674.

[20] Onfray, 58. No one but French philosophers still considers Marx a scientist.

THE SHINING PATH

So a final push is needed to rekindle the flames of the Enlightenment. A little more Enlightenment, more and more Enlightenment![21]

If both God and science are out, then what is left? What remains to provide the moral fabric for the atheist-squared social structure? Onfray declares that philosophy, reason, utility, pragmatism, and hedonism, both individual and social, will suffice to lay the groundwork for the New Enlightenment, which will succeed where the first one failed due to its lack of courage. Onfray is particularly frustrated with Kant, blaming his mother for the philosopher's unwillingness to take the final step and postulate the nonexistence of God and the nonexistence of free will.

He is equally annoyed by Voltaire, Montesquieu, Rousseau, and d'Alembert for their deism and for their refusal to embrace the sensual. In the place of their timid audacity, he states his preference for the dazzling light of Feuerbach, Nietzsche, Marx, and Freud, although Marx is too scientific for him. But their work is central to Onfray's master plan for atheology, which he describes as a "physics of metaphysics, a true theory of immanence, a materialist ontology," intended to complete Georges Bataille's proposed *Summa Atheologica* and serve as the basis for a new secular religion, a new hedonistic morality, and a new social order.

To Onfray, the negation of God inherent in the concept of atheism is not enough, it is merely a halfway measure. Whereas Dawkins and Harris only hint at humanism and a happiness metric as a potential replacement for religion and traditional Western morality while nervously clutching at the latter as a security blanket, Onfray boldly rejects their secular synthesis with all the self-righteous certainty of a Jacobin denouncing a Girondist before the Revolutionary Tribunal. According to Onfray, the New Atheist path leads only to Nietzschean nihilism; his atheology is post-Nietzschean, leading humanity beyond the dialectic of nihilistic struggle and into a hedonistic philosopher's paradise.

In a 2005 interview with Onfray published in *Il Giornale*, Daniele

---

[21] Onfray, 6.

Belloni perceptively saw fit to label Onfray the Robespierre of atheism. When one takes into account how the French philosopher recognizes Satan as being the emblem of the Enlightenment[22] and how
he equates the dialectic between Christian and New Atheist as being
equivalent to God and the devil while simultaneously declaring the
synthesis to be insufficient, one can only conclude that his ontological utopia would lead to an unprecedented Reign of Horror and evils
of a magnitude hitherto unknown by Man. For Michel Onfray demands nothing less than an atheological *auto da fé*, burning Western
civilization on the fiery stake of a New Luciferian Enlightenment.
This would not be worrisome if it were only more inane insanity on
the part of a French philosopher, the problem is that Onfray's proposed new order is not merely the logical extension of the secular
utopia sought by Russell, Dawkins, and Harris, it is the stark, rational articulation of that which the New Atheists do not dare to admit,
either to themselves or to the reading public.

---

[22] Onfray, 15.

XII

HITLER, THE INQUISITION, THE CRUSADES, AND HUMAN SACRIFICE

*Now, you will stay in the Comfy Chair until lunch time,
with only a cup of coffee at eleven.*

—CARDINAL XIMINEZ

IT WOULD BE IMPOSSIBLE TO WRITE A BOOK of this sort without addressing the three subjects that inevitably come up when atheists are contending with Christians. Just as atheists anticipate the need to answer for Stalin and Mao, Christians are expected to answer for the Inquisition and the Crusades. And both sides recognize the need to deal with the Hitler Questio-Like Einstein,[1] the Führer made enough ambiguous statements to

---

[1] I concur with Richard Dawkins on this point, despite a few metaphorical statements about God. It is not reasonable to conclude that Albert Einstein was anything but an agnostic.

leave the matter up for discussion; unlike Einstein,[2] no one is eager to claim Hitler and his National Socialists as members of their intellectual camp. The Unholy Trinity have no choice but to concern themselves with the matter, of course, and they do so largely in the manner that one has come to expect from them.[3] Harris wastes eight pages attempting to tar the Catholic Church and Pope Pius XII with guilt by insufficient opposition,[4] then on the basis of no evidence whatsoever, declares that Auschwitz was a logical and inevitable consequence of the Christian faith.[5] Hitchens also complains about the Catholic Church and relates a few irrelevant anecdotes about Italian Fascists and Irish Blue Shirts, but then shows genuine insight when he notes that the Hitler regime shows us "with terrible clarity what can happen when men usurp the role of gods."

Dawkins, on the other hand, demonstrates that he is perfectly capable of presenting a reasonable case when he chooses to do so and lays out some reasonable evidence for the reader to reach his own conclusion on the matter. He avoids making the common case for Hitler's religious faith on the basis of his abused childhood,[6] wisely, considering that one could apply precisely the same argument to Christopher Hitchens and Dawkins himself. Instead, after quoting Hitler's public statements that state outright that he is a Christian, and a very devout one at that, Dawkins quotes private statements that reveal a deep hatred for Christianity surpassing that possessed by even the most militant New Atheist.

---

[2] What is unexpected, however, is how much the Nazi Martin Bormann's description of a metaphorical God sounds almost exactly like Albert Einstein's as described by Richard Dawkins.

[3] Given the non-polemical nature of his book, Daniel Dennett commendably sees no reason to mention the matter.

[4] Harris, *The End of Faith*, 104. Harris finds it extraordinary that no German Catholics were excommunicated, but then, other than Hitler there were no former Catholics in the Nazi hierarchy. The most notable Catholic, former Reichkanzler Franz von Papen, was jailed after speaking out against Hitler after Kristallnacht and was acquitted at Nuremberg.

[5] How strange that it should happen only once in more than 2,000 years, and at the behest of a few fanatical anti-Christians, no less. I further note that the Buddhist Harris neglects to mention the fact that Professor Walter Wüst, who commanded the SS-Ahnenerbe under Himmler after February 1937, publicly declared that Hitler's ideologies corresponded with those of the Gautama Buddha.

[6] I seem to recall someone informing us that a Catholic upbringing is even worse than sexual abuse for a child.

It is possible that Hitler had by 1941 experienced some kind of deconversion or disillusionment with Christianity. Or is the resolution of the contradictions simply that he was an opportunistic liar whose words cannot be trusted, in either direction?[7]

It is worth noting that most of the statements that indicate Hitler's Christian faith were made in public, prior to 1934, when he was still a politician running for elected office. Given his subsequent actions once he had secured political power, there is no reason to believe that Hitler meant them any more sincerely than George W. Bush intended to keep his promise to pursue a "more humble foreign policy" three years before he launched an invasion to bring democracy and freedom to the Middle East. But Hitler was no atheist, neither was he agnostic; the evidence tends to suggest that he was a pagan[8] who was skeptical, but open to the possibility of acquiring temporal power through supernatural means.

The Thule Society that founded the German Workers' Party that was the predecessor of the Nazi Party, was an esoteric society connected with the occultist Madame Blavatsky and the Theosophists. Hitler was the fifty-fifth member of the DAP, which was renamed the National Socialist German Workers' Party, or NASDAP, only four months after he joined on October 19, 1919. While the Nazis suppressed their early connection with the Thule Society and even arrested its founder, Rudolf von Sebottendorff, when he published a book about the relationship between Hitler and the society, the Nazi interest in esoteric matters, primarily on the part of Heinrich Himmler and the SS, is well-known and has played a role in everything from Charles Stross's excellent novel *The Atrocity Archives* to Wolfenstein 3D and the Indiana Jones movies.

It is not known to what extent Hitler shared Himmler's enthusiasm for the supernatural, but it is reasonable to assume that if he was as skeptical about its existence as the New Atheists are today, he

---

[7] Dawkins, *The God Delusion*, 276. Given that Hitler was not only a politician, but a stunningly effective one, the answer has to be yes.

[8] Hitler once made an interesting statement to Bormann about the foolishness of restoring Odin worship, which he refers to as "our old mythology." As he goes on to talk about getting rid of Christianity, it's apparent that his goal is to create a new and better Teutonic mythology compatible with science and philosophy.

would not have allowed the Reichsführer-SS and founder of the Studiengesellschaft für Geistesurgeschichte, Deutsches Ahnenerbe,[9] an annual budget of the modern equivalent of $5.6 million to spend on occult research, medical experiments, and expeditions to Sweden, Syria, Iraq, Finland, and Tibet.

And yet, if Dawkins is not quite able to definitively conclude that Adolf Hitler was not a Christian, Robert Wistrich, the professor of modern Jewish history at Hebrew University, has no such qualms. In *Hitler and the Holocaust*, Wistrich writes:

> *Indeed, the leading Nazis—Hitler, Himmler, Rosenberg, Goebbels, and Bormann—were all fanatically anti-Christian, though this was partly hidden from the German public.... The conviction that Judaism, Christianity and Bolshevism represented one single pathological phenomenon of decadence became a veritable leitmotif for Hitler around the time that the "Final Solution" had been conceived of as an operational plan.*[10]

But the most convincing proof that Hitler was neither an atheist nor a Christian can be seen in two documents that the various New Atheists and Wistrich were probably not aware of at the time they wrote their books. The first of these was prepared by the Office of Strategic Services in preparation for the Nuremburg trials in 1945. Released to the public in 2001, the report from the archives of Gen. William J. Donovan, special assistant to the U.S. chief of counsel at the Tribunal, is a fascinating description of the Third Reich's methodical plan to coopt, pervert, and ultimately usurp the Catholic and Protestant churches of Germany. As an editor of the Nuremberg Project for the *Rutgers Journal of Law and Religion* described it: "They wanted to eliminate the Jews altogether, but they were also looking to eliminate Christianity."[11]

---

[9] The Study Society for Primordial Intellectual Science, German Ancestral Heritage, usually known as the Ahnenerbe, was an SS department set up by Himmler to investigate the ancestral German heritage. It is this group that attempted to find the Holy Grail and other mystic treasures, as portrayed in the movies. *The Atrocity Archives* is probably the most interesting fictional portrayal of this occultic bureaucracy; my own novella that briefly touches on the subject, "The Lesser Evil," can be downloaded for free from the online archive at http://www.memoware.com.

[10] Wistrich, Robert S. *Hitler and the Holocaust*. New York: Modern Library, 2001. 131–132.

[11] Colimore, Edward. "Papers Reveal Nazi Aim: End Christianity," *The Philadelphia Inquirer*, 9 Jan. 2002.

The first installment, entitled "The Nazi Master Plan; The Persecution of Christian Churches," shows how the Nazis planned to supplant Christianity with a religion based on racial superiority. The report, prepared by the Office of Strategic Services—a forerunner of the CIA—says: "Important leaders of the National Socialist party would have liked...complete extirpation of Christianity and the substitution of a purely racial religion."[12]

The second document is equally significant. It is the thirty-point plan for a National Reich Church, drawn up by Alfred Rosenberg, the Nazi ideologist who was Reich Minister for the Occupied Eastern Territories and head of the Centre of National Socialist Ideological and Educational Research. Three of its more significant points are as follows:

1. *The National Reich Church is determined to exterminate irrevocably and by every means the strange and foreign Christian faiths imported into Germany in the ill-omened year 800.*
2. *The National Reich Church demands immediate cessation of the publishing and dissemination of the Bible in Germany as well as the publication of Sunday papers, pamphlets, publications, and books of a religious nature.*
3. *The National Reich Church does not acknowledge forgiveness of sins. It represents the standpoint which it will always proclaim that a sin once committed will be ruthlessly punished by the honorable and indestructible laws of nature and punishment will follow during the sinner's lifetime.*

One need not be a theologian to recognize that whatever religion happens to lurk behind a church that does not recognize the forgiveness of sins and is determined to suppress the Bible, it is not Christianity.

Although the only logical conclusion is that Hitler was neither a Christian nor an atheist, there are still lessons that Christians and atheists can learn from his pagan totalitarianism. Christians must

---

[12] "Nazi Trial Documents Made Public." BBC News, 11 Jan. 2002. The entire OSS report can be downloaded in four PDF files from http://www.lawandreligion.com/nurinst1.shtml.

recognize that it is possible for their institutions to be infiltrated and utilized for evil purposes even as they religiously attend church and participate in the mainstream of society. Had more German Christians demonstrated the courage of the evangelical Confessing Church and openly opposed Hitler, as did the pastors who signed the 1934 Barmen Declaration,[13] much tragedy might well have been averted. Despite the deception that was undeniably involved, Christians have no excuse for being blind to such things, not when they have been warned in the Bible to be on their guard against deceitful wolves in sheep's clothing.

As for atheists, they must recognize that science is a deadly foundation on which to build future utopias and it should make them more than a little uncomfortable to consider the striking similarities in the following three quotes, one from a Humanist, one from a New Atheist, and the other from a leading Nazi.

- Religion is something left over from the infancy of our intelligence; it will fade away as we adopt reason and science as our guidelines.[14]
- The dogma of Christianity gets worn away before the advance of science. Religion will have to make more and more concessions. Gradually the myths crumble.[15]
- Religion has run out of justifications. Thanks to the telescope and the microscope, it no longer offers an explanation of anything important.[16]

THE SPANISH INQUISITION

It is a curious thing considering how often it is brought up in conversation and Internet debate by lay atheists, but in *The God Delusion*, Rich-

---

[13] "*We reject the false doctrine that the Church could have permission to hand over the form of its message and of its order to whatever it itself might wish or to the vicissitudes of the prevailing ideological and political convictions of the day.*" The Barmen Declaration, The Confessing Synod of the German Evangelical Church, 1934.

[14] Bertrand Russell, attributed: source unknown. <http://www.positiveatheism.org/hist/quotes/russell.htm>.

[15] Adolf Hitler, (transcribed by Martin Bormann) Hitler's Secret Conversations 1941–1944 (H. R. Trevor-Roper, Trans.), (New York, 1953), 49.

[16] Hitchens, 282.

ard Dawkins conspicuously neglects to detail what he describes as the "horrors" of the Spanish Inquisition. Christopher Hitchens and Daniel Dennett both avoid discussing it altogether. Only Reason's clown, Sam Harris, is sufficiently foolish to swallow the old Black Legend, hook, line, and sinker, as he attempts to portray the collective inquisitions as one of the two "darkest episodes in the history of faith."[17]

There was not one historical inquisition, but four, the Medieval, the Spanish, the Portuguese, and the Roman.[18] Of these four, it is the Spanish Inquisition to which most critics commonly refer due to its notorious intensity. It is, therefore, the one worth examining in some detail to determine just how dark this episode in the history of faith truly was and how it compares to the three events to which Harris implicitly compares it: the Holodomor, the Great Leap Forward, and the Holocaust.

On June 9, 721 A.D., Duke Odo of Aquitaine defeated Al-Samh ibn Malik al-Khawlani before the walls of the besieged city of Toulouse. This battle, followed by the victories of King Pelayo of Asturias and Charles Martel at the battles of Covadonga and Tours, brought to an end a century of remarkably successful Islamic expansion. Over the next 760 years, the Umayyads' conquests on the Spanish peninsula were gradually rolled back by a succession of Christian kings, a long process disturbed by the usual shifting of alliances as well as varying degrees of ambition and military competence on both sides of the religious divide. The *Reconquista* was completed with the fall of Muslim Granada[19] in 1492 to the Castilian forces of King Ferdinand.

---

[17] Harris, *The End of Faith*, 79. The other being the Holocaust. Harris is subscribing to a false view of the inquisitions created by sixteenth-century Protestant propagandists and shaped by nineteenth-century novelists. There is no evidence to indicate that the thumbscrews, toe screws, pear-shaped vise, or "Spanish Chair" described by Harris were ever used by the Spanish Inquisition, and amusingly enough, one of the three methods that actually *was* used by the inquisitors, the *toca*, is virtually identical to the use of "water-boarding" torture that Sam Harris defends. "*I am one of the few people I know of who has argued in print that torture may be an ethical necessity in our war on terror.*" Harris, Sam. "In Defense of Torture." *The Huffington Post.* 17 Oct. 2005.

[18] The Roman Inquisition is still around; the current Grand Inquisitor is His Eminence William Joseph Levada, a cardinal from Long Beach, California. Although he doesn't go by "Grand Inquisitor," his actual title is Prefect of the Congregation for the Doctrine of the Faith. I have to say, it's a little disappointing. If I were P of the C for the D of the F in full E-F-F-E-C-T, I would totally wear a black mask and a red cape at all times and insist on being addressed as Grand Inquisitor by everyone, which is probably why I'll never be named a cardinal. That and I'm not Catholic.

[19] Boabdil of Granada had been a tributary king subject to the united Christian kingdoms of Castile and Aragon for eight years at the time of his surrender of Granada. In 1483, he had unwisely decided to invade Castile and was captured.

The Spanish Inquisition, which began in 1481, cannot be understood without recognizing the significance of this epic 771-year struggle between Christians and Muslims over the Spanish peninsula. What took the great Berber general Tariq ibn Zayid only eight years to conquer on behalf of the Umayyad Caliphate required almost 100 times as long to regain, and neither King Ferdinand II of Aragon nor his wife, Queen Isabella of Castile, was inclined to risk any possibility of having to repeat the grand endeavor.

Isabella, in particular, was concerned about reports of *conversos*, Christians who had pretended to convert from Judaism but were still practicing their former religion. This was troubling, as it was reasonable to assume that those who were lying about their religious conversion were also lying about their loyalty to the united crowns and it was known that some Jews were encouraging Muslim leaders to attempt the recapture of al-Andalus.[20] An investigation was commissioned and the reports were verified, at which point the Spanish monarchs asked Pope Sixtus IV to create a branch of the Roman Inquisition that would report to the Spanish crown. The Pope initially refused, but when Ferdinand threatened to leave Rome to its own devices should the Turks attack, he reluctantly acceded and issued *Exigit Sinceras Devotionis Affectus* on November 1, 1478, a papal bull establishing an inquisition in Isabella's Kingdom of Castile.

One tends to get the impression that Ferdinand was less than deeply concerned about the potential *converso* threat and may have even been acting primarily to mollify his wife, as he promptly made use of this hard-won new authority to do absolutely nothing for the next two years. Then, on September 27, 1480, the first two inquisitors, Miguel de Morillo and Juan de San Martín, were named, the first tribunal was created, and by February 6, 1481, six false Christians had been accused, tried, convicted and burned in the Spanish Inquisition's first *auto da fé*.

What happened in between November 1478 and September 1480 to inspire this sudden burst of action? While historians such as Henry Kamen pronounce themselves baffled as to what could have provoked the Spanish crown, the most likely impetus was that on July

---

[20] "*It remains a fact that the Jews, either directly or through their correligionists in Africa, encouraged the Mohammedans to conquer Spain.*" *The Jewish Encyclopedia* (1906). Vol XI, 485.

28, three months before Ferdinand's decision to appoint the two inquisitors, a Turkish fleet led by Gedik Ahmed Pasha attacked the Aragonese city of Otranto. Otranto fell on August 11 and more than half of the city's 20,000 people were slaughtered during the sack of the city. The archbishop was killed in the cathedral, and the garrison commander was killed by being sawed in half alive, as was a bishop named Stephen Pendinelli. But the most infamous event was when the captured men of Otranto were given the choice to convert to Islam or die; 800 of them held to their Christian faith and were beheaded *en masse* at a place now known as the Hill of the Martyrs. The Turkish fleet then went on to attack the cities of Vieste, Lecce, Taranto, and Brindisi, and destroyed the great library at the Monastero di San Nicholas di Casole, before returning to Ottoman territory in November.

It is one of the great ironies of history that three times more people died in the forgotten event that almost surely inspired the Spanish Inquisition than died in the famous flames of the inquisition itself. Despite its reputation as one of the most vicious and lethal institutions in human history, the Spanish Inquisition was one of the most humane and decent of its time, and one could even argue the most reasonable, considering the circumstances. Indeed, there are few historical institutions that have ever been so misunderstood, as the following three facts should clarify:

1. The Spanish Inquisition did not attempt to convert anyone to Christianity. It had no authority over professing Jews, Muslims, or atheists; its sole mission was to distinguish between genuine Christians and those who were falsely pretending to be Christians and were actually practicing another faith.
2. The inquisitors were not slobbering psychotics as portrayed by Dostoevsky and Edgar Allan Poe. They were usually at least partially educated clerics from the more scholarly monastical orders who closely followed the specified rules and procedures, which happened to be the most humane in the world at the time.
3. Torture was rarely used,[21] and only when there was substantial

---

[21] Kamen, 189. Most crimes were not considered serious enough to justify torture. The incidence of torture varied greatly depending on the tribunal, as the lowest rate was at Valencia, where half

evidence to indicate that the accused was lying. Torture could only be used on one occasion for fifteen minutes,[22] and could not cause the loss of life or limb, or shed blood; although there were occasional excesses, the main reason we know about them is because those responsible for committing them were held accountable by the Church authorities.

4. The main reason there was a Spanish Inquisition in the first place is that, unlike in other European kingdoms, Ferdinand and Isabella encouraged Jews and Muslims to convert to Christianity instead of simply expelling them all. In the century leading up to the Spanish expulsion of the estimated 40,000 Jews who did not convert in 1492 and the subsequent expulsion of Muslims ten years later, Jews were expelled from Germany, France (twice), Austria, Switzerland, the Netherlands, Poland, Italy (twice), Lithuania, Portugal, and the Kingdom of Naples. Religion may have been the measure, but the motive behind the Spanish Inquisition was unmasking treason and potential rebellion against the Spanish crown.

In light of its nightmarish reputation, it will surely surprise those who believe that millions of people died in the Spanish Inquisition to learn that throughout the sixteenth and seventeenth centuries, less than three people per year were sentenced to death by the Inquisition throughout the Spanish Empire, which ranged from Spain to Sicily and Peru.[23] Secular historians given access to the Vatican's archives in 1998 discovered that of the 44,674 individuals tried between 1540 and 1700, only 804 were recorded as being *relictus culiae saeculari*.[24] The 763-page report indicates that only 1 percent of the

---

of 1 percent of those tried were tortured; the highest known rate was at Seville, where 11 percent suffered the treatment.

[22] *"According to Professor Agostino Borromeo, a historian of Catholicism at the Sapienza University in Rome and curator of the 783-page volume released yesterday, only 1% of the 125,000 people tried by church tribunals as suspected heretics in Spain were executed.... What the church initiated as a strictly regulated process, in which torture was allowed for only 15 minutes and in the presence of a doctor, got out of hand when other bodies were involved."* Arie, Sophie. "Historians Say Inquisition Wasn't That Bad." *The Guardian*, 16 June 2004.

[23] Kamen, Henry, *The Spanish Inquisition: A Historical Revision*. New Haven: Yale University Press, 1997. 203.

[24] Relinquished to the secular court, a verdict known as "relaxation." Which wasn't all that relaxing, considering how it generally led to being burned at the stake.

125,000 trials recorded over the entire inquisition ultimately resulted in execution by the secular authority, which means that throughout its infamous 345-year history,[25] the dread Spanish Inquisition was less than one-fourteenth as deadly on an annual basis as children's bicycles.[26]

Historical Event	Responsible	Dates	Total Deaths	Deaths per Year
Great Leap Forward	atheists	1958–1963	43,000,000	8,600,000
Holodomor	atheists	1932–1933	3,500,000	1,750,000
Holocaust	pagan theists	1941–1945	6,000,000	1,500,000
Spanish Red Terror*	atheists	1936–1939	72,344	24,114
Children's Bicycles	Schwinn	1920–2007	11,310	130
Spanish Inquisition**	Christian theists	1481–1834	3,230	9
Medieval Inquisitions***	Christian theists	1184–1500	2,000	6
Portuguese Inquisition****	Christian theists	1540–1794	1,175	5

* Colbatch, Hal G. P. "Orwell's Bad Republicans." The American Spectator, 7 Aug. 2007.
** Agostino Borromeo, Vatican Revision on Inquisition History, (Vatican City, 1998). The 3,225 number is based on the assumption that the rate of executions over the final 136 years remained as high as it was for the 160-year period from 1540 to 1700, plus the additional 1,750 burnings that is the average of the estimates provided by Henry Kamen and William Monter based on the records of the local tribunals during the more active period from 1481 to 1530.
*** This includes a number of historical inquisitions. It's worth noting that one of the most notorious inquisitors, Bernard Gui of Toulouse, only executed forty-two people out of the 900 guilty verdicts recorded during his fifteen years in office.
**** Lea, Henry Charles. Book 8. Vol. 3 of A History of the Inquisition of Spain. However, the Vatican report indicates a slightly higher percentage of relaxations, 5.7 percent compared to Lea's 3.7 percent.

If the Spanish Inquisition was, as historian Henry Charles Lea once described it, theocratic absolutism at its worst, one can only conclude that this is an astonishingly positive testimony on behalf of theocratic absolutism. It is testimony to the strange vagaries of history that it should be the Spanish Inquisition that remains notorious

---

[25] Obviously 1481 to 1834 is 353 years, not 345, but the inquisition was briefly abolished on three occasions after 1800.
[26] "In 2002, 130 children ages 14 and under died in bicycle-related crashes. The bicycle injury death rate among children ages 14 and under declined 70 percent from 1987 to 2002." Facts About Injuries To Children Riding Bicycles. Safe Kids Worldwide.

today, even though the 6,832 members of the Catholic clergy murdered in the Spanish Republican Red Terror of 1936[27] is more than twice the number of the victims of 345 years of inquisition.

THE CRUSADES

The New Atheists also don't pay as much attention to the Crusades as one might imagine considering how often the medieval wars come up in casual conversation with everyday atheists. Hitchens mentions it primarily in passing, noting only Raymond of Aguilers's famous account of the bloody aftermath of the First Crusade's siege of Jerusalem and the Fourth Crusade's sack of Byzantium. Dawkins is even more reserved—he not only declines to detail the horrors of the Spanish Inquisition, but those of the Crusades as well. Dennett merely notes that crusades have never been waged over musical traditions—although it's conceivable that Hitchens might be amenable to signing up for one waged in the name of Mozart—and Harris, despite his deep concerns over the danger posed by an expanding Islam, unaccountably leaves out any discussion of those who historically fought against it.

The Crusades, especially the First Crusade, are undoubtedly the foremost Christian example of religious war. They are not only an example of one of the dangers of religion, they also serve as an excellent example of one of the primary dangers to religion, that of being co-opted and used by secular powers for secular purposes. While the First Crusade began as a religious response to an entirely secular plea for military assistance by the desperate Emperor of the Byzantine Empire, by the end, it was dominated by petty warlords scrambling for land and power. And with each subsequent Crusade, the religious influences and motivations were pushed further and further aside, until by the last four Crusades, neither the Pope nor the common people whose fervor propelled so much of the religious zeal to take the Cross were involved in any way.

---

[27] Julio de la Cueva, "Religious Persecution, Anticlerical Tradition and Revolution: On Atrocities against the Clergy during the Spanish Civil War," *Journal of Contemporary History*, 3 (1998): 355–369.

Crusade	Declared By	Objective	Outcome[*]
First Crusade	Pope Urban II	Recapture Jerusalem	Jerusalem recaptured, three Latin principalities established in the Holy Lands.
Second Crusade	Pope Eugene III	Recover the County of Edessa	The Crusaders attacked friendly, wealthy Muslim Damascus instead and lost.
Third Crusade	Pope Gregory VIII	Recapture Jerusalem	Acre and Jaffa recaptured, Richard and Saladin sign treaty to give Christian pilgrims access to Jerusalem.
Fourth Crusade	Pope Innocent III	Recapture Jerusalem	Constantinople sacked, Byzantine Emperor deposed, and Venetian puppet installed.
Fifth Crusade	Pope Honorius	Recapture Jerusalem	Sultan offers Jerusalem, clueless legate turns it down, then is forced to withdraw.
Sixth Crusade	Holy Roman Emperor Frederick II	Recapture Jerusalem	Frederick and Sultan of Egypt sign treaty of 1229, giving Jerusalem to Frederick.
Seventh Crusade	King Louis IX of France	Recapture Jerusalem	Objective changed to Cairo, Sultan of Egypt captures Louis.
Eighth Crusade	King Louis IX of France	Recapture Antioch and relieve Acre	Louis died of disease in North Africa.
Ninth Crusade	Prince Edward of England	Rescue King Louis IX	Truce at Acre in 1272. Acre fell in 1291, ending the crusading era.

[*] Phillips and Axelrod, 1:376–389.

Jerusalem aside, the Crusades were surprisingly irreligious. It was not until the end of the Second Crusade, fifty years after the First Crusade took Jerusalem, that the conflict between the Christian Kingdoms of Outremer and the neighboring Muslim principalities was drawn on religious lines. Strangely enough, the fall of Edessa that inspired the Second Crusade took place only because a careless Christian ruler had taken the greater part of his army to the aid of a Muslim ally. Without that single ecumenical but disastrous error in judgment, the Crusades would probably not be viewed today as the foremost example of religious warfare, and Zengi, who today is regarded as the first great anti-Western jihadist, would have continued to concentrate his efforts on his fellow Muslims.

> *Down to the rise of Zengi, the first prince who began to unite the emir-*
> *ates, the Franks were slowly but surely occupying the cities of the Infi-*
> *del.... The strange battle of Tel-basher in 1108 is worth notice. Tancred of*
> *Antioch and Joscelin, Lord of Tel-basher, had quarreled. So had Ridwan of*
> *Aleppo and Javaly of Mosul. Each allied himself with a stranger against*
> *his own co-religionist, and in the fight Frank fought with Frank and Turk*
> *with Turk. Tancred and Ridwan were victorious.*[28]

The rise of the aggressive atabeg of Mosul still resonates through-out history. Zengi, nominally loyal to the sultan of Baghdad, made war with equal enthusiasm against Muslims and Christians alike; it was for fear of him that the Emir of Damascus made an alliance with the King of Jerusalem. But Zengi was a supreme opportunist, and when Joscelin left Edessa insufficiently garrisoned in 1144 to help the bey of Hasankeyf attack Zengi's city of Aleppo, the atabeg was quick to take advantage, besieging Edessa and taking it in less than a month.[29] Prior to that, for more than a decade, Zengi had been fo-cused on obtaining the riches of Damascus. But despite twice besieg-ing it and arranging for the assassination of its emir, he was unable to take the city due to the military alliance between the Muslim Emir-ate of Damascus, the Christian Kingdom of Jerusalem, the Christian Principality of Antioch, and the Byzantine Empire, before being as-sassinated himself in 1146.

The history of Muslim-Christian cooperation in the Holy Land during the early part of the crusading era only makes the fatal greed and treachery of the Second Crusade all the more deplorable. From the beginning, there was less enthusiasm for reclaiming Edessa than there had been for retaking Jerusalem. The common people were far less interested in the fate of a minor county than the Holy City and Bernard of Clairvaux found it necessary to sell the Crusade as a means of obtaining absolution. St. Bernard's clever marketing did the trick and this time a much more impressive assortment of nobles and even royalty took the cross, including the King and Queen of France, the Count of Flanders, the Count of Toulouse, the Count of Champagne,

---

[28] Oman, 256.

[29] This brilliant military action is considered to mark the start of the anti-Crusader jihad, although there would likely have been no subsequent jihad had the Second Crusade remained on target.

the Earl of Surry, the King of Germany, and the Duke of Swabia.[30]

But royal blood does not flow with any inherent honor, for when the King of Jerusalem's High Court met in Acre on June 24, 1148, representatives from Edessa and Antioch were conspicuously absent. Many crusaders began to think about the tempting wealth of Damascus, with whom King Baldwin III was allied against Zengi's son, the Emir of Aleppo. While the French only wanted to go home, having been badly mauled by the Turks on their long march to Acre, the Germans saw more profit in the idea of conquering one of the Holy Land's wealthiest cities instead of helping Joscelin regain Edessa. In the end, King Baldwin foolishly joined with King Conrad III of Germany in convincing the Christians to attack friendly Muslim Damascus instead of enemy-held Edessa.

The attack was an abysmal failure. The large size of the crusading army left Mu'in ad-Din, the Emir of Damascus, no choice but to reluctantly ask both of Zengi's heirs, Nur ad-Din of Aleppo and Saif ad-Din Ghazi of Mosul, for help. Although the crusaders were driven off after an unsuccessful four-day siege prior to Nur ad-Din's arrival, as Mu'in ad-Din had feared he was forced to acknowledge the Emir of Aleppo as his overlord. The chastened crusaders returned to Europe having gained little wealth and having lost much honor. Less than a year later, Prince Raymond of Antioch found himself fighting against Damascus as well as Aleppo when he was slain by Nur ad-Din at the Battle of Inab. Nur ad-Din died in 1174, whereupon his widow married a brilliant general who also happened to be the governor of Egypt. Her new husband did not hesitate to proclaim himself the Sultan of Egypt, and soon afterward, the Sultan of Syria, too. His name was Saladin.

The wages of the Second Crusaders' sin of treachery was death for Outremer. Jerusalem, Antioch, and Acre did not fall overnight; it would be another thirty-nine years before Jerusalem fell to Saladin and 143 years before Acre was taken by the Mamluk Sultan Kalil. Not all fatal wounds are immediately apparent; during the final siege of Acre in 1291, the Grand Master of the Knights Templar abruptly dropped his sword and turned away from the battle. When his knights protested his apparent cowardice, he replied: "I'm not running

---

[30] The future Holy Roman Emperor, Frederick I Barbarossa.

away; I am dead. Here is the blow." He then showed them the mortal wound that would soon kill him.

The Christian betrayal of a Muslim friend was the mortal wound that transformed the Crusades from a victorious divine mission into two centuries of war between Christianity and Islam. It was not an act motivated by faith, it was an act of supreme faithlessness in violation of every Christian precept. And it was costly—an examination of the eight Crusades that followed the initial recovery of Jerusalem will show that even when they were successful, any gains they made were quickly lost to a Muslim world that had united against them. Sir Stephen Runciman, who wrote the classic history of the crusading era, concluded that in contrast to the astonishing success of the First Crusade, the disasters of the eight subsequent ones are an object lesson in the tragedy that can take place when religious ideals are perverted by Man's sinful nature.

> *The triumphs of the Crusade were the triumphs of faith. But faith without wisdom is a dangerous thing. By the inexorable laws of history the whole world pays for the crimes and follies of each of its citizens. In the long sequence of interaction and fusion between Orient and Occident out of which our civilization has grown, the Crusades were a tragic and destructive episode. The historian as he gazes back across the centuries at their gallant story must find his admiration overcast by sorrow at the witness that it bears to the limitations of human nature. There was so much courage and so little honor, so much devotion and so little understanding. High ideals were besmirched by cruelty and greed, enterprise and endurance by a blind and narrow self-righteousness; and the Holy War itself is nothing more than a long act of intolerance in the name of God, which is the sin against the Holy Ghost.*[31]

But although the Crusades will likely remain the model of Christian holy war for the foreseeable future, the reason that they are no longer at the forefront of atheist attacks on Christianity is because it is difficult, and growing increasingly harder, to shake a disapproving finger at the actions of men who were faced with the challenge of a militant and expanding Ummah at their borders. Overconfi-

---

[31] Runciman, Steven. Vol. 3 of *A History of the Crusades*. Cambridge: The University Press, 1954. 480.

dent due to its success in running roughshod over a wealth-sapped Western Christianity, modern secular society is simply not conceptually suited to dealing with a faith of the sword. The vacuous recommendations of Sam Harris in response to the global jihad would surely be considered laughable by the battle-hardened Byzantines, who watched in despair as their proud, centuries-old civilization was overrun by its historical antecedent.

"Conversational" intolerance is a toothless weapon, and the other alternative suggested by Harris, preemptive mass murder, can only be rejected by every decent human being as more intolerable than the problem it purports to solve. A better answer can be found in the Crusades, in the very failures pinpointed by Runciman. It is faith, but combined with wisdom this time, that can provide what was once Christendom with the spirit that it needs to survive and allow the civilization that it spawned centuries ago to thrive again.

The battle is already being waged, by men such as Peter Akinola, the Archbishop of Nigeria, who leads the fast-growing Anglican Church in Africa,[32] and whose answer to the violent and unprovoked attacks on Christians in his country is as simple as it is astonishingly effective: "Make the church grow."

The secular faith in democracy and material wealth is too weak, too vague, too societally enervating, to provide the post-Christian West with the spiritual steel it requires for survival. Democracy's failures in Algeria, in Turkey,[33] in Iraq, in Pakistan, and in Palestine prove that Enlightenment ideals are not sufficient for the task, either. Just as a doctor cannot inoculate against a specific virus by using a randomly selected vaccine, not any meme is capable of effectively competing with a powerful and highly infectious one. The choice facing Western society today is the same as it was 1,000 years ago: the cross or the crescent.

---

[32] "To modern, liberal, Western eyes, Dr. Akinola is at the most extreme end of fundamentalist Christianity.... More importantly, he is in the front line of relations between Christianity and Islam. In the northern, Sharia states of Nigeria, Christians have been driven from their looted homes, even murdered. The relationship with Islam is central to his ministry and he has found a way to counter Islam without violence: it is called evangelism." "For God's Sake." The Times, 5 July 2007.

[33] Four military coups in forty years is no evidence of democratic success. And the Islamist party known as the AKP just won the parliamentary elections for the second consecutive time.

THE AZTEC EMPIRE AND HUMAN SACRIFICE

If one looks at the history of the world, there are two facts that no reasonable man can deny: first, that people do bad things, and second, that religion has been central to people's lives for as long as history has been recorded. The centrality of religion in past societies means that it has been a mechanism for an amount of these bad things people have done, which occasionally makes it appear that religion is the source of the evil behavior. And while it pains me to make use of a much-overused expression, in this case, it is absolutely true that correlation is not causation.

The Unholy Trinity make no effort to provide any evidence of a causal relationship between religion and the various evils they cite as proof of religion's historically deadly and venomous nature. Instead, they provide a laundry list of historical events that bear varying degrees of tangential relationship to religion, from the *a priori* causal to the entirely oxymoronic. The most famous example of the former is probably the Aztec practice of mass human sacrifice to the gods Huitzilopochtli, Tezcatlipoca, Huehueteotl, Tlaloc, and Xipe Totec, through which the Aztecs were believed to have murdered as many as 250,000 individuals per year toward the end of the fifteenth century. An example of the latter is the ludicrous attempt to blame the brutal atheist repression of religion in the Soviet Union on religious faith.

The correlation between the Aztec religion and the human sacrifices is undeniable. The sacrifices were intended to repay Man's debt to the gods, to maintain the circle of life and death, to postpone the heat-death of the universe, to bring rain, and to avoid plague. However, the need for life, the universe, and everything preceded the massive sacrifices that made Aztec culture so infamous, indeed, such large-scale butchery was not even possible until an empire had been established ruling over hundreds of the city-states known as *altepetl*. Like most empires, the Aztec Empire was ethnically diverse, and the Mexica people who ruled it were outnumbered by their subjects; the Aztec Empire was actually a triple alliance of the Mexica city of Tenochtitlan with the Acolhua people of Texcoco and the Tepanecs of Tlacopán.

A ruling people surrounded and outnumbered by their subjects require a mechanism to enable them to maintain their position of primacy. There is a need to prevent the ratio of the population delta between rulers and ruled from getting out of hand as well as a necessity to inspire enough fear in the subjected populace to prevent it from rebelling on a regular basis. In light of these imperial necessities, it is important to note that the Mexica decision to ally with the Acolhua and Tepanec people occurred sixty years before the bloody reconsecration of the Great Pyramid at Tenochtitlan by the Aztec leader Ahuitzotl, and that it was the fifteen years of Ahuitzotl's reign that marked the high point of the Aztec Empire. Nor should it come as a surprise that the people who made up most of the involuntary sacrifices were not Mexica, Acolhua, or Tepanec, but rather prisoners taken from their subject peoples and the surrounding enemy tribes.

It is even more significant that according to Bernardino de Sahagún, the Franciscan missionary to the Nahua now known as the father of modern ethnography, the Aztecs did not defend the practice of human sacrifice on religious grounds, but instead argued that it was no different than the European method of waging warfare. This attitude strongly suggests that the primary impetus behind their mass human sacrifice was, as Clausewitz once described warfare, diplomacy by other means. This does not completely exonerate religion from its intimate involvement in the abominable practice, of course, but indicates that the matter must be considered more deeply before we can realistically conclude that religion was or was not the cause of Aztec human sacrifice.

The important question is this: Is it religion or the establishment and maintenance of empire that is more often accompanied by the mass slaughter of a recently subjected people? If we consider the worst examples of religious slaughter other than the sacrifices at Tenochtitlan, such as the massacres of the French Huguenots, the harrying of the Jews, the witch burnings, the sack of Jerusalem, and the indiscriminate violence of the Thirty Years' War, none of them can really be described as lethal violence inflicted by a ruling elite on a more numerous subject people.[34] However, there are many

---

[34] Except, of course, for the Peasants' War aspect of the Thirty Years' War. But that was only one part of the whole.

historical examples of imperial massacres committed for reasons of policy with no apparent religious component, such as Temujin's innovation of wiping out a substantial proportion of his new subjects, a governing technique he developed in order to solve the problem of the inconclusive nature of steppe warfare while reducing potential threats to Mongol supremacy.

> *The Khan's intention to wipe out his enemies on a large scale came as a shock to them, since it went beyond anything to which they were accustomed.... [The linchpin] was a not unknown procedure, though it had never been applied on quite such a vast scale. Prisoners were led past the wheel of a wagon. Those who were taller than the linchpin were beheaded; the children, who were smaller, survived to be taken into the Mongol armies when they grew up.*[35]

And yet his treatment of the Jurkin was gentle in comparison with the vengeance he took upon the Tangut for their refusal to aid him in his war against the Khwarezmian Empire. Nor was the Great Khan the only ruler to make a habit of taking massive measures intended to shock potentially disloyal subjects into abject submission. When Julius Caesar wished to teach the insufficiently pacified Celts a lesson during the Gallic Wars, he rounded up all 53,000 members of the defeated Aduatuci tribe and auctioned them off as slaves in a single giant auction.

He was even crueler when dealing with the German tribes of the Usipetes and Tenctheri; when the Germans defeated a force of his cavalry, Caesar feared that the Roman defeat might inspire the many conquered tribes of Gaul to further rebellion and took effective, but brutal measures to forestall them. Caesar's infantry burst into the huge German camp, taking them by surprise. The women and children ran, but instead of being permitted to flee unmolested as was normally the case, they were pursued by the Roman cavalry who had been given orders to hunt them down. The sound of their families being slaughtered destroyed the morale of the German warriors and permitted them to be routed easily by the outnumbered Roman infantry. Caesar writes that of more than 400,000 Germans, "a large

---

[35] Lister, R. P. *Genghis Khan*. New York: P. Davies, 1969.

number were killed, and the rest plunged into the water and perished" while the Romans didn't lose a single legionary.[36]

These are three of many historical examples. From King Sargon II's enslavement of the 27,290 Israelites that brought an end to the rebellious kingdom of Israel to Alexander the Great's slaughter of the 7,000 surrendered Indians at Massaga and Sherman's March through Georgia, empires have made use of mass violence to send an unmistakable message to their conquered subjects. Given this historical reality, the most reasonable conclusion is that the Aztecs' massive human sacrifices probably had as much, if not more, to do with imperial policy than with genuine religious motivation. The history of imperialism suggests that when faced with a diverse group of subjects known to be prone to rebellion, some form of mass slaughter is highly probable; it is only surprising that such actions were not more often cloaked in religion.

> *Heaven brings forth innumerable things to help man.*
> *Man has nothing with which to recompense Heaven.*
> *Kill. Kill. Kill. Kill. Kill. Kill. Kill.*

This was the inscription with which Chang Hsien-chung commemorated the savage bloodbath that baptized his reign as the emperor of the Great Western Kingdom in 1644. His capital city of Chengdu, which had once been home to 400,000 inhabitants, was nearly devoid of humanity by 1685. And although Chang's inscription has religious overtones, it is more properly understood as the despairing cry of a nihilist who has been driven to the point of madness by his overriding will to power. Three centuries later, the Yellow Tiger's lament was echoed by the slogan of the Moscow-ordered policy with which the Chinese Communist Party inspired the Hunan Uprising of 1928. "Burn, burn, burn! Kill, kill, kill!"[37]

It is not religion, but the desire to obtain power over others and the need to maintain it that is the common theme throughout these historical tales of horror. Religion is one of many guises under

---

[36] Caesar, Gaius Julius. *The Conquest of Gaul*, Penguin Classics, 1983. 94. The 430,000 is almost surely a large exaggeration, but there's no reason to doubt Caesar's claim to have wiped out both of the German tribes.

[37] Chang and Halliday, 72.

which this drive can be cloaked, but judging by the comparatively few examples that can be assigned to it, it is not one of the more effective ones. And even when religion does happen to be used in this way, it is inevitably intertwined with the secular power of government. It was the Spanish Crown, not the Church, which conceived and controlled the Spanish Inquisition, and the Aztec priests would have had no sacrifices to offer if they were not provided large quantities of victims captured in the Flower Wars of the Aztec kings.

Even the most obvious modern example of religion-inspired harm is ultimately a matter of secular power. Bin Laden and the al-Qaeda terrorists have attacked the West to achieve a specific military goal, the withdrawal of Western troops from Saudi Arabia and Iraq. And the Muslims now inhabiting the former Christendom are not agitating for the right to practice their religion, but rather to achieve greater political influence in those countries to which they have immigrated.

There is an institution that has caused great harm to humanity, which is responsible for nearly all the wars, all the mass atrocities and untold human suffering throughout history, but it is not religion. That institution is government. And regardless of whether you consider government to be a necessary evil or the source of all that is good in society, it cannot be denied that it is the institution of government that bears the direct responsibility for every tangible evil that the New Atheists have accused religion of committing.

If religion vanished today, the vast majority of human conflicts would still exist. Furthermore, the basis for the moral systems upon which most of humanity depends for guidance would be gone; the great twentieth-century experiment with godlessness suggests that this would cause many new conflicts to explode where one religion-based conflict had been before.

The New Atheist argument against religion is a category error. Whether God exists or not, whether people believe in the concept of a deity or not, religion is simply incapable of causing great harm to humanity. It can only be a scapegoat, because it does not provide the primary motivation or the means for crime, for war, or for repression and massacre. One might as reasonably blame plate tectonics for creating the physical geography that has played such a significant role in determining historical patterns of conflict. Even on the rare

occasions when religion can be positively correlated with the incidence of great harm, a closer examination will usually show that it is neither the controlling nor the causal factor. The individual will to power does not exist because of religion, nor does the institution of government. In neither case is religious motivation required to inspire them to murderous action and there are more historical examples of religion acting as a mitigating force on their lethal proclivities than as an exacerbating one.

One might protest that it is impossible to conceive of a world without government, but then, the idea is no more far-fetched than the vision of a world without religion. And there are certainly far fewer individuals with an exceptional will to power and the ambition to control the lives of others than possess a modicum of faith in God.

XIII

THE RED HAND
OF ATHEISM

Atheism is the core of the whole Soviet system.

—ALEKSANDR I. SOLZHENITSYN, "The Oak and the Calf"

ACH MEMBER OF THE UNHOLY TRINITY demonstrates some level of concern with finding a way to assert that atheism is in no way to blame for the murderous atrocities of Communism, deservedly infamous for committing the worst mass murders in Man's history. Dawkins and Hitchens are both fully aware of how badly the lethal record of atheists holding absolute power undermines their case against religion and they are eager to find some way of explaining this record in a manner that allows them to separate the actions of the responsible individuals from their denial of the existence of God.

The bumbling Harris, on the other hand, appears to be genuinely surprised in his afterword to the paperback edition (published a year after the hardcover) that his single paragraph blaming the actions of Stalin and Mao on "unjustified belief" is insufficient to convince anyone that the correlation between their atheism and their murderous acts is nothing more than unfortunate coincidence. But while Harris's minimalist case was dismissed on logical and syntactical grounds in Chapter VII,[1] the related arguments made by Dawkins and Hitchens require more consideration.

Hitchens begins with integrity and historical competence by confessing that the charge that secular and atheist regimes have committed worse crimes than their religious counterparts cannot be avoided and even admitting that it would be reasonable to say that secular totalitarianism is "the *summa* of human evil." Unfortunately, instead of looking at the obvious question of why secular totalitarianism should have proved to be much worse than religious-inspired evils, Hitchens drifts off into a tangential discussion on totalitarianism from which he never returns. This tangent is particularly unfortunate for Hitchens, as he makes an elementary logical error of the sort that one normally expects of Harris. After explaining how the concept of totalitarianism was coined by a Marxist describing Stalin's rule and was popularized by Hannah Arendt in *The Origins of Totalitarianism,* and noting that the term is useful because it distinguishes between ordinary despotism and absolutist systems, Hitchens promptly turns around and begins arguing with himself on the very next page:

> For most of human history, the idea of the total or absolute state was intimately bound up with religion. . . . We now value the few exceptions from antiquity—such as Periclean Athens with all its deformities—precisely because there were a few moments when humanity did not live in permanent terror of a Pharaoh or Nebuchadnezzar or Darius whose least word was holy law.[2]

But the divine right of kings, even the antique notion of divine royalty, didn't begin to approach the total domination of all aspects of the state exhibited by the Soviet and Nazi regimes. This is why a

---

[1] In case you've forgotten, Harris first claimed that the actions of history's two most infamous atheists were due to "unjustified belief" and then on "an absence of rationality" without ever demonstrating either. Even worse, he was trying to confuse the reader by substituting "unjustified belief" and "an absence of rationality" with "religious faith." It boils down to a logically fallacious No True Atheist argument.

[2] Hitchens, 230–231.

separate term was required in the first place, and why Hitchens himself rightly declares it to be useful. His example of Darius is particularly strange, as the great Persian king was a worshipper of Ahura Mazda who tolerated other faiths enough to pay for their shrines and allow the Jews to rebuild their temple in Jerusalem, who ruled over a decentralized empire with hereditary satraps, and dutifully accepted his subjugation to the historic laws of the Medes and Persians. In pointing to Darius as a totalitarian ruler, Hitchens was apparently thinking of the biblical stories of Esther and Daniel, both of which refer to the way in which the king's every written and signed decree was deemed unalterable law.[3] But setting aside the fact that a written public decree is not a "least word," these examples show that not even the Persian king was above the Persian law, thus providing more evidence that Darius the Great was not an absolutist ruler presiding over a totalitarian state.

Hitchens's statement that there were few exceptions to totalitarianism in antiquity is equivalent to asserting that most historical states were totalitarian. This is obviously untrue; of his eight specific examples, the monarchies of China, India, and Persia, the Aztec and Inca Empires, and the medieval courts of Spain, France, and Russia, the only one that could even remotely be described as totalitarian is the latter. Hitchens has it entirely backward, as most of humanity did not live in permanent terror of its kings and emperors, indeed, for most of history, the inhabitants of any ancient or medieval kingdom tended to look to the person of their supreme ruler to protect them from the depredations of their local officials, assuming they even knew who he was. Professor Frithjof Kuhnen of the University of Göttingen cites numerous examples from Moghul India and medieval Korea showing how weak rulers who lost control over their tax collectors inadvertently caused oppression of the peasants so vicious that it forced them to flee the land, sometimes to the point of depopulating entire regions.[4]

---

[3] "Now, O king, issue the decree and put it in writing so that it cannot be altered—in accordance with the laws of the Medes and Persians, which cannot be repealed." Daniel 6:8. This was how the king was manipulated into throwing Daniel into the lions' den. It is impossible to imagine Hitler or Stalin executing anyone they did not want to simply because the law demanded it. The whole point of being a totalitarian dictator is to be above the law, after all.

[4] Frithjof Kuhnen, "The Development of Man-Land Relations in Asia." Quarterly Journal of International Agriculture, 1 (1989). 64–79.

If one accepts Arendt's definition of totalitarianism, as Hitchens does, one must also recall that she traced its origins back to the early nineteenth century. This is a strong indication that the ancient and medieval rulers were not totalitarian, however cruel and capricious some of them may have been. The significant difference between the nature of the modern totalitarian state and that of history's many tyrants is the very reason for Arendt's coining the new term in the first place. A particularly important element of Arendt's work is her recognition that despite the racist elements of Nazism, totalitarian rule tends to be fundamentally opposed to the concept of national sovereignty,[5] which was one of the factors that led her to correctly conclude that the Italian Fascists were not totalitarians, their close ideological kinship to the Communists and National Socialists not-withstanding.

Hitchens himself goes even further astray with the Fascists, to say nothing of the Moonies, the Afrikaners, the Shah of Iran, and the Taliban, as the seven pages he spends discussing them—30 percent of his chapter entitled "The 'Case' Against Secularism"—have little to do with either secularism or mass murder by the atheist state, and he raises the internationally sophisticated reader's eyebrows by praising the African National Congress for saving South African so-ciety from complete barbarism and implosion. As the mordant African joke now has it, "What's the difference between Mugabe and Mbeki?"[6] "About ten years." One concludes that Hitchens must not have visited Sun City in a while, at least not since South Africa surpassed Colombia to become the murder capital of the world in 2002, eight years after the end of apartheid.[7]

And while attempting to draw a link between the Catholic aph-orism "*extra ecclesiasm, nulla salus*"[8] with what he tells us is one of Fidel Castro's favorite sayings—"Within the revolution anything. Outside of the Revolution—nothing."—Hitchens unexpectedly fails to recognize that the Cuban dictator's saying is actually inspired by the phrase that Benito Mussolini used to describe the heart of the

---

[5] Another warning sign about the grand humanist project known as the European Union. And the African Union. And the North American Union. . . .

[6] The dictator of Zimbabwe and the President of South Africa, respectively.

[7] Phillips, Barnaby. "Living in SA's crime capital." BBC News, 11 April 2002.

[8] "*Outside the Church there is no salvation.*"

Fascist philosophy: "*Tutto nello Stato, niente al di fuori dello Stato, nulla contro lo Stato.*"[9]

Hitchens also leaves out the fact of Mussolini's atheism and former Communism, and that the Fascists' Lateran Treaty with the Vatican was a truce between two hostile and powerful Italian organizations, not the mutually admiring alliance he portrays. He also makes a factual error in declaring that Mussolini "had barely seized power" before reaching the accord with the Church; actually, the March on Rome that gave Mussolini the Prime Ministership took place seven years before the Lateran Treaty was signed on June 7, 1929, almost ten years to the day after Mussolini published the manifesto in which he called for the Church's abolition.[10]

The scare quotes in the chapter's name would have been much more appropriate had Hitchens entitled it "A 'Defense' of Secularism," as it is not so much an ineffective defense against the argument that secular atheism is a direct cause of the heights of human evil as it is a nonexistent one.

As for Dawkins, the Oxford scientist deals with the matter by engaging in his customary bait-and-switch. The seven pages of the section entitled "What About Hitler And Stalin? Weren't They Athiests?" is almost entirely dedicated to Hitler, with only a single paragraph addressing the uncomfortable fact of Stalin's atheism. While Dawkins manfully confesses that the Soviet dictator was without question an atheist, he does not neglect to mention Stalin's seminary training and equates the significance of the incorrect presumption that Hitler and Stalin were both atheists with the fact that they, like Saddam Hussein, both also possessed mustaches.

What matters is not whether Hitler and Stalin were atheists, but whether atheism systematically influences people to do bad things. There is not the smallest evidence that it does.[11]

---

[9] "*Everything in the State, nothing outside the State, nothing against the State.*"

[10] The second point of the fourth plank in the Fascist Manifesto, written and published by Mussolini on June 6, 1919, declares: "*The seizure of all the possessions of the religious congregations and the abolition of all the bishoprics, which constitute an enormous liability on the Nation and on the privileges of the poor.*"

[11] Dawkins, *The God Delusion*, 273.

Again Dawkins reveals his historical ignorance, and again, he demonstrates that he is not so much a bad scientist as an atheist propagandist who has abandoned science altogether. For there is not only the smallest evidence that atheism correlates with people doing very bad things, the evidence is so strong that it is almost surely causal. Dawkins, like Harris, focuses on the wrong question. Like medieval philosophers they focus on the explanatory logic of the perceived problem, and they do so ineptly, instead of examining the matter in a scientific manner by observing the relevant evidence. Dawkins cannot think of why a war would be fought in the name of atheism—a more relevant question would be to wonder why millions of individuals would be slaughtered by their own government in the name of atheism—but this is putting the cart well before the horse.

No one really cares why atheists kill innocent people *en masse*. People are primarily concerned with the undeniable fact that atheists do it with such an astonishing degree of regularity on the rare occasions that they find themselves in a position to do so.

And now for a few microscopic pieces of the evidence that Dawkins cannot seem to locate. Christendom may be considered to have begun in 392, when the Roman Emperor Theodosius the Great established Christianity as the official state religion of the empire. From that date, there were approximately 126 emperors of the Western and Eastern empires until the fall of Byzantium in 1453. If one adds to that total the roughly sixty-five kings who ruled over each of the twenty-seven member states of the geographical area formerly known as Christendom since Charlemagne was crowned Holy Roman Emperor in 800 A.D., one calculates a very conservative estimate of 1,781 Christian kings and emperors ruling as theocratic monarchs over their royal or imperial subjects. This number is probably too small by at least an order of magnitude, given Jared Diamond's previous estimate of 1,000 European principalities, but it is more than sufficient to prove the point and it would take far too long to do the research required to calculate the precise number. Although those 1,781 Christian rulers, like rulers everywhere, engaged in wars and indulged in murders and committed plenty of other deplorable deeds, very, very few of them ever engaged in a systematic act of mass murder that can be reasonably described as anything approaching the crimes of the sort committed by Stalin. Nor did most of their later successors, who did not rule by blood and divine decree but instead governed with varying degrees of consent from the populace, with the singular exception of a certain German Reichskanzler.[12]

By all accounts, the slaughter of the Protestant Huguenots known as the St. Bartholomew's Day Massacre was the most infamous of medieval Christendom.[13] It was the low point of the thirty-six years of the Wars of Religion, which in addition to the religious component was a struggle between the House of Guise and the House of Bourbon for the throne of France. And while the massacre was not ordered by King Charles IX—it was at the instigation of his mother, Catherine de' Medici, of the famously ruthless Italian family—it was blessed with his approval. The murder of an estimated 10,000 Frenchmen over the period of several months by the French crown horrified all Christendom. Even the king's father-in-law, the Holy Roman Emperor, denounced it, and the young king went to his early grave crying out "What evil council I have followed! O my God, forgive me!"

And yet, had this worst of all the medieval monarchs of Christendom been an atheist, and had he been responsible for killing twice as many of his subjects as he in fact was, he would still not be numbered among the ranks of the fifty most lethal atheist leaders in history. This is not to excuse or justify Charles IX's historical villainy, but it is necessary to view such acts in perspective, especially when the New Atheists are claiming that it is religion's potential to inspire murderous violence that justifies their attacks on it.

There has only been one officially atheist country in history, the Albanian dictatorship of Enver Hoxha, which declared itself to be

---

[12] I considered the propriety of including Robert Mugabe, who was raised Catholic and married in a Catholic ceremony, but is an avowedly Marxist dictator, on either side, but finally concluded it would be best just to leave him out. The allegiance of modern African leaders to their nominal ideologies and religions is seldom as cleanly defined as one would like.

[13] While it would be irresponsible to fail to remark on the infamous medieval slaughters of the Jews by Christian mobs, it must be recalled that Jews were seldom numerous in any Christian kingdom; there were only 80,000 Jews in all of Spain after eight centuries of Muslim tolerance. Jewish persecution simply wasn't murder on the modern scale; for example, the worst attack in the history of English Jewry, the Clifford's Tower massacre, resulted in the deaths of 150 Jews. Moreover, these attacks seldom took place with royal approval—after the anti-Jewish riots at Westminster in 1189, Richard I hanged three of the instigators.

the world's first atheist state in September 1967.[14] However, there have been twenty-eight countries in world history that can be confirmed to have been ruled by regimes with avowed atheists at the helm, beginning with the First French Republic and ending with the four atheist regimes currently extant: the People's Republic of China, the Democratic People's Republic of Korea, the Lao People's Democratic Republic, and the Socialist Republic of Vietnam. These twenty-eight historical regimes have been ruled by eighty-nine atheists, of whom more than half have engaged in democidal[15] acts of the sort committed by Stalin and Mao and are known to have murdered at least 20,000 of their own citizens.[16]

The total body count for the ninety years between 1917 and 2007 is approximately 148 million dead at the bloody hands of fifty-two atheists, three times more than all the human beings killed by war, civil war, and individual crime in the entire twentieth century combined.[17] The historical record of collective atheism is thus 182,716 times worse on an annual basis than Christianity's worst and most infamous misdeed, the Spanish Inquisition. It is not only Stalin and Mao who were so murderously inclined, they were merely the worst of the whole Hell-bound lot. For every Pol Pot whose infamous name is still spoken with horror today, there was a Mengistu, a Bierut, and a Choibalsan, godless men whose names are now forgotten everywhere

---

[14] "*The closing of 2,169 churches, mosques, monasteries and other religious institutions during the past six months represents the concluding phase of the campaign against formal religious institutions and at the same time the intensification of the final phase aimed at eliminating the informal manifestations of religion in Albania.*" "Albania Claims: 'First Atheist State in the World,'" Radio Free Europe, 9 Oct. 1967.

[15] Prof. Rummel's term coined to describe government-instigated mass murder of its own citizens.

[16] All numbers taken from Prof. Rummel's estimates at http://www.hawaii.edu/powerkills/SOD. TAB16A.1.GIF with some minor updates from newer Rummel figures. The calculations provided are the mid-range for a total of 148 million victims of Communism, although death tolls as high as 260 million in the twentieth century have been estimated. Note that some known Communist countries are not listed here, for example, the state murders committed by the Nicaraguan Sandinista regime and the People's Republic of South Yemen numbered 5,000 people or less. In some cases, such as Kampuchea and Laos, the numbers reflect the victims of more than one Communist regime, for example, the Khmer Rouge ruled Kampuchea from 1975–1978, after which the Vietnamese-installed puppet government ruled until 1991. Both regimes committed mass murders, although the Khmer Rouge were ten times as deadly as their successors.

[17] Prof. Rummel estimates 38.5 million people killed in all the wars and civil wars throughout the twentieth century. Averaging the published murder rates for the four largest "countries" in the world, China, India, the U.S.A., and the EU, at their respective high points, I calculated an approximate global murder rate of 3.12 per 100,000 population and multiplied it by an average twentieth-century population of 3.82 billion to reach an estimated 11.9 million private murder victims in the twentieth century. See chapter VII, footnote 39.

Country	Dates	Murders
Afghanistan	1978–1992	1,750,000
Albania	1944–1985	100,000
Angola	1975–2002	125,000
Bulgaria	1944–1989	222,000
China/PRC	1923–2007	76,702,000
Cuba	1959–1992	73,000
Czechoslovakia	1948–1968	65,000
Ethiopia	1974–1991	1,343,610
France	1793–1794	40,000
Greece	1946–1949	20,000
Hungary	1948–1989	27,000
Kampuchea/Cambodia	1973–1991	2,627,000
Laos	1975–2007	93,000
Mongolia	1926–2007	100,000
Mozambique	1975–1990	118,000
North Korea	1948–2007	3,163,000
Poland	1945–1948	1,607,000
Romania	1948–1987	438,000
Spain (Republic)	1936–1939	102,000
U.S.S.R.	1917–1987	61,911,000
Vietnam	1945–2007	1,670,000
Yugoslavia	1944–1980	1,072,000

but in the lands they once ruled with a red hand.

Is a 58 percent chance that an atheist leader will murder a noticeable percentage of the population over which he rules sufficient evidence that atheism does, in fact, provide a systematic influence to do bad things? If that is not deemed to be conclusive, how about the fact that the *average* atheist crime against humanity is 18.3 million percent worse than the *very worst* depredation committed by Christians, even though atheists have had less than one-twentieth the number of opportunities with which to commit them. If one considers the statistically significant size of the historical atheist set and contrasts it with the fact that not one in a thousand religious leaders have committed similarly large-scale atrocities, it is impossible to conclude otherwise, even if we do not yet understand exactly why this should be the case. Once might be an accident, even twice could be coincidence, but fifty-two incidents in ninety years reeks of causation! No doubt this is why the Unholy Trinity attempt to limit the discussion of secular evil to Stalin and Mao.

In *god is not Great*, Christopher Hitchens makes a halfhearted attempt to suggest that the lethality of the modern atheist leader could only be an artifact of the availability of more efficient means of killing people,[18] but this lackluster defense falls apart when confronted by the staggeringly vicious slaughters committed by technologically challenged killers such as Chang Hsien-chung, Genghis Khan, and Selum the Grim,[19] to say nothing of the lack of interest shown by most non-atheist leaders in making similar use of their own advanced weaponry. But the former Marxist, who presumably knows one strain of socialism from another, ventures upon more fruitful ground when he mentions that in his opinion, the ostensible Communism of the mad butchers of the North Korean mortocracy is less Marxist ideology than it is a "debased yet refined form of Confucianism and ancestor worship."

This variance from the creed is true of most Communisms: the ideology of the Peruvian Shining Path differs from the pure Maoism of its Chinese originator, which in turn bears little resemblance to the Ethiopian Communism of the Derg regime or the extreme anti-intellectual ruralism of the Khmer Rouge. Even within a single regime, communist ideology tended to vary greatly. For example, the Leninist revision that perverted the industrial vision of Marx and substituted a backward rural peasantry for an urban proletariat after the October Revolution saw further modification once the battle between the internationalist Trotsky and the author of the "socialism in one country" doctrine, Stalin, was decided in favor of the latter. As much as I dislike agreeing in any way with revisionist Communist apologists, I must confess they have a legitimate point when they question the accuracy of applying the same ideological label to the international post-industrial scientific socialism of Marx and the nationalist pre-industrial peasant socialism of Mao.

---

[18] Thanks, science!

[19] It's bad enough when your ruler is known as "the Great." If he's called "the Grim," a change of address might be in order.

But no matter how far a murderous Communist dictator departs from the formal creed of scientific socialism, one factor always remains the same: his conviction that there is no God to whom he must ultimately answer for his deeds and that any evidence of that God must be destroyed.

> *The program of the Communist International also clearly states that Communists fight against religion. . . . Remember that the struggle against religion is a struggle for socialism.*
>
> —EMILIAN YAROSLAVSKY,
> Pravda editor and Chief of the Union of the Militant Godless[20]

G. K. Chesterton wrote that once Man ceases to believe in God, he does not believe in nothing, but will instead find himself capable of believing almost anything. This is why, as Christopher Hitchens notes in *god is not Great*, Communists in the Soviet Union and North Korea sought to replace religion, although it is demonstrably incorrect to insist, as Hitchens does, that they were not trying to negate it as well. For if it were merely a matter of substituting one religion for another, Lenin would not have insisted that "Atheism is a material and inseparable part of Marxism," Trotsky would not have asserted that the "very essence" of religion "is the mortal enemy of Communism,"[21] and the Bolsheviks would not have seen fit to honor the first atheist philosopher, Jean Meslier, in Moscow soon after the October Revolution.[22] The complete negation of religion was an explicit Soviet goal, for as the Russian Commission for the Rehabilitation of the Victims of Political Repression reported in 1995, 200,000 clergy were massacred as a part of Lenin's program of "merciless terror" against the Church.[23]

---

[20] "A not entirely enthusiastic participant last week was Dictator Joseph Stalin at the celebration by massed Communist delegations from all over Russia of the tenth anniversary of the founding in Moscow of the Union of the Militant Godless. This unprecedented Jubilee of Godlessness could only be compared to that celebrated by Bolsheviks in honor of the tenth anniversary of the Legalization in Russia of Abortion." "Godless Jubilee": Time Magazine, 17 Feb. 1936.

[21] Trotsky, Leon. Pravda, 24 June 1923.

[22] Onfray, Michel. "Jean Meslier and 'The Gentle Inclination of Nature.'" Translated by Marvin Mandell. New Politics, 2006.

[23] "Documents relate how clergymen, monks, nuns were crucified on royal gates and shot in the basements of the Cheka, scalped, strangled, drowned and submitted to other bestial tortures." Alexander Yakovlev, Chairman, Commission for the Rehabilitation of the Victims of Political Repression.

But what is the connection? What did Lenin and Trotsky see that Dawkins does not? Why should a belief in the nonexistence of God cause one individual to kill another, much less make it possible to predict that it will cause political leaders to liquidate large numbers of their own citizenry? How was it that Bertrand Russell was able to foresee the inevitable bloodshed to come in 1920, two years before Stalin became General Secretary and four years before he consolidated his power by banishing Trotsky? And even more importantly, why did the atheist Russell believe that the civilized world not only would, *but should*, risk a descent into barbarism by following the awful Soviet example?

> *The civilized world seems almost certain, sooner or later, to follow the example of Russia in attempting a Communist organization of society. I believe that the attempt is essential to the progress and happiness of [M]ankind during the next few centuries, but I believe also that the transition has appalling dangers. I believe that, if the Bolshevik theory as to the method of transition is adopted by Communists in Western nations, the result will be a prolonged chaos, leading neither to Communism nor to any other civilized system, but to a relapse into the barbarism of the Dark Ages.[24]*

The answer is that without a belief in that which transcends the natural, Man's ambition is limited to the material. These ambitions take many different forms, but intellectuals seem particularly drawn toward the idea of modifying human society according to their personal preferences. It may only be a coincidence, but it is interesting to note that many totalitarian rulers were not merely intelligent individuals, but intellectuals and the authors of what at times are still surprisingly insightful books. Hitler's critique of the irrelevant futility of Marx's obsession with class in *Mein Kampf* is more accurate than the objections posed by most contemporary economists, Christopher Hitchens comments favorably on Trotsky's prescience regarding future European developments, and both Lenin and Mussolini showed an unusual ability to turn a phrase. One of the great benefits of this literary loquacity on the part of modernity's most notorious

---

Fletcher, Philippa. "Inquiry Reveals Lenin Unleashed Systematic Murder of 200,000 Clergy." *Hobart Mercury*, 29 Nov. 1995.

[24] Russell, Bertrand. *The Practice and Theory of Bolshevism* (New York, 1920), 169.

killers is that it provides us with the ability to see into their thought processes decades after they have departed from the scene. And the one constant theme revealed in these various thought processes is the idea that Man can somehow be improved.

Lenin wished to create a New Soviet Man. Hitler declared that as Germany was built anew, the greatest task of the Volk was to raise a New Man. Mao's ambition was to build a new society and a new nation from the ancient Chinese people. Bertrand Russell wrote that man's salvation could only be *built* upon the firm foundation of "unyielding despair." Sam Harris informs us that there is no alternative to dictatorship—imposed, but benign—to bridge the gap from today's religious societies to tomorrow's secular utopia.[25]

In his book *Intellectuals*, the British historian Paul Johnson observes that intellectuals tend to focus on the abstract rather than tangible reality. While this is a useful and positive attribute when one is developing an entirely abstract concept such as string theory, constructing evolutionary stable strategies or creating a virtual world out of mathematics, art, and C compilers, it is rather less harmless when the abstract vision intersects with the harsh reality of human behavior. Human behavior seldom makes sense. In a rational world, no wealthy wife and mother would risk losing both her children and her comfortable life by dabbling with drugs, no professional football star would run the chance of injuring his body and voiding his multi-million dollar contract in order to ride a motorcycle, and no investment advisor would risk his gravy train in order to cheat a wealthy client out of a petty sum. And yet, every day, all around us, we see humans behaving in stupid, self-defeating, self-destructive, short-sighted, and nonsensical ways.

Christianity teaches that this is because man is hopelessly prone to evil, and that war and poverty will always be his curse due to his fallen nature. The Christian cannot hope to end these things, so he is content to work to ameliorate them where and when he can, according to the biblical commands. Islam, Hinduism, and Buddhism are even more fatalistic, teaching that worldly evils are respectively inevitable, merited, or illusion. In any case, none of the major religions offer any justification for attempting to fix Man's nature, since any

---

[25] Harris, *The End of Faith*, 151.

effort to do so is doomed to futility for a variety of reasons.

The atheist knows no such limits. Where the theist sees the inherent restrictions of human nature as created by God, the atheist sees nothing but the potential for human progress. What this progress is ultimately directed toward depends entirely on the particular vision; the ambitions of Pol Pot were certainly different than those of Lenin, Russell, or Harris, but regardless of what the final end is, the means and the stages through which the atheist visionary progresses will tend to be very similar, if not entirely the same. At each stage, most visionaries fail, indeed, few intellectuals ever even manage to articulate a semi-coherent vision, but even so, the process is a recognizable one that tends to proceed in six stages:

1. Persuasion
2. Deception
3. Ascension
4. Decision
5. Destruction
6. Renunciation

The initial stage of Persuasion is never very successful except in drawing a small band of true believers to share the dream. This is a peaceful attempt to convince others to see the vision and voluntarily join the cause and is the stage at which the humanists are today. The second stage, Deception, involves presenting targeted and misleading appeals to larger groups capable of being deceived into allying with or otherwise supporting the cause. This is the stage where the socialist greens pushing global warming as an excuse for stronger central government currently are, as well as the eurocrats of the European Union, although the latter, being more successful, are much further along in the process.

The third stage is Ascension, in which the visionary makes alliances with rival groups and consolidates his hold on political power. In a mostly peaceful transition to power, such as the Fascists and National Socialists managed, this stage primarily involves bluff and clever diplomacy. In a violent one, it usually involves fighting within and without the movement, as can be seen in the vicious struggle between the Bolsheviks and Mensheviks before, during, and after the October Revolution, until Lenin finally banned the Mensheviks in 1921.

It is the fourth stage, Decision, that is the crucial one, as it involves the hitherto successful visionary being forced to confront the reality that his abstract model simply does not function in the real world, either due to the idiosyncrasies of human behavior or fundamental flaws in his design. The visionary is thus presented with a choice to either abandon the model, adjust it to fit humanity, or attempt to force humanity to fit the model. Mussolini is a good example of an atheist visionary who adjusted his model, compromising his vision of a pure Fascist Italy in order to avoid direct confrontation with the Vatican and the large corporations. Because the original Fascist model was an improvement on its socialist predecessor, constructed to take advantage of human nature rather than war against it, there was little need for violence in order to fit the Italian population into the revised vision, thus aborting the fifth stage. Had Mussolini been more circumspect in his imperial ambitions or had the British government not alienated him over his invasion of Ethiopia,[26] Italy would likely have fought World War II on the side of the Allies, possibly prevented Hitler's takeover of Austria, and would probably still be Fascist today.

The reason Communism has so habitually devolved into violence is because it is an impressively stupid vision that violates both basic human nature in the form of the individual's desire for material betterment as well as the economic law of supply and demand. Its early institution was such a disaster that Lenin was quickly forced to revise some of his more dysfunctional policies, but he was the first in a long, lethal line of Communist leaders who made a practice of always attempting to force their populations to fit the Communist mold instead of adjusting the utopian vision to fit humanity. Indeed, the deadliest atheists are those who recognize the need to do away

---

[26] Manchester, William. *Alone 1932–1940*. Vol. 1 of *The Last Lion: Winston Spencer Churchill*. Boston: Little, Brown and Company, 1988. 160–161. Incompetent British foreign policy all but drove Mussolini into his Pact of Steel with Hitler. The ridiculous thing is that after irritating Mussolini into withdrawing from the Stresa Front, which was an alliance between Britain, France, and Italy against Nazi Germany, the French and British governments ended up offering him far more Ethiopian territory than his forces had been able to conquer in the first place. So, they managed to sell out Ethiopia and lose a vital ally at the same time.

with those who are not capable of fitting the mold long before they reach the fourth stage, which is why the mass killing begins as soon as the visionary has the capability to begin the slaughter. Pol Pot is the premier example of this particularly ruthless breed.

The fifth stage is Destruction. Those building a new man or a new society cannot permit human liberty or even the freedom of thought, because such things will always stand in the way of the vision by offering competition with it. They especially cannot permit religion. Kim Jong-il sounds very much like Sam Harris in his insistence that Christianity is one of the greatest threats to his rule; it is reported that many, if not most, of the estimated 200,000 prisoners being held in the twelve concentration camps throughout the Hermit Kingdom are Christians imprisoned for their faith. And the North Korean dictator's actions show that once the decision has been made that the vision must take precedence over those who either threaten it or simply cannot be made to fit within it, the killing begins.

This slaughter in the name of atheist progress is neither theoretical nor a thing of the past, it is occurring today, in places such as Camp 22, the largest concentration camp in North Korea. One defector was a former military attaché at the North Korean Embassy in China who had previously worked in management at the camp:

"I witnessed a whole family being tested on suffocating gas and dying in the gas chamber," he said. "The parents, son and a daughter. The parents were vomiting and dying, but till the very last moment they tried to save kids by doing mouth-to-mouth breathing."

Hyuk has drawn detailed diagrams of the gas chamber he saw. He said: "The glass chamber is sealed airtight. It is 3.5 [meters] wide, 3m long and 2.2m high. [There] is the injection tube going through the unit. Normally, a family sticks together and individual prisoners stand separately around the corners. Scientists observe the entire process from above, through the glass."

He explains how he had believed this treatment was justified. "At the time I felt that they thoroughly deserved such a death. Because all of us were led to believe that all the bad things that were happening to North Korea were their fault; that we were poor, divided and not making progress as a country."[27]

---

[27] Barnett, Anthony. "Revealed: the Gas Chamber Horror of North Korea's Gulag." *The Observer*, 1 Feb. 2004.

But destruction never works, as the human spirit never dies. The courage of the persecuted inspires those who see them die, the resistance continues, and finally, the sixth stage, Renunciation, is reached. Sometimes a pretense is made that the vision is still in place even though no one actually believes it, occasionally a genuine transformation toward a more functional model is attempted, and sometimes the entire edifice collapses under the burden of its structural contradictions. Soviet *Glasnost* was an example of Renunciation; the People's Republic of China appears to currently find itself in this stage, caught between pretense and attempting to transform a formerly Communist society into a modern neofascist one.

Bertrand Russell was not the only one to foresee the inevitable result of Communism. In much the same way that John Locke foresaw the probable consequences of atheist rule, Julien Benda recognized the connection between the belief that science is mankind's only means of determining truth of any kind and a hatred for human liberty in his 1927 book, *La Trahison des Clercs*.[28] In the same year that a petty revolutionary named Mao Tse-Tung fought his first campaign, the Autumn Harvest Uprising, Benda pointed out that the partisans of arbitrary authority always preach the idea of progress.[29] And a decade before Benda, Lord Acton was giving lectures at the University of Cambridge explaining how liberty without religious belief is only partial liberty and anticipating Hitchens by nearly a century in noticing the way in which Communism's atheist antecedents were attempting to replace God.[30]

The particular deadliness of Communism is not due to any peculiar aspect unique to Marxism, but because it requires retrofitting humanity to suit its atheist, utopian vision. Any creed or ideology that similarly violates the long-established patterns of human behavior

---

[28] It was published in English as *The Betrayal of the Intellectuals*, although "The Treason of the Learned" is a less misleading translation.

[29] Benda sounds as if he is prophetically referring to the New Atheists when he writes: "It remains to discover whether those who brandish this doctrine believe in it or whether they simply want to give the prestige of a scientific appearance to passions of their hearts, which they perfectly know are nothing but passions."

[30] "*They had two enemies, the aristocrat and the priest; and they had two passions, the abolition of an upper class and the abolition of religion.... [T]he originality of these men is that they sought a substitute for it, and wished to give men something to believe in that was not God.*" John Emerich Edward Acton, *Lectures on the French Revolution* (London, 1999 ed.), 224.

in the name of progress will bear a high probability of leading to the same bitter harvest. Due to their ability to think in the abstract, their rejection of religious and societal traditions and their total focus on the material, atheists are uniquely susceptible to embracing utopian visions that conflict with these historical patterns. The ultimate answer to Richard Dawkins's question is that it is not atheism alone, but the lethal combination of atheism with an ambitious vision of secular progress that inevitably leads to the guillotine, the gulag, and the gas chamber.

Man requires God, whether He exists or not, because in His absence Man becomes a devil.

XIV

OCCAM'S CHAINSAW

Rational ignorance cannot explain why people gravitate toward false beliefs, rather than simply being agnostic. Neither can it explain why people who have barely scratched the surface of a subject are so confident in their judgments—and even get angry when you contradict them.

—BRYAN CAPLAN, *The Myth of the Rational Voter*

S INCE RICHARD DAWKINS WAS THOUGHTFUL enough to devote an entire chapter to arguments for God's existence, I thought it was only right to return the favor and take a look at some of the most common arguments one hears from atheists. Some of these are arguments justifying their belief in God's nonexistence, others are those made in counterpoint to various theistic arguments. All of them are at least partially logically fallacious. However, I don't intend to precisely follow Dawkins's example, as I shall focus on current arguments made by living atheists, not archaic ones made by long-dead men and refuted by famous philosophers more than 200 years ago.

THE ARGUMENT FROM AUTHORITY

There are three versions of this. The first is based on the partially accurate but misleading claim that atheists are more intelligent than theists, a claim that depends on altering the definition of atheist from "an individual who does not believe in God" to "an individual who calls himself an atheist." This is an implicit argument from authority because there is no point to making any reference to this theoretical superiority except to put pressure on the non-atheist to stop thinking for himself and accept the view of his intellectual superiors.

Sam Harris makes the second version of this argument in *Letter to a Christian Nation* when he writes that 93 percent of the members of the National Academy of Sciences do not accept the idea of God.[1] Again, this has no significance regarding the fact of God's existence or nonexistence, it is simply intended to pressure the non-atheist to accept the opinion of the elite academy members in lieu of his own. Harris might as meaningfully report that 84 percent of the academy prefers the color blue. Dawkins puts even greater weight behind this argument, spending four pages citing everything from the National Academy of Sciences members, a survey of the Royal Society, the negative correlation of religion with education, and Mensa meta-studies.[2]

The third variant, of course, is the invocation of famous atheist scientists such as Albert Einstein, James Watson, and Richard Dawkins.

THE ARGUMENT FROM LACK OF EVIDENCE

This argument is particularly superficial, given the obvious impossibility of personally examining all the evidence relevant to the matter and the equally obvious reality that every individual unquestioningly accepts information without demanding supporting evidence every single day. Daniel Dennett observes that the division of labor

---

[1] Note that Harris doesn't state that they are atheists, only that they *"do not accept the idea of God."*

[2] Speaking as a member of Mensa myself, I can state with some authority that most of my fellow Mensans are functional idiots, their high IQs notwithstanding. These are the same sort of clueless intellectuals who were convinced that a centrally planned socialist economy was a great idea fifty years ago. Intelligence is like firepower: unless you learn how to use it properly, you'll never do anything with it but shoot yourself in the foot.

is applauded when it comes to the delegation of decision-making in everything from science and politics to legal and medical issues, to which I add that most of this delegation is based on an unquestioning faith in the authority to which the decision is delegated.

No normal individual actually examines more than a very small percentage of the authoritative information that he or she is provided on a daily basis, as evidenced by the explosion of low-fat foods that was soon followed by the ongoing obesity epidemic. Even though the evidence was easy to obtain—I'm eating this fat-free food, but I'm getting fatter instead of losing weight—millions of people chose to blindly trust scientific studies rather than their mirrors and weight scales.

The fact that you may not have seen any evidence of God is meaningless; you probably haven't seen any evidence of evolution or quantum mechanics, either, and aside from a very few highly intelligent, well-educated exceptions, you're not capable of accurately judging the evidence even if you did examine it yourself. There is no shortage of those who testify to their personal experience of God, and it is both ironic and an error of logic to argue that their evidence is irrelevant due to your blind faith in something else for which you have seen no evidence. While it is reasonable to state that you have not seen any evidence for God's existence, it is illogical and incorrect to assert that no such evidence exists. One can certainly state that no scientific evidence for God exists, based on its absence from the scientific literature. But then, there is no scientific evidence that your mother exists, either, much less that she loves you. From my perspective, there's not even any scientific evidence that you exist. Science is an excellent tool for increasing knowledge, but it is far from the only means of obtaining it because scientific evidence is only one of the various forms of evidence.

In almost every case, an argument from lack of evidence merely indicates in whom one has elected to place one's unquestioning trust.

THE ARGUMENT FROM HALLUCINATION

This is the atheist's counter to the theistic argument from personal experience. In *The God Delusion*, Dawkins puts scare quotes around "experience," by which he means to indicate that evidence based on personal experience is unreliable and even irrelevant. He bases this argument, amusingly enough, on psychology, which is one of the few scientific fields that makes even less use of the scientific method than evolutionary biology. But to simply state, on the basis of no evidence whatsoever, that "mass hallucination" caused 70,000 people in Portugal to simultaneously see the sixth apparition of the Lady of Fatima is not an explanation, it is merely an evasion. Dawkins's invocation of David Hume proves nothing, except that from the atheist's perspective Hume might as well have ended his statement at the comma: "No testimony is sufficient to establish a miracle." This isn't logic, it's merely a demonstration of a mind shuttered closely to ward off any evidence it cannot explain in terms it understands.

Being one who has personally experienced both what appears to have been a supernatural phenomenon as well as a few chemically induced hallucinations, I can testify that the two are about as likely to be confused as *Halloween* and Christmas. And by *Halloween*, I mean the movie, not the holiday. It is certainly reasonable to doubt any one individual's perceptions, but it is intellectual cowardice to arbitrarily declare all human perception itself to be completely meaningless outside of the scientific researcher's laboratory.

THE ARGUMENT FROM TEMPORAL ADVANTAGE

One of the obvious weaknesses in the atheist concept of the conflict between science and religion is the fact that many, if not most, of the great scientists in history were religious men. Even the first great martyr of science, Galileo Galilei, was not an atheist but a Christian. For every Watson and Einstein, there is a Newton, a Copernicus, a Kepler, and yes, a Galileo. Atheists deal with this in two ways, either by simply co-opting them—I have seen lists of famous atheists on the Internet that include Galileo—or by claiming them *post facto*. Dawkins, for example, implies that had these great religious scientists only been privy to the information available today, they would have abandoned their faith; other atheists come right out and state this directly.

What this argument neglects to take into account is that nearly all of the great religious scientists were not merely religious, but Christians, and that there were far fewer scientists than there are today. The first fact is significant because it indicates that there is likely a difference between the Christian worldview that supported a search for scientific truth and the various non-Christian worldviews that did not. The second fact is even more interesting, as it suggests that the non-Christian worldview of today's science may in fact be hindering the pace of scientific development rather than helping it. The fact that today there are far more scientists accomplishing far less in terms of significant scientific developments could indicate, as John Horgan has suggested, that science is close to its goal of explaining nature and that there is simply not much more for scientists to do except learn how to make practical use of their theoretical knowledge. Alternatively, one could argue that the religious scientists of the past had it easy, working with a relatively blank slate, and have left only the most difficult tasks for their secular successors.

But the more we learn, the less we actually seem to know. Just this year, we were informed that what had been the accepted model of gene regulation may be less complete than was previously thought when researchers on the Encyclopedia of DNA Elements project discovered twice as many RNA transcripts and ten times more DNA transcripts than expected. Astrophysicists tell us that either 96 percent of the universe is missing or there is something wrong with our understanding of how gravitation affects the 4 percent we can see. And few can manage to keep up with adaptive devo punk-echthroi neo-quasi-Darwinism, or whatever the evolutionary biologists are calling this week's spin on St. Darwin's dangerous idea.

To assert that the greatest minds of the past, the original thinkers who weren't afraid to challenge either orthodox dogma or the intellectual conventions, would automatically abandon their faith in favor of a status quo professed by the masses of over-specialized, under-achieving scientific mediocrities of today is not only a completely baseless assumption, it is egotistic wishful thinking.

THE ARGUMENT FROM FICTION

This argument states that because the Bible and every other sacred text are wholly man-made and as fictitious as anything written by Shakespeare or any other classic from the literary canon, there is no reason to take them seriously, much less base moral systems or societal structures upon them. The problem here is that the Bible has not only proven to be a more reliable guide in many instances than the current state of secular science as well as an accurate historical document, but sometimes a better predictor of future events than the experts on the subject. I bought euros back when they were worth just over ninety cents on the dollar because of the eschatological interpretations of the Book of Revelation that the European Common Market would one day become a single political entity, the endless vows of the European elite to the contrary notwithstanding. Now, the EUR/USD rate is bouncing around 1.45. Maybe it was just a fortuitous coincidence, but on the other hand, if a northern country shows signs of invading Israel, let's just say I won't hesitate to short their currency.

It is not an ability to explain past events, but its predictive value that proves the value of a model. And whether one considers geopolitics, psychology, or child development, the ancient text repeatedly proves itself to be a better predictive model than those supplied by the scientific experts.

Nowhere in the Bible does it say that the Earth is flat. But Jesus's statement in John 8:58, "before Abraham was born, I am!" is a very strange thing for an itinerant first-century rabbi to say,[3] given the way it presages the twentieth-century concepts of multiple universes and existence outside the space-time continuum.

THE ARGUMENT FROM THE UNFAIRNESS OF HELL

This argument takes the possibility of the supernatural a little too seriously for any of the New Atheists, but one probably encounters it more often from Low Church atheists than one hears all the previous

---

[3] One could argue that "I am that I am" is an even stranger thing for a burning bush to say.

five arguments combined. And since it's a Low Church argument, it is naturally a particularly stupid one that manages to ignore huge quantities of readily available evidence pertaining to human behavior while simultaneously assuming perfect long-term rationality on the part of every individual human being. This argument states that because Heaven is really good and Hell is really bad, the purported choice that God offers between the two really isn't a choice, because what sort of idiot would choose to go to Hell? Therefore, it would be unfair for God to send anyone to Hell, and therefore neither God nor Hell can possibly exist.

The answer is the same sort of idiot that chooses to buy lottery tickets, smokes meth, has premarital sex, gambles in Vegas, buys technology stocks, or cheers for the Minnesota Vikings. In short, human idiots, which we all are to greater or lesser degrees. Everyone makes foolish decisions that combine short-term pleasure with long-term pain, and the fact that a correct choice should be completely obvious to any rational individual doesn't mean that the choice is not a genuine one. Therefore, God is being fair in presenting the choice... which is really neither here nor there since God's theoretical fairness or unfairness has nothing to do with the fact of His existence or nonexistence.

Just as the fact that an argument is ridiculous doesn't mean it doesn't exist or that you're not going to hear it again and again.

THE ARGUMENT FROM GOD'S CHARACTER

This is another superficial argument popular with Low Church atheists, although it pops up from time to time among the more militant High Church breed. It states that even if God exists, the morality He dictates is so abhorrent to the atheist and inferior to the atheist's own moral sensibilities that the atheist cannot believe in Him. And in the unlikely event that the atheist is ever confronted by God, he will refuse to acknowledge His divine status let alone His right to rule over Mankind.

I find it very difficult to take this argument seriously, given how the first words out of every angel's mouth seems to be "Fear not!" I am as arrogant as anyone (and more than most, I'm told), but on the day when I meet my Maker, the Creator Lord of the universe, I fully intend to set new speed records in performing a full proskynesis complete with averted eyes.[4] It's not so much the biblical confidence that "every knee shall bow" that makes me skeptical about this theoretical atheist machismo in the face of the Almighty, it's the part about how even the demons believe...and tremble. I don't know what it takes to make a powerful fallen angel shake with terror just thinking about it, but I have a feeling that neither Richard Dawkins nor Bertrand Russell will be wagging their fingers at God and criticizing Him for insufficient evidence on the day their disbelief is conclusively destroyed.

The argument is totally specious from the logical perspective, of course, because the fact of God's existence no more depends on the quality of His character than does Charles Manson's. Things exist or don't exist regardless of whether we wish them to be or not.

THE ARGUMENT FROM MORAL EVOLUTION

The idea that morals are not defined by sacred texts but have instead evolved naturally is the subject of much pseudo-scientific speculation and a few books, such as Marc Hauser's *Moral Minds,* have been written about it. Christopher Hitchens is the foremost advocate of this idea among the New Atheists. While they admit that morality exists, they argue that it has evolved naturally through a material process, therefore it cannot have been acquired through divine revelation. However, like Richard Dawkins's concept of the meme, the idea of moral evolution is little more than the use of an applied metaphor, a fundamentally unscientific concept that appears to be increasingly popular in the softer sciences today. Hauser articulates a concept of "primitive detectors" that are suspiciously similar to Dawkins's imaginary "original replicators" that he supposes to have started the process of our moral evolution.[5] But referring to these

---

[4] No doubt this is why God prefers the faith of little children. A little girl once told me that when she goes to Aslan's country, she will run to him and give him a big hug because she loves him so much. Shocking abuse on the part of her parents, I thought. Those books should be banned, really.

[5] Hauser, Marc D. *Moral Minds: How Nature Designed Our Universal Sense of Right and Wrong.* New York: Ecco, 2006. 314.

principles as DNA—Darwinian Nodes of Action—only makes them sound scientific, it does not magically endow them with the material properties of Deoxyribonucleic acid.

There are a number of problems with the idea of moral evolution if we pretend that it is not a metaphor but literal evolution. First, if the mechanism of evolution takes place at the gene level, it is very difficult to understand how one moral would mutate and replicate itself genetically. Second, it is easy to observe that the pace of moral transformation is rapidly accelerating. Less than forty years ago, homosexuality was universally considered an immoral action. Today, there is a substantial minority in the West that insist the belief in either the immorality or the psychological abnormality of homosexuality is itself immoral, a rapid notional transformation that is consistent with neither past moral transformations nor biological evolution. Furthermore, moral evolution depends upon the group selection aspect of evolutionary theory that has largely fallen into disfavor among modern evolutionary biologists.

Either Mankind should expect to start sprouting wings within the next century or the process of human moral development cannot be reasonably described as evolution.

THE ARGUMENT FROM THE GOLDEN RULE

It is often asserted that Christian morality is no different than other ethical systems that are based on the Golden Rule. And it is true that one can find pre-Christian examples of the same concept in the *Analects of Confucius*, in the Mahabharata, the Dhammapada, the Udanavarga, and even the histories of Herodotus. Still, there are two errors in this argument because Christian morality is not based on the Golden Rule, and because the Golden Rule, which states that a man should not do to others what he would not have them do to him, cannot provide a basis for a functional moral system.

Jesus Christ's version of the Golden Rule, given in Matthew 7:12, is merely summary advice, not the basis of Christian morality. "So in everything, do to others what you would have them do to you, for this sums up the Law and the Prophets." This is practical advice given in the context of a general admonishment and it cannot possibly be the essence of Christian morality, for in the very same chapter, Jesus informs his listeners that "only he who does the will of my Father who is in heaven" will enter that kingdom. He did not say, "only he who does to others what he would have them do to him." This mention of the Heavenly Father's will, which also appears in the Lord's Prayer, foreshadows the true foundation of Christian morality, which was articulated when Jesus answered an expert in Jewish law in Matthew 22:37:

> *"Teacher, which is the greatest commandment in the Law?" Jesus replied: "'Love the Lord your God with all your heart and with all your soul and with all your mind.'" This is the first and greatest commandment. And the second is like it: 'Love your neighbor as yourself.' All the Law and the Prophets hang on these two commandments.'"*

Obviously, a moral system based on loving the Lord your God and obediently submitting your will to His is a very different moral system and a far more objective one than the Golden Rule, which is not only entirely subjective, but incapable of accounting for either rational calculation or human psychopathy. It provides no moral basis to criticize a man for crawling into Adriana Lima's bed unannounced so long as he harbors no desire to bar Miss Lima from doing the same to him, and sanctions a thief to steal on the grounds of a belief that he wouldn't miss that which was stolen were the thief himself the prospective victim. The Golden Rule is also too easily transformed into the idea of doing unto others as you believe they wish to do unto you, which was the basis for the Holocaust as well as Sam Harris's proposed ethic of mass murder in preemptive self-defense.

THE ARGUMENT FROM SUPERIOR MORALS

There are many atheists who live lives that are morally exemplary according to religious standards. This causes some atheists to claim that this exemplary behavior is evidence of atheist moral superiority, because the atheist is behaving in a moral manner of his own volition, not due to any fear of being eternally damned or zapped by a lightning bolt hurled by an offended sky deity. However, this is a logical error, because while motivation plays a role in how we judge immoral actions, there are no similar gradations of that which is morally correct. There are many evils, there is only one Good.

For example, the act of stealing a loaf of bread is considered more immoral if the theft was committed by a rich thief who simply didn't feel like paying for it than if the bread was stolen by a poor man who needed to feed his two hungry children. But the act of driving an injured person to the hospital is no more right when performed by a good Samaritan who just happened to be passing by than by a paramedic team who will be financially compensated for their actions. We may find the one more admirable, being less expected, but it cannot be more morally correct because that would imply that there was some degree of moral incorrectness to a correct action. To do right is to do right, the amount of rightness in the action no more depends upon the motivation than the amount of a woman's pregnancy depends upon whether she is a married woman whose third round of I.V.F. treatment has finally proven the charm or a high school senior knocked up by the varsity quarterback on prom night.

An atheist can certainly behave better than a theist by the theist's own moral reckoning. But it is logically incorrect to insist that identical moral behavior on the part of an atheist and a theist is proof of the atheist's moral superiority.

THE IRRATIONALITY OF ATHEISM

Our actions generally satisfy us. . . . But that does not mean they are rational in a narrower sense: the product of serial reasoning.

—DANIEL C. DENNETT, *Consciousness Explained*

High Church atheists regard themselves as supremely rational individuals. They have from the very start. History's first confirmed atheist, Jean Meslier, wrote that banishing the "vain chimeras" of religion would be enough to cause rational opinions to fill the minds of the formerly faithful, and anticipated Sam Harris by several centuries with his announcement that the moral precepts of Christianity were no better than those that every rational man could imagine.[6]

---

[6] Meslier, Jean. *Superstition in All Ages*, Anna Koop trans. (1878 ed.).

Almost 300 years later, forty-three commenters at the militant-ly atheist science blog Pharyngula reported the results of an online personality test they had taken. Similar to the Myers-Briggs Type Indicator survey, the test was hopelessly transparent and subjective, but provided a useful means of examining how these predominantly atheist individuals view themselves. They reported an average Rational rating of 94 out of 100, compared to an Extroverted rating of 32 and an Arrogance rating of 49. They do not see themselves so much as champions of reason, but paragons! Is this a justified belief?

While the atheist may be godless, he is not without faith, because he puts his trust in the scientific method and those who use it whether he understands their conclusions with regards to any given application or not. But because there are very few minds capable of grasping higher-level physics, for example, let alone understanding their implications, and because specialization means that it is nearly impossible to keep up with the latest developments in any of the more esoteric fields, the atheist stands with utter confidence on an intellectual foundation comprised of things he himself neither knows nor understands.

In fairness, he cannot be faulted for this because there is simply too much information available for all of it to be processed by any individual. He can, however, be legitimately criticized when he fails to admit that he is not actually operating on reason in most circumstances, but is instead exercising a faith that is every bit as blind and childlike as that of the most thoughtless, Bible-thumping fundamentalist. Still, it can be argued that this is not necessarily irrational, it is only ignorance and a failure of perception.

The fundamental irrationality of the atheist can primarily be seen in his actions, and it is here that his general lack of intellectual conviction is also exposed. Whereas Christians and the faithful of other religions have rational reasons for attempting to live by their various moral systems, the atheist does not. Both ethics and morals based on religion are nothing more than man-made myth to the atheist, he is therefore required to reject them on rational materialist grounds. He can, of course, make a perfectly rational decision to abide by ethics and morals to which he does not personally subscribe because it would be dangerous to do otherwise in a society where he is outnumbered. This is W. Somerset Maugham's semi-rational atheism, which states "do what thou wilt, with due regard for the policeman around the corner."

So the atheist seeks to live by the dominant morality whenever it is convenient for him, and there are even those who, despite their faithlessness, do a better job of living by the tenets of religion than those who actually subscribe to them. But even the most admirable of atheists is nothing more than a moral parasite, living his life based on borrowed ethics. This is why, when pressed, the atheist will often attempt to hide his lack of conviction in his own beliefs behind some poorly formulated utilitarianism, or argue that he acts out of altruistic self-interest. But this is only *post facto* rationalization, not reason or rational behavior.

One need only ask an atheist what his morality is and inquire as to how he developed it and why it should happen to so closely coincide with the dominant societal morality to discover that there is nothing rational about most atheists' beliefs. Either he has none and is "immorally" practicing Dennett's doxastic division of labor[7] by unquestioningly accepting the societal norms that surround him, or he is simply selecting which aspects to credit and which to reject on the basis of his momentary desires. In neither case does anything that can legitimately be described as reason enter into the picture. The same is often true of his atheism itself; it is telling to note that Hitchens and Dawkins became atheists after long and exhaustive rational inquiries into the existence of God, both at the age of nine.[8] The idea that there is any rational basis for atheism is further damaged by the way in which so many atheists become atheists during adolescence, an age that combines a tendency toward mindless rebellion as well as the onset of sexual desires that collide with religious strictures on their satisfaction.[9]

---

[7] Immoral in Dennett's eyes, not mine. Dennett, *Breaking the Spell*, 295.

[8] Atheism didn't initially take in Dawkins's case, as he bought in to the Argument from Design until he was sixteen. No wonder he's so obsessed with the topic. Apparently I was significantly "brighter" than both Hitchens and Dawkins, my father tells me that I was five years old when we came home from church one afternoon and I told him that "I don't believe that." After having twenty-one years to think about it and learn how the world operates, I changed my mind.

[9] Is there any doubt that most college-age atheists would have no problem believing in a God who permitted them to get laid at will? This is why even the most idiotic forms of paganism compete so favorably with atheism.

With this in mind, it's interesting to note that intelligent men of intellectual repute such as Francis Collins and Antony Flew should have rejected atheism at the tender ages of twenty-seven and eighty-one, respectively. Atheism is not only irrational, it is quite literally childish in many instances.

But the ultimate atheist irrationality is the idea that Man himself is rational. Despite the fact that many of our behavioral sciences are founded on this principle, including the dismal science so dear to me, almost all the observable evidence, scientific and anecdotal, forces one to conclude otherwise. Consider how the way in which the educated Western voting class manages to combine total ignorance with fundamental misconceptions to achieve a higher state of irrational consciousness that is breathtaking in its delusionary confidence, the miracle of aggregation notwithstanding.[10] And in *Consciousness Explained*, Daniel Dennett describes a Multiple Drafts model of consciousness that renders the most basic concept of Man's rationality suspect; he notes that the closer one examines the human mind, the more its fragmented and internally competitive nature becomes apparent.[11]

You need only look around to see hundreds of examples of totally irrational human behavior every single day. Indeed, you need only spend a moment of honest introspection to find dozens of examples in your own life. Perhaps you bought an Internet stock in late 1999, or are dating a girl who cheated on her last boyfriend with you. The chances are good that you spent tens of thousands of dollars on a college degree that not only cost you five years' worth of wages and work experience, but has nothing to do with your job now. You probably vote in presidential elections even though it is statistically improbable and logically impossible for your one vote to have any impact on the final result.[12] And yet despite the irrationality of your activities, you will continue to vote, invest, love, and live because

---

[10] Caplan, Bryan. "The Myth of the Rational Voter: Why Democracies Choose Bad Policies." Cato Unbound. 29 May 2007.

[11] *"The intentional stance presupposes (or fosters) the rationality, and hence the unity, of the agent—the intentional system—while the Multiple Drafts model opposes this central unity all the way."* Dennett, *Consciousness Explained*, 458.

[12] Regardless of whether your candidate wins or loses by more than one vote, your vote was irrelevant. In the highly unlikely circumstance that your candidate happens to win by the one vote you cast, the courts will arbitrarily determine the outcome.

you are not a robot, you are a human being. Man is not a rational animal, he is a rationalizing one who uses his intellect to construct reasons in *post facto* defense of his irrational desires.

Predicated on an unreliable human attribute that may not even exist, rejecting the foundation of Man's most successful civilization, trusting a notoriously quixotic institution for a miracle as a means of replacing that foundation and refusing to learn from its past disasters, atheism is not so much the basis for an irrational philosophy as for an insane one. Attempting to build a society on reason is like waging a war on terror; the effort is doomed to failure because it's a category error. There is no evidence, scientific or historical, that any human society can survive its establishment on an atheist foundation, let alone thrive, and a fair amount of evidence to the contrary.

We are fortunate, therefore, that so many atheist individuals nevertheless continue to openly adhere to conventional religious morals and ethics that they have no rational grounds for respecting. This irrational, if pragmatic, compromise between a public nod to morality and its private dismissal is an ancient one. When Socrates taught his students that knowledge is the only good and ignorance the only evil more than 2,000 years ago, he was fully aware of the potentially dangerous repercussions of this teaching and argued in *The Republic* that it was necessary to keep such virtuous knowledge to the ruling elite. The knowledge of the nonexistence of morality was the great secret to which only the rulers were to be privy and the justification for keeping their subjects in ignorance for their own good, lest the herd break out into rebellion.

The ever-practical Romans understood this, too. Seneca the Younger described religion as being regarded as true by the common folk, false by the wise, and useful by the rulers. But as an aristocrat in a cruel and brutal culture, he may have understated religion's importance to social stability, because it is more than useful for the peaceful maintenance of a civilized society, it is a downright necessity. Even the greatest champions of reason reluctantly accepted this bitter reality. Despite his distaste for Christianity and contempt for the Catholic Church, Voltaire regarded the belief in God and in an afterlife of rewards and punishments to be the basic requisites of ethical behavior.

Still, the irrationality of the New Atheists and their faithless flock does not mean that there are no atheists who are rational, or that there are none who are true to their godless convictions. Friedrich Nietzsche is the foremost example, but there is certainly no shortage of other individuals who do not fear to determine their own moral compass in the absence of God. We call them sociopaths and suicides.

THREE RATIONAL ATHEISMS

His nature being what it is, man is born, first, with a desire for gain. If this nature is followed, strife will result and courtesy will disappear. Second, man is born with envy and hate. If these tendencies are followed, injury and cruelty will abound and loyalty and faithfulness will disappear.

—HSÜN TZU

While most atheisms are irrational regardless of whether they are considered from an individual or a societal perspective, this is not always the case. There are three variants of atheism that can be considered at least partly rational: these can be described as Somerset atheism, Nietzschean atheism, and post-Nietzschean atheism.

Somerset atheism is the common practice of moral parasitism described in the previous section. It is a partially rational atheism that functions perfectly well on an individual level but cannot function on a societal level because it depends entirely on the existence of an external morality to support it. In the West, it amounts to Christian atheism, in which the atheist accepts the entire body of traditional Christian morality less whatever elements do not appeal to him, so long as the subtraction does not land him in jail. This is entirely rational behavior for the atheist who wishes to participate in society as a member in good standing, but it cannot reasonably be described as having its ultimate basis in reason because it has no essential foundation of its own.

Somerset atheism is a pragmatic variant of the atheism of Aleister Crowley and Friedrich Nietzsche, which takes no account of society's mores in stating that "do what thou wilt" based on the individual's will to power is the whole of the law. This is entirely rational from the individual's perspective and it is the variant to which history's great killers have subscribed. Three years before he joined the Communist Party, Mao Tse-Tung articulated his personal morality in his commentaries on Friedrich Paulsen's *A System of Ethics*:

> *I do not agree with the view that to be moral, the motive of one's actions has to be benefiting others. Morality does not have to be defined in relation to others. . . . [People like me want to] satisfy our hearts to the full and in doing so we automatically have the most valuable moral codes. Of course there are people and objects in the world, but they are all there only for me. . . . I have my desire and act on it. I am responsible to no one.*[13]

Mao is unconsciously echoing the pagan philosophy of the Noble Soul, which Nietzsche adopted and transformed into his doctrine of the *übermensch*, thus he wrote "Egoism is the very essence of a noble soul." The Nietzschean atheist refuses to recognize the limits of either God or Man on his desires, the very possession of which is proof of his superiority and inherent right to fulfill them regardless of the cost to others. Although not an atheist, Hitler fully subscribed to this philosophy, which is why he is often confused with one; in truth, his paganism was more true to the philosophy's source than the atheist variants of Lenin, Mao, and the many other communist killers.

This philosophy is rational, but it is literally psychopathic in the sense described by Dr. Robert Hare, developer of the Psychopathy Checklist-Revised, a clinical scale used to diagnose psychopathy. He describes psychopaths as predators who use intimidation and violence to satisfy their own selfish needs. "Lacking in conscience and in feelings for others, they take what they want and do as they please, violating social norms and expectations without guilt or remorse."[14]

While it is not possible to diagnose the mental health of a dead man, the tens of millions of Chinese murdered by the Mao regime tend to indicate that the close correspondence between the words of the twenty-four-year-old philosophy student and Dr. Hare's description of psychopathy is not entirely coincidental.

---

[13] Chang and Halliday, 15.

[14] Robert D. Hare, "Psychopaths: New Trends in Research." *The Harvard Mental Health Letter*. Sept. 1995.

The post-Nietszchean atheism of Michel Onfray is also entirely rational. Onfray recognizes that if one rejects the source of a moral system, one has no logical basis for retaining that which derives from it. For example, if all men are created equal, removing the Creator from the equation therefore requires abandoning the idea that men are equal unless another basis for that equality can be provided. This is the reason for his contempt for the irrational New Atheists, who attempt to maintain most of the traditional Christian moral structure while simultaneously kicking out its support. Onfray may be completely unreliable when it comes to facts, but his logic is much stronger than any of the New Atheists, including that of his fellow philosopher, Daniel C. Dennett.

But where Nietszchean atheism limits its psychopathy to the individual, however powerful he might be, post-Nietszchean atheology expands the primacy of desire to a societal level. It is social psychopathy that is an order of magnitude beyond that envisioned by the most rabidly psychopathic intellectual. Not even Leon Trotsky's vision of an international Communism is as ambitious in its ghastly grandeur as Onfray's sociopathic philosophy of desire. Nietzsche only wished to slay God and rule over His Creation, the post-Nietzschean dreams of total destruction so that he may build a new creation from the ashes.

It is not the irrational atheist who is dangerous to those around him; the very unreason that makes him a part of the human race renders him mostly harmless. It is the towering narcissism that follows from his strict and logical devotion to pure rational materialism which causes the rational atheist to disavow his connection to humanity and calmly embark on a well-reasoned descent into inhuman madness.

XV

MASTER OF PUPPETS OR GAME DESIGNER?

She was an atheist, but she was a Lutheran atheist, so she knew
exactly what God she didn't believe in.

—GARRISON KEILLOR, "Wobegon Boy"

DOUBTS ABOUT THE EXISTENCE OF GOD, particularly the existence of a good and loving God, often stem from great emotional pain. While doubts are naturally bound to occur to any rational individual in moments of somber reflection, it is particularly hard to imagine that a loving God who loves us would choose to intentionally inflict pain upon us, especially if He is all-powerful. When one surveys the long list of horrors that have engulfed countless men, women, and children throughout the course of history, the vast majority of them innocent and undeserving of such evil fates,[1] one finds it easy to sympathize with the individual who concludes that God, if He exists and is paying attention to humanity, must be some sort of divine sadist.

---

[1] From the point of view of any human individual, you understand. We haven't gotten to the theology yet.

Because doubts are reasonable, normal, and inevitable, they should never be brushed aside, belittled, or answered with a glib phrase, for not only does decency demand that they receive a sensitive hearing, but they can also have powerful ramifications that resonate long after the doubter himself has had them resolved one way or another. Randal Keynes, a descendant and biographer of Charles Darwin, asserts that it was the death of Darwin's beloved daughter Annie, at the age of ten after a long illness, that convicted the great evolutionist of his dangerous idea that neither divine intervention nor morality had anything to do with the operation of the natural laws.[2] And if this tragic loss was not the only element involved in Darwin's transition from an accomplished student of theology to the inventor of what today is the primary driving force behind the anti-theist New Atheism, it is widely considered to have been the final blow that pushed him over the edge.[3]

One would not be human if one could not sympathize with Darwin's anguished rejection of the notion that there was any justice or even a silver lining to be found in the death of his beautiful little girl. And perhaps there was some consolation, if any consolation was to be found, in viewing his terrible loss as taking place within the context of a mechanistic universe, wherein one was not subject to the ineffable caprice of an unpredictable deity, but to the predictable operation of natural laws that one could at least hope to understand and attempt to utilize.

But if God exists, it is a basic theological error to attempt to place the blame for earthly tragedies on Him. In fact, it is not only a theological error, but also a fundamental error of logic to conclude that God, even an all-powerful God, must be to blame for every evil, accident, or tragedy that befalls us.

THE CONTRADICTION OF DIVINE CHARACTERISTICS

In a chapter considering the arguments for God's existence, Richard

---

[2] Keynes, Randal. *Darwin, His Daughter, and Human Evolution*. New York: Riverhead Trade, 2002.
[3] Desmond, Adrian and James Moore, *Darwin: The Life of a Tormented Evolutionist*. New York: W. W. Norton & Company, 1991. 272–279.

Dawkins muses briefly upon what he considers to be a logical contradiction. He writes:

> Incidentally, it has not escaped the notice of logicians that omniscience and omnipotence are mutually incompatible. If God is omniscient, he must already know how he is going to intervene to change the course of history using his omnipotence. But that means he can't change his mind about his intervention, which means he is not omnipotent.[4]

As Dawkins surely knows, this is a silly and superficial argument; indeed, he follows it up with a little piece of doggerel by Karen Owens before promptly abandoning the line of reasoning in favor of a return to his attack upon Thomas Aquinas. While the argument appears to make sense at first glance, it's merely a variation on the deeply philosophical question that troubles so many children and atheists,[5] of whether God can create a rock so heavy that He cannot lift it.

First, it is important to note that the Christian God, the god towards whom Dawkins directs the great majority of his attacks, makes no broad claims to omniscience. Although there are eighty-seven references to the things that the biblical God knows, only a single example could potentially be interpreted as a universal claim to complete knowledge.[6] Among the things that God claims to know are the following:

He knows the way to wisdom and where it dwells, he knows the day of the wicked is coming, he knows the secrets of men's hearts, he knows the thoughts of men and their futility. He knows the proud from afar, he knows what lies in darkness, and he knows what you need before you ask him. He knows the Son, he knows the day and the hour that the heavens and the earth shall pass away, he knows the mind of the Spirit and that the Apostle Paul loved the Corinthians. He knows who are his, he knows how to rescue godly men from

---

[4] Dawkins, *The God Delusion*, 78.

[5] The frequency with which atheists mention it on their Web sites makes it look that way, anyhow.

[6] "*Dear children, let us not love with words or tongue but with actions and in truth. This then is how we know that we belong to the truth, and how we set our hearts at rest in his presence whenever our hearts condemn us. For God is greater than our hearts, and he knows everything.*" (1 John 13:18).

trials, and perhaps most importantly, he knows that the thoughts of the wise are futile.

The only straightforward claim to omniscience is made on God's behalf by the Apostle John, who clearly states "he knows everything." However, the context in which the statement is made also indicates that this particular "everything" is not intended to encompass life and the universe, but rather everything about human hearts. Not only does this interpretation make more sense in light of the verse than with an inexplicable revelation of a divine quality that appears nowhere else in the Bible, but it is also in keeping with many previous statements made about God's knowledge.

After all, when Hercule Poirot confronts the murderer in an Agatha Christie novel and informs the killer that he knows everything, the educated reader does not usually interpret this as a statement that the Belgian detective is confessing that he is the physical manifestation of Hermes Trismegistus, but rather that he knows everything about the crime he has been detecting.

In keeping with this interpretation, Dr. Greg Boyd, the pastor at Woodland Hills Church and the author of *Letters to a Skeptic*, has written a book laying out a convincing case for the Open View of God,[7] which among other things chronicles the many biblical examples of God being surprised, changing His mind, and even being thwarted. Moreover, it would be very, very strange for a presumably intelligent being such as Satan to place a bet with God if he believed that God knew with certainty what Job's reaction to his torments would be.

But in addition to the fact that it is based on a false assumption, the problem with the Contradiction of Divine Characteristics, as we shall henceforth refer to the logical conundrum posed by Dawkins, is that omniscience, or the quality of knowing everything, is the description of a capacity, it is not an action. Likewise, omnipotence, being all-powerful, is a similar description, which is why these nouns are most often used in their adjectival forms modifying other nouns, for example, an omniscient god is a god who knows everything, i.e., possesses all knowledge. But capacity does not necessarily indicate full utiliza-

---

[7] Boyd, Gregory A. *God of the Possible: A Biblical Introduction to the Open View of God.* Baker Books.

tion and possession does not dictate use; for example, by this point it should be clear that an intelligent scientist is nevertheless perfectly capable of writing something that is not intelligent at all.

Lest you think that this distinction between capacity and action is somehow tantamount to avoiding the question, note that Dawkins himself refers to God "using his omnipotence" in constructing the supposed contradiction.

Now, as I write this sentence, I am holding the book entitled *The God Delusion* in my hand. I paid cash for it at the bookstore prior to reading it through in its entirety, so I now possess the book in a very real and legally binding sense, and I feel sure that the reader will readily acknowledge that I therefore possess all the knowledge contained within it in every relevant meaning of the term. But can I tell you the precise wording of the first sentence on the seventh page? Well, no, not without taking the action required to actually look at it.[8]

This illustrates the difference between capacity and action, and the distinction is a vital one. Possession may be nine-tenths of the law, but it is not synonymous with use. Unless one clings stubbornly to an overly pedantic definition of both omniscience and omnipotence, an inherent incompatibility simply doesn't exist between the two concepts. Indeed, if Daniel Dennett is correct and "knowledge really is power,"[9] then logic not only dictates the compatibility of all-knowledge with all-power, but requires that the two superficially distinct concepts are actually one and the same. In this case, there not only is no contradiction between God's omniscience and omnipotence, there is not even the theoretical possibility of a contradiction.

Regardless, a God who stands outside of space and time and who possesses all knowledge as well as all power is not bound to make use of his full capacities, indeed, who is going to shake his finger at him for failing to live up to his potential? Only the likes of Dawkins and Owens, one presumes, as their ability to logically disprove God's existence by this method depends upon His abiding by their rigid definitions of His qualities...at least one of which He does not even

---

[8] You might argue that I am applying a different meaning of the word "possess" here than the one you would like me to use in order to claim that my statement is illogical. Exactly.

[9] Dennett, *Breaking the Spell*, 48.

claim in His Word.

When considered in this light, the Contradiction of Divine Characteristics can't help but bring to mind a scene from the novel *Catch-22*, in which Joseph Heller wrote of an aptly named atheist called Frau Scheisskopf.[10] "'I don't believe,' she sobbed, bursting violently into tears. 'But the God I don't believe in is a good God, a just God, a merciful God. He's not the mean and stupid God you make him out to be.'"

Furthermore, there is no theological significance whatsoever to a reduced form of omniscience and omnipotence that would satisfy even the most pedantic critical application of the logic. If one accepts the hypothesis that God is bound by logic and thereby imagines a God possessing qualities of tantiscience and tantipotence[11] equating to omniscience and omnipotence minus the amount of knowledge and power required to avoid conflicting with the logical incompatibility, one is still left with a God whose theoretical capabilities are sufficient to fulfill the various claims about His knowledge and power made in His Word. Moreover, from the human perspective, this logically acceptable tantiscient God would be completely indistinguishable from the omniscient one.

When it's time to feed my Viszla, I don't magically summon food from the mysterious bag of plenty. But my dog doesn't know that. From his perspective, there's no difference between my buying it at the store or my summoning it into material existence by the magic force of my divine will. Likewise, we are incapable of perceiving the difference between a god who knows everything and a god who merely knows a whole lot more than we do, moreover, the latter is the god that more closely fits the description of the biblical God.

Dawkins, of course, knows that it is as pointless to logically consider the potential contradiction between two arbitrarily defined concepts as it is to argue over the score of the 1994 World Series; would that his acolytes understood as much themselves.

---

[10] It is usually a bad sign if your argument bears close similarities to a fictional one made by a character bearing a name that translates as possessing a head full of excrement.

[11] Lots of knowledge and lots of power. It's a silly neologism, but useful here. Of course, by the ontological argument, the mere act of imagining such a god is tantamount to proving it exists, so we had probably all better pray that the tantipotent god and the omnipotent god play nicely together. If not, well, I'd lay odds on the omnipotent one and short the stock market.

OMNIDERIGENCE

DERIGO -rigere -rexi -rectum [to set straight, direct]; of placing [to order, dispose]; milit. [to draw up]; Transf., [to direct, aim, guide]

—*Latin Dictionary and Grammar Aid*, University of Notre Dame

Though it may at first seem to be a waste of time to analyze an argument to which Dawkins himself doesn't assign much value, it is important to remember that all things, even specious and superficial arguments for His nonexistence, may prove useful in serving the greater glory of God. That's true in this case, for in considering the Contradiction of Divine Characteristics argument, we were forced to draw a distinct line between capacity and action, the confusion of which is also the root of a much more serious theological error. Interestingly, this theological error is committed by Christians as readily as atheists, perhaps even more often, as they trust in God's plan for their lives instead of making use of their God-given[12] intelligence and free will.

There are a variety of phrases that contain the same inherent implication about a certain view of God. Many evangelical Christians refer to "God's perfect plan" for their lives. This concept is reinforced with children's songs such as "He's Got the Whole World in His Hands" and echoed by sports stars who compete in the assurance that their victory has been divinely secured ahead of time. It is held by American Exceptionalists who believe that God has uniquely blessed the United States of America and has authored a Manifest Destiny for it, and by Christian Zionists who see a divine hand in every violent twist and turn of the Mideast Peace Process.

These various evangelicals have an unexpected ally in Sam Harris, who declares it to be an obvious truth that "if God exists, he is the most prolific abortionist of all"[13] due to the fact that 20 percent of all known pregnancies miscarry, and then asserts that those who believe in God should be obliged to present evidence for his existence in light of "the relentless destruction of innocent human beings that we witness in the world each day."

---

[12] Feel free to insert "presumably" if you like. Or even "supposedly."
[13] Harris, *Letter to a Christian Nation.*

276 THE IRRATIONAL ATHEIST

What the evangelical and the atheist have in common here is a belief that because God is omnipotent, omniscient, and compassionate, he is somehow responsible for these events, although Harris would qualify that with the necessary "if he exists." And in fairness, it must be pointed out that when Harris cites Hurricane Katrina and the 2004 Asian tsunami as God's failure to protect humanity, he is really doing rather better than the "perfect plan" evangelical who would assert that these tragedies were sent by God for some ineffable higher purpose intended to benefit humanity.

This belief in an all-acting God, who not only guides the grand course of events but actually micromanages them, is the result of the same confusion between capacity and action that we saw in the Contradiction of Divine Characteristics. When God asserts that He cares about the sparrows and knows when one falls from its branch, this is very different from an assertion that He only happens to know about it because He personally struck the sparrow down. An omniscient God knows the number of hairs on your head and an omnipotent God is capable of changing their color, but it requires an active Master Puppeteer to personally pluck them, one by one, from your balding head, in the desired order.

Sadly, the English language appears to lack a word describing such a god, even though this is the way that many individuals, even those who do not believe in Him, believe God behaves. So, as Richard Dawkins coined the very useful word "meme," it appears to have fallen to me to invent a word that is, despite its undeniable utility, rather less likely to be dropped into conversations at coffeehouses for sheer effect.

Hence the term *omniderigence*, which I define as: the infinite use of unlimited or universal power, authority, or force; all-controlling; all-dictating. Less formally, one can think of it as über control-freakdom or ultimate puppet-mastery.

Harris shows how this mistaken belief in God's omniderigence is part and parcel of the atheist case against God, and the following dialogue will demonstrate how it leads inevitably to doubts on the part of the religious believer. Two years ago, my cousin's four-year-old son Andrew was diagnosed with leukemia. At the request of Andrew's grandfather, I posted a prayer request on my blog, asking my readers to pray for the recovery of the little boy.

It was heartening to see how many people, of varying religious faiths and even a complete lack of faith, wrote to tell of their prayers and best wishes for Andrew. And as nearly everything does on the blog, it sparked a heated discussion, in this case regarding precisely who was responsible for the leukemia. The omniderigent position was best summarized by the following e-mail from a Christian reader:

> God didn't give Andrew leukemia, but He did allow it to happen, knowing full well what the outcome will be, and hiding the outcome from Andrew and his family. This makes God seem awfully cruel, when one word from His mouth would take Andrew's leukemia away and spare his God-fearing family greater pain.

My reply was as follows:

> I wholeheartedly disagree, and while I'm not particularly enamored of what will no doubt be the can of worms this will open, I will attempt to explain why. Regardless of how badly this twists your panties, do try to keep in mind that belief in the existence or nonexistence of God's power has nothing to do with one's Christian faith. After all, it is written that the demons, too, believe. And tremble.
>
> There are two possibilities. Either evil is part of God's plan and has been from the beginning, or God is somehow constrained in his ability to unleash his power upon this Earth. The biblical account describing how God gave Man dominion over the Earth, a dominion which the Scriptures explain was subsequently handed over in turn to Satan, strongly suggests the latter.
>
> Jesus Christ himself states that Man possesses certain authority over evil in his own right. If evil is from God, then Man must have authority over God, a more fundamentally heretical notion than the idea that God's hand is somehow constrained. This limited human authority is underlined by the situation in which his disciples complained that they could not cast out certain demons and Jesus explained that only prayer would suffice to address that sort. In other words, the disciples were required to make an appeal to God's authority instead of simply making use of their own.
>
> So, my conclusion is that the leukemia inflicted on Andrew is either a random occurrence or intentionally inflicted by the evil being that both Paul and Jesus Christ recognized as the ruling power of this world. I believe that doctors, secular and Christian alike, are doing God's work as they war against sickness and disease, just as Jesus Christ commanded his disciples.

Indeed, to assert that a child suffering leukemia is God's will is to imply that those attempting to heal him are doing evil by defeating it. The problem of evil is not a difficult one, once one is able to accept the notion that God is not a cruel and easily bored puppeteer. Omniderigence leads inevitably to doubt, because it requires accepting the idea that all evil stems from God. But if everything is in God's hands and moving according to God's plan, then what need would there have ever been for Jesus Christ to come to and die on a cross?[14]

Even so, despite the evidence and the logic presented here, the skeptical reader may well ask if there isn't at least some element of omniscience or even omniderigence implied in the assertion of God's omnipotence. How can an all-powerful god not know what is going on around him? And is it really conceivable to imagine an all-powerful being sitting idly by and refusing to intervene in the affairs of humanity as they unfold? The answer, surprisingly enough, is suggested by Daniel C. Dennett in one of his more technical books.

GODS OF THE MACHINE

First, there is the activity of our hacker Gods, who are free to cast their eyes and minds over huge manifolds of possible Life worlds, trying to figure out what will tend to work, what will be robust and what will be fragile. For the time being, we are supposing that they are truly God-like in their "miraculous" interactions with the Life world—they are not bound by the slow speed of glider-light; they can intervene, reaching in and tweaking the design of a creation whenever they like, stopping the Life world in mid-collision, undoing the harm and going back to the drawing board to create a new design.

—DANIEL DENNETT, *Freedom Evolves*

I am, as you may recall from the introduction, a game designer.[15] Most of my experience has been with designing and producing computer games for the DOS/Windows platform, and I think it would

---

[14] There's a happy ending to the story. Andrew was cured and remains a healthy little boy today. For which God, the medical team, and the scientists who developed the medicines prescribed are all to be greatly praised.

[15] Actually, according to one of the industry mags, I am a "Game Design Expert." They've capitalized it, so it must be true.

be safe to say that the best adjective to describe my career would be "innovative" rather than "successful." In 1996, following the release of id Software's Quake, my partner and I began designing our first true 3D game for GT Interactive. Our two previous games had been of the 2.5D first-person shooter[16] variety, and although we managed to do some interesting and lucrative things with speech recognition technology and hardware bundling deals, we had not yet achieved the sort of market success or recognition within the game industry that we sought.

Youthful hubris, combined with a desire to surpass id's legendary pair of John Carmack and John Romero, led us to create a supremely ambitious design. Not only would we create our own 3D engine, but we would also create a multi-tiered artificial intelligence system that would allow for complete cooperation and two-way verbal interaction[17] with AI-controlled squadmates fighting an opposition force made up of separate artificial intelligences in a three-dimensional, non-Euclidean world. The insane impracticality of this design can be seen in the way that ten years later, no electronic game has yet demonstrated even half of the technologies required to fully realize the concepts with which we were working. Nor are they likely to any time soon, as the success of Valve's Half-Life showed that gamers were perfectly happy playing through pre-programmed scripted scenarios, which require neither sophisticated artificial intelligences nor complex synthetic speech systems.[18]

The financial collapse of our publisher forced us to abandon this design, but not before we had managed to develop a significant chunk of both the TacAI, which governed individual activities such as ducking, dodging, and laying down covering fire, as well as the StratAI, which made decisions about larger-scale, goal-related matters such as what target its troops should be attacking first, when reinforcements should be summoned, and when to fall back to a stronger position. Ironically, considering the topic of this book, we made use of a genetic programming approach in developing these

---

[16] Like *Wolfenstein 3D* and *Doom*, in other words.

[17] Combining speech recognition with synthetic text-to-speech technology provided the verbal interaction with the AIs.

[18] Happily, this is beginning to change with the AI middleware from AI Implant, Kynogon, and my own third-tier PsyAI system.

artificial intelligences, a technique that makes use of evolutionary algorithms in an unnatural selection scheme favoring the survival of the optimally performing, or if you will, the fittest.

In this game world the lead programmer, Big Chilly, reigned supreme. He was, precisely as Dennett describes the hacker gods of the Life world, quite literally omnipotent from the perspective of its denizens, able to create thunder, hurl lightning, shake the Earth, create sickness, or grant health according to his whim. He could perform miracles such as stopping time or even making time flow backward, he could grant one character invulnerability while striking another dead in an instant. He was omniscient, too, able to peek into an AI's "mind" to see what actions it intended as well as taking in the entire world at a glance. That which was unseen by the characters was not hidden from him, and he operated entirely outside their temporal references. Whereas they moved about in conventional time on a second-by-second basis, he had the ability to examine their movements in time-slices ranging from one-quarter to one-thirty-fifth of a second.

In short, Big Chilly was not only their creator, he was their God.[19]

And while it would have been incredibly interesting had these artificial intelligences become self-aware and begun worshipping him, the project unfortunately came to an end before that could happen thanks to circumstances beyond our control. However, it didn't end before something of relevance to the subject of this chapter took place.

Not long before our publisher, GT Interactive, went out of business, we were demonstrating the game to our executive producer and a few other GT employees. Big Chilly was playing through a POW rescue mission, a mission which he and others on the development team had played hundreds of times before throughout the course of playtesting. The mission involved one fireteam of AI troops making a diversionary attack on one side of the enemy base while the player led a second team around the other side to rescue the prisoners. Being the lead programmer, Big Chilly of course knew where all the enemy troops were located because he was responsible for assigning their starting positions, and while the specific results of the scenario

---

[19] This chapter does seem to be taking a strange turn toward a George R. R. Martin horror story, doesn't it. Shades of *Sandkings*... anyhow, bear with me, it all makes sense.

varied from one playing to another, the degree to which both friendly and enemy troop behavior varied from the norm was well-known.

During the demo, Big Chilly and the three AI-controlled members of his fireteam had successfully taken out both the wide patrol and the guards, and they were just beginning to lay the explosives to blow the door that held the prisoners captive when there was a sudden burst of bright laser fire that caused him to jump in his seat and emit a startled shriek loud enough to make everyone else in the room jump, too. While his AI squadmates shot down the intruder before anyone's battlesuits took too much damage, what shocked Big Chilly was that for the first time in hundreds of playings, an enemy AI had taken it upon itself to circle around behind the rescue force and attack it from an unexpected direction.

But how could this happen? How could a lowly artificial intelligence surprise a lead programmer who was demonstrably omniscient and omnipotent in the AI's world? How can the created do what the creator did not will? The answer, when viewed in this context, should be obvious.

Surprise was possible because the programmer was not choosing to exercise either his knowledge or his power at that particular point where real-time intersected game-time. While he could have easily provided that particular character with a scripted path and prevented the character from being able to depart from it, he had already elected not to do so. He could have constructed the character in such a way that its head would have exploded for the sin of attempted deicide, or even as punishment for the sin of merely daring to look upon him in all his pasty geek glory, but he did not do that, either. And finally, while he could have been scanning that particular AI's "thought" processes and known what it intended to do in the very instant the intention was born, instead he refrained and so learned about its actions through entirely "natural" means.

If it is not difficult to accept that an omniscient and omnipotent programmer can reject omniderigence, why should it be hard to imagine that an all-powerful God might choose to do the same? Even human lovers know that the lover cannot control the beloved, so it should not be difficult to believe that a loving God would permit His creatures to choose freely how they will live.

As for why He might elect to do so, it is worth considering philosopher Nick Bostrom's idea that we are living in a posthuman computer simulation. His concept offers the bizarre possibility of combining diverse elements of the Singularity, evolution, and the Bible. Bostrom, the director of the Future of Humanity Institute at Oxford, suggests that because the amount of processing power continues to increase at a rapid rate, the ability to simulate environments containing virtual humans with fully developed virtual nervous systems is inevitable.[20] Once that ability exists, the number of simulated humans would soon exceed the number of actual ones; consider, for example, how many virtual people exist on the average gamer's various systems over the course of a year. Even if you play nothing more than *Madden*,[21] *Call of Duty*, and *World of Warcraft*, you're still probably looking at more than 10,000 virtual individuals for every actual person. Actual, that is, from our perspective; because the ratio of virtual to actual humanity in our particular universe indicates that from a futuristic posthuman perspective, the probability is extremely high that any one individual in our "time" must be a "virtual ancestor" rather than a real one.[22]

But posthumans are not the only ones who might conceivably be interested in running full-blown simulations. As I mentioned, when we were developing TacAI's in the mid-'90s, we made use of an evolutionary approach in developing our algorithms. Instead of providing the AI with a detailed script, we gave it a few simple rules designed to encourage it to preserve itself while trying to destroy its enemies and then released it in the little virtual war lab. The AIs that acquitted themselves well were saved, those that didn't were junked. Over time, this unnatural selection led to increasingly effective algorithms that we then incorporated into the game, which allowed the AI-controlled characters to behave in the desired manner, seeking shelter, laying down covering fire for friendly characters, and even anticipating enemy movements.

---

[20] Tierney, John. "Our Lives, Controlled From Some Guy's Couch" *The New York Times*, 14 Aug. 2007.

[21] John Madden NFL Football, for the uninitiated. I have, of course, been down with Madden since 1992.

[22] I'm just going to go out on a limb and suspect that both drugs and PS2 were involved in the development of this particular hypothesis.

This AI development process is remarkably similar to the biblical description of the harvest of souls, of the separating of the wheat from the chaff. This metaphor is central to the New Testament; Jesus Christ mentions it on several occasions and in several different forms, such as the distinction between sheep and goats. While the "God as game designer" hypothesis might reasonably be described as literally making God in one's own image, especially when it comes from a game designer, it does offer the potential of explaining the importance of obedience to God's will as well as the seemingly arbitrary nature of what is in line with that will and what is not. If we are AIs in God's laboratory, then we cannot expect to have any more understanding of His ultimate purpose for us than the AIs in Big Chilly's war lab did.

If one combines the concept of the biblical harvest of souls with Bostrom's ideas about posthuman simulation, one can even develop an interesting and completely heretical concept of theodicy. From the posthuman perspective, our universe looks exactly like a zero-player Massive Multiplayer Online game, an oxymoronic concept I conceived in the process of patenting a design for the Artificial Player Character, or APC. An APC is similar to a Non-Player Character, except that it possesses its own individual motivations that provide it with the volition required in order to behave proactively in the MMO environment. This is known as third-tier artificial intelligence, or PsyAI. When seen from the posthuman point of view, we are all nothing more than APCs running around the virtual environment of an MMO called the World of Man.

Like all game characters, we are bound by the limits set by the MMO's posthuman designer. However, if another posthuman managed to hack into the MMO, this second posthuman would have the ability to begin interacting with the APCs, corrupting the virtual environment, and generally creating havoc within the game world. Perhaps he would tell some of his friends how to break in, then let them take over APCs and play as proper player-characters, but with amped-up stats and abilities that the regular APCs can't match.

Faced with a maliciously corrupted game, the posthuman designer can either turn it off or attempt to fix it. He could simply manually scrub each aspect of the game, but this brute force solution would risk creating new problems and would certainly warn the mischievous interloper. A more elegant solution would be to trap the malicious posthuman and his friends in the game without warning, then insert a viral APC designed to infect other APCs with the ability to resist the malice of the posthuman intruder. His purpose in doing so would be to salvage those APCs whose emergent behavior suits his original plan to develop AIs capable of demonstrating the behaviors required for the real game.

In other words, Heaven is where the action begins.

This may be little more than over-caffeinated techno-speculation, but it is, I think, an exciting way to view the universe as well as providing a reasonable solution for those pesky problems of evil and ultimate purpose. If it also happens to be a near mathematical certainty, then so much the better. It is a fundamentally optimistic perspective, because if this is only the 3D war lab, imagine what the real game in all its multi-dimensional glory must be like! Even if we are immaterial simulations, we are immaterial simulations with a genuine purpose and a future more radical than we can possibly imagine in front of us. Accepting the idea that we are not only the gods of the machine, but also the machines of God, gives us the wherewithal to face the prospect of death with enthusiastic anticipation instead of courage, resignation, or even terror.

If it's in the game, it's in the game. But are you ready for the next level?

XVI

"I BELONG TO JESUS"

Al termine della partita Milan-Liverpool, finale di Champions' League disputata due settimana fa ad Atene e vinta dalla squadra italiana, ci sono stati anche momenti di spiritualita'.... le telecamere hanno portato in diretta sui teleschermi di tutto il mondo la sua maglietta "I belong to Jesus," ma quel che la televisione non ha mostrato e' la sua preghiera in mezzo al campo, in mezzo all'esultanza dei compagni e alla desolazione degli avversari.[1]

O N THE EVENING OF MAY 23, 2007, a young man removed his jersey at the end of a soccer game. This is not an uncommon occurrence at such events. What was unusual was how important the game was and how many people saw what the shirt underneath his jersey said. An estimated 209 million viewers around the world watched the Champions League final between AC Milan and Liver-

---

[1] At the end of the game between AC Milan and Liverpool, the Champions League final played two weeks ago in Athens and won by the Italian team, there were also moments of spirituality.... (T)he cameras brought directly to TV screens throughout the world the message on his t-shirt, "I belong to Jesus," but what the cameras did not show was his prayer, in the middle of the field, amidst the celebration of his teammates and the disappointment of his opponents.

pool, a rematch of the 2006 final won by the famed English club. In addition to seeing the Italians take revenge for their previous defeat with a 2–0 victory, they witnessed Milan's brilliant attacking midfielder, Kaká, declare his Christian faith with a T-shirt that read "I BELONG TO JESUS."

It was a striking statement that made an even bigger global impact when a photo montage of the Brazilian international dropping to his knees and praying with his back to his team's celebration was published by the *Corriere della Sera*, entitled "La preghiera di Kaká." One photo in particular was a beautiful and iconic image, the handsome young player kneeling with his head thrown back, his arms spread wide, and an unashamed declaration of faith on his chest.

That *auto da fé* will likely have a greater impact on the world than all the books published by the New Atheists ever could, because Ricky Kaká is not only an Italian and European champion, he is a genuine soccer god. Only twenty-five, he was the leading scorer in the Champions League, netting ten goals in twelve games. He was voted the UEFA fans player of the year with 31 percent of the vote and named the best player in the world by the *Gazetto dello Sport* as well as by leading German and English publications. By the time this book is published, he will almost certainly have won the sport's most prestigious individual award, the *Ballon d'Or*, given annually to the European Footballer of the Year.

Last season, ten of the twenty-four boys on the club team I coach sported the red and black stripes of the *rossoneri* at practice. Eight of them wear number 22.

The reason Kaká's prayer resonated so profoundly with Christians and non-Christians alike was because it testified to a higher purpose in life. Very, very few of us will ever know such a moment of complete triumph, almost no one can hope to reach the pinnacle of his profession and know that the eyes of all the world are upon him at the very height of his youth and beauty. In a world full of paparazzi, celebrity magazines, and shallow people releasing sex tapes in a desperate bid for fifteen minutes of fame, it is astounding to see a man reject the mass public adulation he has merited in order to humbly give God the glory.

Bertrand Russell, Richard Dawkins, and other men without faith have expended millions of words in telling Man that there is no purpose to his existence except that which he invents, and that merely to inquire as to that purpose is to ask a stupid question. Ricky Kaká, with four simple words, told Man that he has a purpose that is higher than any riches, fame, or earthly success. He offers living proof that there is something more fulfilling than the very best the world can offer. It is Kaká's argument that is the more compelling by far. The fool confounds the wise.

Man needs role models. He seeks them out throughout his life. Not long after I became a Christian, I watched Evander Holyfield walk fearlessly into the ring to meet Iron Mike Tyson, singing "Glory to Glory" and clearly unafraid of the terrible beating every boxing expert was sure he was about to receive. Like millions of fight fans, I watched Holyfield's confident demeanor before the opening bell with fascination. It wasn't his unexpected victory, but his entrance that made me want to understand the boldness exemplified by the faithful warrior that night.

Holyfield's fearlessness before battle came from the source that inspired the history-changing courage of the martyrs who died in Rome twenty centuries ago and today animates the indomitable spirit of the martyrs who are dying for the name of Jesus Christ of Nazareth in China, Iraq, Nigeria, Laos, and North Korea. It comes from faith, from a religious faith in a living God.

For you did not receive a spirit that makes you a slave again to fear. . . .

The Unholy Trinity are deeply and profoundly afraid. They fear faith, they fear those who possess it, and they fear what science has created. They fear everything that cannot be forced to fit within their material reductionist model. They fear the future and they fear God even though they do not believe in Him. And most of all, they fear that which they cannot control and do not understand. The light shines in the face of their dark reason and the darkness comprehendeth it not.

Bertrand Russell once said that he had spent his entire life searching in vain for evidence that Man is a rational animal. What the Unholy Trinity have failed to take into account in constructing their collective case against religion is the fact that Man is not, and never will be, entirely rational. Even if it were to be conceded that Man is nothing but a talking beast evolved through natural selection from a common ancestor shared with fish, squirrels, and monkeys, observation tells us that human beings seldom, if ever, act on a completely rational basis. Reason is a useful tool, but it will never suffice to define Man in his entirety, nor, by will or by force, can Man convert himself into a being of pure rationality this side of the Singularity. Indeed, for conclusive proof of Man's fundamental irrationality, one need look no further than *The God Delusion*, *The End of Faith*, and *god is not Great*.

Richard Dawkins, Sam Harris, and Christopher Hitchens are living evidence that Man's dreams will always rule his intellect; he will always possess faith, hope, and love. Reason is no substitute for religion; it can never be.

Revelation 22:20–21

APPENDIX A

MURDERER'S ROW

THIS IS THE LIST of the fifty-two atheist leaders who personally presided over the non-martial murders of at least 20,000 human beings. Most, though not all, served as the heads of the regime responsible for the slaughters; for example, d'Herbois and Billaud-Varenne were only two members of the nine-man Committee of Public Safety that launched the revolutionary Reign of Terror in France. Some names that one might expect to see, such as Nicaraguan Sandinista leader Daniel Ortega, are missing because the confirmed number of government killings do not rise to the 20,000 mark. In other cases, such as that of Zimbabwean dictator Robert Mugabe, there is sufficient evidence to indicate a leader is not an atheist despite his nominal Marxism.

Afghanistan	Nur Muhammad Taraki, Babrak Kamal
Albania	Enver Hoxha
Angola	Agostinho Neto, José Eduardo dos Santos
Bulgaria	Vulko Chervenkov, Todor Zhivkov
Cambodia	Pol Pot, Heng Samrin

China	Mao Tse-Tung, Hua Guofeng, Deng Xiaoping, Jiang Zemin, Hu Jintau
Cuba	Fidel Castro
Czechoslovakia	Klement Gottwald, Antonín Zápotocký, Antonín Novotný, Gustáv Husák
East Germany	Walter Ulbricht, Erich Honecker
Ethiopia	Tafari Benti, Mengistu Haile Mariam
French Republic	Jean-Marie Collot d'Herbois, Jacques Nicolas Billaud-Varenne
Greece	Nikolaos Zachariadis
Hungary	Mátyás Rákosi
Laos	Kaysone Phomvihane, Khamtai Siphandone
Mongolia	Khorloogiin Choibalsan, Yumjaagiin Tsedenbal
Mozambique	Samora Machel
North Korea	Kim il-Sung, Kim Jong-il
Poland	Władysław Gomułka, Boleslaw Bierut
Romania	Gheorghe Gheorghiu-Dej, Nicolae Ceausescu
Soviet Union	Vladimir Lenin, Joseph Stalin, Nikita Khrushchev, Leonid Brezhnev
Spain	Manuel Azaña, Francisco Largo Caballero
Vietnam	Ho Chi Minh, Le Duan, Truong Chinh, Nguyen Van Linh, Do Muoi, Le Kha Phieu, Nong Duc Manh
Yugoslavia	Josip Broz Tito

APPENDIX B

TWO
DIALOGUES

M UCH OF THE DEBATE BETWEEN CHRISTIANS
and atheists revolves around what might be termed
atheidicy, or the problem of atheist amorality.
While I addressed three of the most common atheist responses in Chapter XIV, there is one other response that, while less common, deserves a more detailed refutation.
Since most High Church atheists are well-educated, it should come
as no surprise that their favorite anti-theistic arguments tend to be
those they picked up in college. This means that when the subject of
morality comes up, the name of Socrates is never far behind, specifically the Socratic dialogue known as Euthyphro which concerns the
relationship between religion and ethics.

While I like the Socratic method and have been known to make use of
it on occasion, I've never been terribly impressed with the examples
Socrates uses in the dialogues recorded by Plato. They tend to strike
me as doing little more than setting up incompatible strawmen, then
asserting that the incompatibility proves something, which, upon
closer look, isn't actually the case. Fortunately, this sort of argument
is easy enough to pick apart as it merely requires demonstrating that

the base assumptions are false.

The Euthyphro dilemma, as it is known, is constructed thusly: "Is the pious dear to the gods because it is pious, or is it pious because it is dear to the gods?" At first glance, this looks easy enough, as simply substituting "obedience" for "the pious" will destroy the dilemma because it eliminates the tautology posed. One can't do this since it's not right to simply substitute whatever terms one likes and declare the problem solved, and yet this does point toward a way to one possible resolution of the dilemma. Consider the first half of the construction: Socrates' postulate that Euthyphro affirms, that the pious is dear to the gods because it is pious. This is known as the first horn of the dilemma.

> Soc.: Tell me what is the nature of this idea, and then I shall have a standard to which I may look, and by which I may measure actions, whether yours or those of anyone else, and then I shall be able to say that such and such an action is pious, such another impious.
>
> Euth.: I will tell you, if you like.
>
> Soc.: I should very much like.
>
> Euth.: Piety, then, is that which is dear to the gods, and impiety is that which is not dear to them.

Here the Christian must immediately disagree, at least within the context of the modern meaning of the term piety. (We'll get to the definition agreed upon by Euthyphro and Socrates soon.) In this context, the Bible is clear on OBEDIENCE being God's priority, not piety, as there are several examples of pious sacrifices to God being rejected due to their being rooted in disobedience one way or another, beginning with the story of Cain and Abel in Genesis. And Jesus Christ's low opinion of the pious Pharisees is proverbial. From the Christian perspective, the question "*Is obedience loved by God because it is obedience, or is it obedient because it is loved by God?*" only poses a problem for omniderigistes who reject free will and believe that God is directly controlling those who exhibit the behavior He loves. (As well, one is forced to assume, of those who behave in a manner He does not love.) So, unless one subscribes to the notion of an omniderigent god, there is no contradiction whatsoever involved in positing a god who holds obedience dear, who loves that which conforms voluntarily to His will.

This is a known objection to the dilemma, in fact, which is described as being problematic only because "it implies that what is good is arbitrary, based merely upon God's whim; if God had created the world to include the values that rape, murder, and torture were virtues, while mercy and charity were vices, then they would have been."[1]

But this can only be considered a genuine problem for those who insist that a fixed principle cannot be arbitrary. In other words, for those paying absolutely no attention to reality. There are a panoply of fixed variables which, if they were different than they are, would radically alter the reality of our universe. They are the very reason Richard Dawkins was forced to face the Argument from Design and construct his Ultimate 747 argument in response to the improbability of all of those variables being fixed in a manner that permits life on this planet. If it were Moloch who were the Creator God, then no doubt child-killing would be considered a virtue; this is hardly unthinkable let alone a logical impossibility considering how abortionettes here in the United States already hold the murder of unborn children to be a genuine moral good.[2]

The fundamental weakness of clinging to this "problem" as proof of the surviving applicability of the dilemma can be seen in the phrase "then they would have been." But since the variables are not fixed that way in the specific universe that we are currently inhabiting, it's not an issue. In the universe next door, we can presume that if there is a different Creator God, then there will also be a different morality, just as a different nuclear weak force would alter the amount of hydrogen and helium in that neighboring universe.

How can it possibly be assumed that physics of the universe next door WILL be different, but that the Creator God next door CANNOT be? That's not a logical failure, it's a complete logical meltdown complete with radiation leak. One suspects that this is the sort of irrational blunder caused by today's intellectual overspecialization.

---

[1] Some random editor on Wikipedia. But it's a fair summary.

[2] It is not within the scope of this book to debate abortion. I merely note that very few would argue that a prenatal human entity of nine-month development is not a child, while abortion activists regard late-term and partial-birth abortions as not only moral goods, but sacred rights

But back to Euthyphro, as Socrates points out a problem with Euthyphro's definition that doesn't affect our case in the slightest:

Soc.: And the quarrels of the gods, noble Euthyphro, when they occur, are of a like nature?

Euth.: Certainly they are.

Soc.: They have differences of opinion, as you say, about good and evil, just and unjust, honorable and dishonorable: there would have been no quarrels among them, if there had been no such differences—would there now?

Euth.: You are quite right.

Soc.: Does not every man love that which he deems noble and just and good, and hate the opposite of them?

Euth.: Very true.

Soc.: But, as you say, people regard the same things, some as just and others as unjust—about these they dispute; and so there arise wars and fightings among them.

Euth.: Very true.

Soc.: Then the same things are hated by the gods and loved by the gods, and are both hateful and dear to them?

Euth.: True.

Soc.: And upon this view the same things, Euthyphro, will be pious and also impious?

Euth.: So I should suppose.

Soc.: Then, my friend, I remark with surprise that you have not answered the question that I asked. For I certainly did not ask you to tell me what action is both pious and impious: but now it would seem that what is loved by the gods is also hated by them. And therefore, Euthyphro, in thus chastising your father you may very likely be doing what is agreeable to Zeus but disagreeable to Cronus or Uranus, and what is acceptable to Hephaestus but unacceptable to Hera, and there may be other gods who have similar differences of opinion.

Euth.: But I believe, Socrates, that all the gods would be agreed as to the propriety of punishing a murderer: there would be no difference of opinion about that.

Needless to say, none of this is of any concern whatsoever to either a monotheist or the Christian who believes in multiple gods but worships only the One whose opinion on the matter happens to be relevant. At this point we can reach three conclusions:

1. The Euthyphro "dilemma" is defeated by shifting the focus from "the pious" to "obedience," therefore it is an inappropriate criticism of Christian morality that is founded on obedience to God's Will.
2. The dilemma relies upon the false assumption that a fixed variable cannot be arbitrarily fixed.
3. The section about disagreement between gods regarding the pious and impious does not apply to a monotheistic god or a Supreme God who rules over other, lesser gods and defines their morality for them.

Here we reach the weak point in Socrates' argument, where he reveals the devious and intellectually dishonest aspect of his character:

SOC.: There was a notion that came into my mind while you were speaking; I said to myself: "Well, and what if Euthyphro does prove to me that all the gods regarded the death of the serf as unjust, how do I know anything more of the nature of piety and impiety? For granting that this action may be hateful to the gods, still piety and impiety are not adequately defined by these distinctions, for that which is hateful to the gods has been shown to be also pleasing and dear to them." And therefore, Euthyphro, I do not ask you to prove this; I will suppose, if you like, that all the gods condemn and abominate such an action. But I will amend the definition so far as to say that what all the gods hate is impious, and what they love pious or holy; and what some of them love and others hate is both or neither. Shall this be our definition of piety and impiety?

EUTH.: Why not, Socrates?

SOC.: Why not! Certainly, as far as I am concerned, Euthyphro, there is no reason why not. But whether this admission will greatly assist you in the task of instructing me as you promised, is a matter for you to consider.

EUTH.: Yes, I should say that what all the gods love is pious and holy, and the opposite which they all hate, impious.

In order to narrow the definition to suit his egalitarian polytheist environment, Socrates first removes the possibility of all individual preferences from the gods. This means that war cannot be pious and holy even though Ares and Athena love it, since Aphrodite objects, while happiness and love cannot be held sacred either if grim Hades takes exception to it. Therefore, Socrates' definition of what is pious must be a vastly reduced subset of what any one particular god loves.

So, the idea of "the pious and the holy" being equated with what the Christian God loves is a bait-and-switch even as Socrates and Euthyprho have defined the term. Whether piety is defined as the modern theist would define it, or as Socrates and Euthyphro do, in either case it cannot possibly be applied to the Christian God.

More importantly, the equation of "pious" with "what all the gods love" is an entirely arbitrary assignation by Socrates, who even admits that he is "amending the definition." To use one famous counterexample, David was loved by God although his actions in seducing Bathsheba and murdering Uriah were notoriously impious by our definition (obedience to God's Will) or by Socrates' definition (that which all the gods love). Either God ceased to love David, which we are informed was not the case, or Socrates' amended definition is merely a subset of "the pious and holy" as I have already proven.

Now, the "dilemma" is founded upon the principle that one cannot logically define "the pious and holy" in a circular manner, since that would not be a definition but rather a tautology. "Is the pious loved by the gods because it is pious, or is it pious because it is loved by the gods?" But now that we recognize how Socrates has twice artificially narrowed the definition of "the pious," all that is necessary to avoid the tautology and destroy the dilemma in the philosopher's own terms is to show that there is a reasonable definition of "loved by the gods" that is not covered by the narrowed definition of "the pious."

> Soc.: And what do you say of piety, Euthyphro: Is not piety, according to your definition, loved by all the gods?
> Euth.: Yes.
> Soc.: Because it is pious or holy, or for some other reason?
> Euth.: No, that is the reason.
> Soc.: It is loved because it is holy, not holy because it is loved?
> Euth.: Yes.

Soc.: And that which is dear to the gods is loved by them, and is in a
  state to be loved of them because it is loved of them?
Euth.: Certainly.

At no point does Socrates convincingly limit "what is loved by the
gods" to the narrowed definition of "the pious." Nor is it difficult to
cite specific divine loves outside of the boundaries set for "the pious." Zeus was reputed to fall in love with various individuals on a
regular basis, this love obviously fell outside Socrates' narrow definition since Hera, being a jealous god, did not approve and often
took vengeance upon the Thunderer's unfortunate beloveds. In like
manner, Poseidon and Athena hated Troy, while Ares and Aphrodite
fought for their favored Trojans.

This is all applicable to the Christian dismissal of Euthyphro as
well, but in order to smash the last remaining shards of the philosophical dilemma on its own terms, we must still find something
that "all the gods love" that cannot reasonably be described as "the
pious." Therefore, I propose the following dialogue with Socrates:

Vox: My dear friend Socrates, do inform me, so that I might better un-
  derstand the nature of Man's proper relation with the gods, what
  the nature of that relationship might be?
Soc.: I believe the custom is for me to ask the questions, sport.
Vox: Humor me, o wisest of the wise.
Soc.: (squeezes arm) Thundering Zeus, you must live at the gym! You
  were saying?
Vox: I was asking you about the nature of our relations with the gods.
  But speaking of Zeus, would it be correct to say that Zeus might
  love a woman?
Soc.: I am given to understand that he is most indiscriminate in this
  regard.
Vox: And would it be likewise correct to state that Zeus could also
  love a man?
Soc.: Mount Olympus would be less one attractive young cup-bearer
  if he could not.
Vox: And is the Thunderer's love limited to these carnal desires, or
  is he also capable of loving men and women in a platonic sense as
  well?

Soc.: I should say he has been known to love those with whom he has no intimate relations.

Vox: Tell me, Socrates, could that platonic love be said to stretch so far as to include all humanity?

Soc.: I think it must, else he would surely have allowed Deucalion and Pyrrha to drown rather than cause the waters to recede and give them safe landing on Mount Parnassos. Moreover, he did eventually free Prometheus once his ire over the fire incident had passed.

Vox: I would not dream of disputing your conclusion, Socrates. As for Aphrodite, does she love humanity any less than the Thunderer?

Soc.: Surely you jest! Is she not the Goddess of Love?

Vox: But what of her red-handed lover, Ares? He glories in chaos and war. Surely he must hate all humanity to bring such terrible suffering upon it?

Soc.: Ah, but there you are wrong, my young friend! Ares loves Mankind most of all, for without it he would have no plaything. Does not a child love his toys?

Vox: Yes, to be sure.

Soc.: Then so, too, does Ares love Man.

Vox: Thank you, Socrates, I see now the limits of my imagination. As for Athena, we know well that she loves the Athenians. But what of the rest of humanity? Did she not hate the Trojans? And what of the Lacedaemonians, whose arms caused the Long Walls to fall?

Soc.: You are confusing anger at a specific offense with a general animus for humanity. The gray-eyed would have harbored no ill will for either Troy or Sparta had they only shown her the proper reverence that is her due. Consider how she granted her favor to all the Hellenes, even the Spartans, at Ilium. Nor did she spurn the men of Syracuse, even when the Athenian forces were shattered against its walls.

Vox: You are wise beyond your many years, Socrates. But surely Artemis, who loathes all men so much that she is known to hunt them, cannot be said to love humanity, but rather, to despise it!

Soc.: Are you so confused as to consider men and women to be entirely different species? Her loathing for men is but a reflection of her peculiar nature, and without men, there would be no women for her to love. As for her love of the chase, would you say that the hunter hates the deer he pursues?

Vox: I stand corrected, Socrates. But then, are there no gods that can be said to hate humanity?

Soc.: Certainly not, or mortal man would perish before the force of an undying Olympian hatred, even were that god to act alone. Not even Zeus and Apollo could spare Troy from the wrath of Athena, Hera, and Poseidon, you may recall. And those the gods hate, they destroy, as you may witness by the Titans imprisoned to this very day in Tartarus.

Vox: So then, you would say that the gods love humanity.

Soc.: Yes.

Vox: All the gods.

Soc.: Yes, that is the point I have been endeavoring to eventually lead you toward.

Vox: Thank you, Socrates, you are most patient and kind. So then, as I have heard that with the assistance of Euthyphro, you have defined "the pious and holy" as "that which all the gods love," may we therefore conclude that humanity is pious?

Soc.: I should say we must.

Vox: And holy?

Soc.: Indubitably.

Vox: And that every man and woman comprises a part of that humanity?

Soc.: That is so, is it not?

Vox: I, too, am given to understand that, Socrates. So then, must we not conclude that every man and woman is pious and holy and loved by the gods?

Soc.: It is certain, we must.

Vox: Including you and me?

Soc.: Was there ever a doubt of it? Now, may I buy you a cup of wine?

Vox: Indeed you may, my learned friend. Let us drink to knowledge, its pursuit, and our hopes of enjoying continued Divine favor.

Of course, it is as pointless to "prove" that every man is pious as it is to "prove" that the pious can be entirely defined as being loved by all the gods. The ability to construct a tautological trap does not serve as a definitive proof of anything; in my dialogue, the weak point is the agreement upon the point that that which applies to collective humanity therefore can be transitively applied to each individual human, but this is still a much more defensible conclusion than several of the agreements reached in Euthyphro.

In his questioning, Socrates is constantly guiding Euthyphro toward the tautological trap, which is perhaps more obvious in my stripped-down version of this form of argument. But since Socrates' narrowed definition is as arbitrary as that which anyone else might devise, and since it manifestly fails to cover the vast majority of things that we are informed, beyond any shadow of a doubt, that the Greek gods loved, Euthyphro's "dilemma" is far more an exercise in rhetorical manipulation than it is a genuine philosophical challenge, still less an intelligent objection to the rationale underlying Christian and other religious moralities.

BIBLIOGRAPHY

Acton, John Emerich Edward. *Lectures on the French Revolution*. London: Batoche Books, 1999.

Adams, Scott. *God's Debris: A Thought Experiment*. Kansas City: Andrews McMeel Publishing, 2004.

Armstrong, Karen. *Islam: A Short History*. New York: Modern Library, 2000.

Arrian. *The Campaigns of Alexander*. Translated by Aubrey de Sèlincourt. New York: Barnes & Noble Books, 1993.

Barro, Robert and Rachel M. McCleary. "Which Countries Have State Religions?" Harvard University, 2005.

Bary, Wm. Theodore de (editor). *Introduction to Oriental Civilizations*. Vol. 1, Sources of Chinese Tradition. New York: Columbia University Press, 1963.

Bondanella, Peter and Mark Musa. *The Portable Machiavelli*. New York: Viking Penguin, 1985.

Boorstin, Daniel J. *Cleopatra's Nose: Essays on the Unexpected*. New York: Vintage, 1994.

Boyd, Gregory A. *God at War: The Bible & Spiritual Conflict*. Downers Grove: InterVarsity Press, 1997.

Bury, J. B. (editor). *The Cambridge Medieval History*. Vols. I–VIII. Cambridge: The University Press, 1964.

Caesar, Gaius Julius. *The Conquest of Gaul*. Translated by S. A. Handford.

London: Penguin Books, 1982.

Carcopino, Jérôme. *Daily Life in Ancient Rome*. Translated by E. O. Lorimer. New Haven: Yale University Press, 1955.

Chang, Jung and John Halliday. *Mao: The Unknown Story*. London: Vintage, 2007.

Clausewitz, Carl von. *On War*. Edited by Anatol Rapoport. London: Penguin Classics, 1982.

Dawkins, Richard. *The Blind Watchmaker: Why the Evidence of Evolution Reveals a Universe Without Design*. New York: W. W. Norton & Company, 2006.

———. *A Devil's Chaplain: Reflections on Hope, Lies, Science and Love*. Boston: Houghton Mifflin, 2003.

———. *The God Delusion*. London: Bantam Press, 2006.

———. *The Selfish Gene*. Oxford: Oxford University Press, 2006.

———. *Unweaving the Rainbow: Science, Delusion and the Appetite for Wonder*. Boston: Mariner, 1998.

Dennett, Daniel C. *Breaking the Spell*. New York: Penguin Books, 2007.

———. *Consciousness Explained*. London: Penguin Books, 1993.

———. *Darwin's Dangerous Idea: Evolution and the Meanings of Life*. London: Penguin Books, 1996.

———. *Freedom Evolves*. London: Penguin Books, 2004.

Diamond, Jared. *Guns, Germs, and Steel: The Fates of Human Societies*. New York: W. W. Norton, 1999.

Dunnigan, James F. *How to Make War*. New York: William Morrow & Company, 1993.

Eco, Umberto. *Apocalypse Postponed*. Edited by Robert Lumley. London: Flamingo, 1995.

———. *Art and Beauty in the Middle Ages*. Translated by Hugh Bredin. New Haven: Yale University Press, 1986.

———. *Art and Beauty in the Middle Ages*. Translated by Alastair McEwen. San Diego: Harcourt, 2000.

———. *La Bustina di Minerva*. Milano: Bompiani Overlook, 2000.

———. *Faith in Fakes: Travels in Hyperreality*. Translated by William Weaver. London: Vintage, 1998.

———. *Kant and the Platypus: Essays on Language and Cognition*. Translated by James Fentress. London: Fontana Press, 1997.

———. *Mouse or Rat? Translation as Negotiation*. London: Phoenix, 2003.

———. *The Search for the Perfect Language*. Translated by James Fentress. London: Fontana Press, 1997.

Finley, M. I. *The Portable Greek Historians*. New York: Penguin Books, 1982.

Gaury, Gerald de. *The Rulers of Mecca*. New York: Dorset Press, 1991.

Geissbühler, Simon. "No Religion, No (Political) Values? Political Attitudes of Atheists in Comparison." *Journal for the Study of Religions and Ideologies.* No. 2, Summer 2002.

Geoffrey of Monmouth. *The History of the Kings of Britain.* Translated by Lewis Thorpe. London: Penguin Classics, 1982.

Gibbon, Edward. *The Decline and Fall of the Roman Empire.* Vols. I–III. New York: The Modern Library.

Gilson, Étienne. *The Philosophy of St. Thomas Aquinas.* Translated by Edward Bullough. New York: Barnes & Noble Books, 1993.

Glynn, Patrick. *God: The Evidence: The Reconciliation of Faith and Reason in a Postsecular World.* Rocklin: Forum, 1999.

Guerri, Giordano Bruno. *Fascisti: Gli italiani di Mussolini, Il regime degli italiani.* Milano: Oscar Mondadori, 1995.

Hanson, Victor Davis. *Carnage and Culture: Landmark Battles in the Rise of Western Power.* New York: Doubleday, 2001.

Harris, Sam. *The End of Faith.* New York: W. W. Norton & Company, 2004.

——. *Letter to a Christian Nation.* New York: Alfred A. Knopf, 2006.

Hauser, Marc D. *Moral Minds: How Nature Designed Our Universal Sense of Right and Wrong.* New York: HarperCollins, 2006.

Hitchens, Christopher. *god is not Great.* New York: Twelve, 2007.

Johnson, Paul. *Intellectuals.* New York: HarperCollins, 1989.

——. *Modern Times: The World from the Twenties to the Nineties.* New York: Harper Perennial, 2001.

Kamen, Henry. *The Spanish Inquisition: A Historical Revision.* New Haven: Yale University Press, 1997.

Keegan, John. *The Face of Battle.* New York: Barnes & Noble Books, 1993.

Kornai, János. *The Socialist System: The Political Economy of Communism.* Princeton, Princeton University Press, 1992.

Lewis, C. S. *Mere Christianity.* London: Fount, 1977.

Lister, R. P. *Genghis Khan.* New York: Dorset Press, 1969.

Livius, Titus. *The History of Rome Vol. I.*

Manchester, William. *The Last Lion: Visions of Glory 1874–1932.* Boston: Little, Brown, 1982.

——. *The Last Lion: Alone 1932–1940.* Boston: Little, Brown, 1988.

Mendel, Arthur P. *Essential Works of Marxism.* New York: Bantam, 1963.

Mises, Ludwig von. *Human Action: The Scholar's Edition.* Auburn: The Ludwig von Mises Institute, 1998.

Mommsen, Theodore E. "Petrarch's Conception of the 'Dark Ages'." *Speculum.*

Newton, Isaac. *The Principia: Mathematical Principles of Natural Philosophy.* Translated by Cohen and Whitman. New York: University of California Press, 1999.

Norwich, John Julius. *Byzantium: The Early Centuries*. New York: Alfred A. Knopf, 1989.

——. *Byzantium: The Apogee*. New York: Alfred A. Knopf, 1999.

——. *Byzantium: Decline and Fall*. New York: Alfred A. Knopf, 1995.

——. *A History of Venice*. New York: Vintage, 1989.

——. *The Middle Sea: A History of the Mediterranean*. Chatto & Windus, 2006.

Ockley, Simon. *The History of the Saracens; Comprising the Lives of Mohammed and His Successors, to the Death of Abdalmelik, the Eleventh Caliph*. London: Henry G. Bohn, 1847.

OFFICE OF STRATEGIC SERVICES Research and Analysis Branch. *The Nazi Master Plan, Annex 4: The Persecution of the Christian Churches*. Draft for the War Crimes Staff. R&A No. 3114.4. 1945.

Oman, Charles. *The Art of War in the Middle Ages A.D. 378–1515*. Oxford: Horace Hart, Printer to the University, 1885.

——. *A History of the Art of War in the Middle Ages*. Vol. 1, 378–1278 A.D. London: Greenhill Books, 1991.

——. *A History of the Art of War in the Middle Ages*. Vol. 2, 1278–1485 A.D. London: Greenhill Books, 1991.

Onfray, Michel. *In Defense of Atheism: The Case Against Christianity, Judaism and Islam*. Translated by Jeremy Leggatt. London: Serpent's Tail, 2007.

Payne, Robert. *The History of Islam*. New York: Dorset Press, 1989.

Pegis, Anton C. *Basic Writings of St. Thomas Aquinas*. Vol. 1. New York: Random House, 1945.

——. *Basic Writings of St. Thomas Aquinas*. Vol. 2. New York: Random House, 1945.

Phillips, Charles and Alan Axelrod. *Encyclopedia of Wars*. Vols. I–III. New York: Facts on File, 2005.

Pipes, Richard. *Communism: A History*. New York: Modern Library, 2001.

Plutarch. *Makers of Rome*. Translated by Ian Scott-Kilvert. London: Penguin, 1987.

Quigley, Carroll. *Tragedy and Hope: A History of the World in Our Time*. New York: MacMillan, 2000.

Rawlinson, George. *Ancient History: The Great Civilizations from 3000 B.C. to the Fall of Rome*. New York: Barnes & Noble Books, 1993.

Rohl, David M. *Pharaohs and Kings: A Biblical Quest*. New York: Crown Publishers, 1995.

Runciman, Steven. *A History of the Crusades*. Vol. I, *The First Crusade and the Foundations of the Kingdom of Jerusalem*. Cambridge: The University Press, 1951.

——. *A History of the Crusades*. Vol. II, *The Kingdom of Jerusalem*. Cambridge:

The University Press, 1952.

———. *A History of the Crusades.* Vol. III, *The Kingdom of Acre and the Later Crusades.* Cambridge: The University Press, 1954.

Russell, Bertrand. *Icarus: or, the Future of Science.* London: Kessinger, 2004.

———. *The Practice and Theory of Bolshevism.* London: George Allen & Unwin, 1921.

———. *Religion and Science.* New York: Oxford University Press U.S.A., 1997.

———. *Unpopular Essays.* London: Routledge, 1996.

Schumpeter, Joseph A. *Capitalism, Socialism and Democracy.* New York: HarperCollins, 1977.

———. *History of Economic Analysis.* Oxford: Oxford University Press, 1963.

Smith, Adam. *The Theory of Moral Sentiments.* Oxford: Oxford University Press, 1976.

———. *The Wealth of Nations.* New York: Modern Library, 1994.

Smith, John Maynard. *Evolution and the Theory of Games.* Cambridge: Cambridge University Press, 2006.

Stephenson, Neal. *The Confusion.* New York: William Morrow, 2004.

———. *Quicksilver.* New York: William Morrow, 2003.

———. *The System of the World.* New York: William Morrow, 2004.

Wishart, Ian. *Eve's Bite.* North Harbor: Howling at the Moon, 2007.

Wistrich, Robert S. *Hitler and the Holocaust.* New York: Modern Library, 2001.

ABOUT THE AUTHOR

Vox Day is a game design expert and libertarian opinion columnist. He left the frozen tundra of Minnesota for the sunny shores of the Mediterranean more than a decade ago, speaks three languages, and is a member of the SFWA, IGDA, and Mensa. He is the author of numerous games, books, and graphic novels in the fantasy and science fiction genres and is the inventor of the WarMouse™. For more information about Vox Day, join the spirited discussion that takes place daily at his blog, Vox Popoli, at voxday.blogspot.com.